21st-Century Modernism

Blackwell Manifestos

In this new series major critics make timely interventions to address important concepts and subjects, including topics as diverse as, for example: Culture, Race, Religion, History, Society, Geography, Literature, Literary Theory, Shakespeare, Cinema, and Modernism. Written accessibly and with verve and spirit, these books follow no uniform prescription but set out to engage and challenge the broadest range of readers, from undergraduates to postgraduates, university teachers and general readers – all those, in short, interested in ongoing debates and controversies in the humanities and social sciences.

Published

The Idea of Culture
Terry Eagleton

Reading After Theory
Valentine Cunningham

The Future of Christianity
Alister E. McGrath

21st-Century Modernism: The "New" Poetics
Marjorie Perloff

Forthcoming

The Death of Race
David Theo Goldberg

The Future of Society
William Outhwaite

The Future of Theory
Jean-Michel Rabaté

The Idea of Black Culture
Hortense J. Spillers

Post/Modern Religion
Graham Ward

21st-Century Modernism

The "New" Poetics

Marjorie Perloff

First published 2002

2 4 6 8 10 9 7 5 3 1

Blackwell Publishers Inc.
350 Main Street
Malden, Massachusetts 02148
USA

Blackwell Publishers Ltd
108 Cowley Road
Oxford OX4 1JF
UK

Library of Congress Cataloging-in-Publication Data

Perloff, Marjorie.
21st-century modernism / Marjorie Perloff.
p.   cm. – (Blackwell manifestos)
Includes bibliographical references and index.
ISBN 0-631-21969-2 (alk. paper) – ISBN 0-631-21970-6 (pbk.: alk. paper)
1. Literature, Modern – 20th century – History and criticism.   2. Modernism (Literature)   I. Title: Twenty-first-century modernism.   II. Title.   III. Series.

PN771 .P46 2002
809'.9112–dc21   2001002633

British Library Cataloguing in Publication Data

A CIP catalogue record for this book is available from the British Library.

Typeset in 11½ on 13½ pt Bembo
by Best-set Typesetter Ltd, Hong Kong
Printed in Great Britain by T.J. International, Padstow, Cornwall

This book is printed on acid-free paper

Contents

List of Plates   vi

Acknowledgments   vii

Introduction   1

1   Avant-Garde Eliot   7

2   Gertrude Stein's Differential Syntax   44

3   The Conceptual Poetics of Marcel Duchamp   77

4   Khlebnikov's Soundscapes: Letter, Number, and
the Poetics of *Zaum*   121

5   "Modernism" at the Millennium   154

Notes   201

Bibliography   206

Index   216

Plates

3.1 Marcel Duchamp, *The Bride Stripped Bare by her Bachelors, Even* or *The Large Glass*, 1915–23.   80

3.2 Marcel Duchamp, *Box of 1914*, 1913–14.   82

3.3 Marcel Duchamp, *Tzanck Check*, 1919.   90

3.4 Marcel Duchamp, *The*, 1915.   92

3.5 Marcel Duchamp, *Rendezvous of Sunday 6th February 1916*, 1916.   96

3.6 Marcel Duchamp, *With Hidden Noise (A bruit secret)*, 1916.   100

3.7 Marcel Duchamp, *With Hidden Noise*
   (a) detail of bottom plaque;   104
   (b) detail of top plaque.   105

3.8 Marcel Duchamp, *Fresh Widow*, 1920.   106

3.9 Marcel Duchamp, *The Bride Stripped Bare by her Bachelors, Even* in the Brooklyn Museum Exhibition of 1926.   112

3.10 Marcel Duchamp, *By or of Marcel Duchamp or Rrose Sélavy*, Series A, 1943.   114

5.1 Extract from Susan Howe's *Thorow*.   169

5.2 Steve McCaffery, "Four Versions of Pound's 'In a Station of the Metro'," panel 1.   193

5.3 Steve McCaffery, "Four Versions of Pound's 'In a Station of the Metro'," panel 2.   194

5.4 Steve McCaffery, "Four Versions of Pound's 'In a Station of the Metro'," panel 3.   196

5.5 Steve McCaffery, "Four Versions of Pound's 'In a Station of the Metro'," panel 4.   198

Acknowledgments

A manifesto could not exist without dialogue – dialogue with those who hold very different positions as well as with friends. I have had the good fortune to get excellent feedback on specific passages in this book from lecture and conference audiences at very different venues, so that writing has been a process of Steinian "beginning again and again." In the case of specific chapters, I should single out the following for special thanks: Charles Altieri and Claude Rawson for responses to the Eliot discussion; David Antin, Ulla Dydo, and Joan Retallack for their assessments of Gertrude Stein; Stamos Metzidakis for his elucidation of some difficult Duchamp passages; and Michael Heim and Gerald Janacek for their heroic help with Russian translation and transliteration in the case of Khlebnikov. For the larger conception of modernism, I owe a debt to conversations with Jean-Michel Rabaté and Richard Sieburth, as well as to Advisory Board Discussions led by Geoffrey O'Brien on the occasion of selecting the poetry to be included in the Library of America volumes on twentieth-century poetry published in 2000. And for comparable discussions about the "state of the art" today, I must single out Craig Dworkin and Ming-Qian Ma who commented and listened every step of the way, as well as Susan Stewart for some wonderful debates about the nature of poetry. My husband Joseph Perloff read the entire manuscript with his eagle eye and made countless helpful suggestions.

But my greatest debt is to my editor Andrew McNeillie, whose expertise on poetry and poetics proved to be the inspiration behind the book. Without his continuing encouragement and confidence, this book, quite simply, would not exist.

A section of chapter 2 was published in rather different form in *American Literature*, 62, no. 4 (December 1990); the short section on Lyn Hejinian's "Happily" was published in the April–May 2001 issue of *Boston Review*.

Marjorie Perloff
Los Angeles

The author and publishers gratefully acknowledge permission to reproduce copyright material as follows:

Ashbery, John, *Self-Portrait in Convex Mirror* (Viking, New York, 1975, copyright Penguin Putnam Inc., New York); Bernstein, Charles, *Dark City* (Sun & Moon Publishing, Los Angeles, 1994); Cabanne, Pierre, *Dialogues with Marcel Duchamp*, trans. Michael Shaw (University of Minnesota Press, 1984, copyright Penguin Putnam Inc., New York); Castillo, Anna, "Seduced by Natassja Kinski" from *Anthology of Modern American Poetry*, ed. Cary Nelson (Oxford University Press, New York, 2000); Duchamp, Marcel, *The Essential Writings of Marcel Duchamp: Marchand du sel – Salt Seller*, ed. Michel Sanouillet and Elmer M. Peterson (Thames and Hudson, London, 1975); Eliot, T. S., *Collected Poems 1909–1962* (Harcourt Inc., New York, 1970); Eliot, T. S., *Inventions of the March Hare*, ed. Christopher Ricks (Harcourt Inc., New York, 1996); Eliot, T. S., *Selected Essays* (Faber and Faber, London, 1958); Eliot, T. S., *The Letters of T. S. Eliot vol. 1 (1898–1922)*, ed. Valerie Eliot (Harcourt Inc., New York, 1988); Eliot, T. S., *The Wasteland: A Facsimile and Transcript of the Original Drafts including the Annotations of Ezra Pound*, ed. Valerie Eliot (Faber and Faber, London, 1971); Howe, Susan., "Thorow" from *Singularities* (Wesleyan University Press, Hanover, NH, 1990); Jakobson, Roman, "Subliminal Verbal Patterning in Poetry" from *Language and Literature*, ed. Krystyna Pomorska and Stephen Rudy (Harvard University Press, Cambridge, MA, 1987, copyright the Jakobson Trust);

Acknowledgments

Khlebnikov, V. V., *Collected Works of Velimir Khlebnikov*, 3 vols., trans. Paul Schmid, ed. Charlotte Douglas (vol. 1) and Ronald Vroon (vols. 2–3), reprinted by permission of the publisher, Harvard University Press, Cambridge, MA, copyright © 1987, 1989, 1997 by the Dia Art Foundation; Khlebnikov, V. V., *Snake Train: Poetry and Prose*, ed and trans. Gary Kern (Ardis Publishing, Ann Arbor, MI, 1976); Khlebnikov, V. V., *Sobranie sochinenii (Collected Writings)* (Wilhelm Fink, Munich, 1968); Louis, Adrian C., "Petroglyphs of Serena" from *Anthology of Modern American Poetry*, ed. Cary Nelson (Oxford University Press, New York, 2000); McCaffery, Steve, *Seven Pages Missing, vol. 1: Selected Texts 1969–1999* (Coach House Books, Toronto, 2001); Mac Cormack, Karen, "French Tom" from *The Tongue Moves Talk* (Chax Press, Tucson, AZ, 1997); Perelman, Bob, "The Marginalization of Poetry" from *Selected Poems* (Wesleyan University Press, Hanover, NH, 1999); Pound, Ezra, *Personae: The Shorter Poems*, revd. edn., ed. Lea Baecheler and A. Walton Litz (New Directions, New York, 1990); Pound, Ezra, *The Cantos of Ezra Pound* (New Directions, New York, 1993); Robinson, E. R., reprinted with the permission of Scribner, a division of Simon and Schuster, Inc., from *Collected Poems of Edwin Arlington Robinson* (Macmillan, New York, 1937); Ruthven, K. K., *A Guide to Ezra Pound's Personnae 1926* (University of California Press, Berkeley, 1969); Schwartz, Delmore, "Tired and unhappy. You think of Houses" from *In Dreams Begin Responsibilities* (1938); Stein, Gertrude, "The Fifteenth of November," *New Criterion*, January 4, 1926; Stein, Gertrude, *Writings 1903–1932* (The Library of America, New York, 1998); Wershler-Henry, Darren, *the tapeworm foundry andor the dangerous prevalence of imagination*, copyright 2000 by Darren Wershler-Henry; reprinted by permission of House of Anansi Press; Zinko, Carolyne, "Toll Takers Don't Let Their Job Take Its Toll" © *San Francisco Chronicle*, May 31, 1999, reprinted with permission.

The publishers apologize for any errors or omissions in the above list and would be grateful to be notified of any corrections that should be incorporated in the next edition or reprint of this book.

Introduction

I would be happy to say that the two Steins [Gertrude and Wittgen-] are the Adam'n' Eve of Language poetry. Or De Man, Derrida, and Dylan; Ashbery, Cage, and Picasso; or Walter Abish and Apollinaire. Maybe it's all about Benjamin and Roussel. But really it's Husserl and Beckett, or maybe Jabès and Zukofsky; maybe whoever first inverted "No ideas but in things!" or invented the term L=A=N=G=U=A=G=E poetry. Connecting a whirl of historical dots into a certain shape is like overlaying a constellation on a bunch of stars in the heavens.

> Joshua Clover, "The Rose of the Name,"

This witty genealogy by a young American poet has it exactly right: Language poetry, together with its related "experimental" or "innovative" or "oppositional" or "alternative" poetries in the US and other Anglophone nations, has often been linked to the two Steins – Gertrude Stein and Wittgenstein (as I myself have argued in *Wittgenstein's Ladder*) – to Guillaume Apollinaire and William Carlos Williams, the Objectivists and New York poets, Samuel Beckett, the Frankfurt School, and French poststructuralist theory. But further: it is interesting that Clover pays no lip-service to the tired dichotomy that has governed our discussion of twentieth-century poetics for much too long: that between *modernism* and *post-*

modernism. Indeed, at the beginning of the twenty-first century, the latter term seems to have largely lost its momentum. How long, after all, can a discourse – in this case, poetry – continue to be considered *post-*, with its implications of belatedness, diminution, and entropy?

In this respect, we are now a long way from 1960, when Donald Allen published his ground-breaking anthology *The New American Poetry*. For Allen and his poets, especially the Charles Olson of "Projective Verse," modernism was finished. As James E. B. Breslin put it in his classic study *From Modern to Contemporary* (1984): "In the ten years following the Second World War, literary modernism like an aging evangelical religion, had rigidified into orthodoxy." The "end of the line," for Breslin, was represented by such "New Critical" poets as Karl Shapiro and Delmore Schwartz, Richard Wilbur and Hayden Carruth. Fortunately, so this narrative would have it, by the late 1950s the "hermetically sealed space of the autonomous symbolist poem" was giving way to the radical "new energies" of Black Mountain and San Francisco, the New York poets and the Beats – "The Postmoderns" as Allen called them in the title of his revised edition of *New American Poetry* (1982). With their "open-form," "authentic," process-oriented, improvisatory, colloquial, vernacular poetry, the New American Poets positioned themselves against the conservatism, formalism, and suspect politics of modernism, from Eliot (the American transplanted to Britain) and Auden (the Englishman transplanted to the US) to Randall Jarrell and the Robert Lowell of *Lord Weary's Castle* (1947).

Allen's anthology introduced the literary public to some of the most exciting poets coming of age in the late 1950s: Frank O'Hara and John Ashbery, Robert Creeley and Robert Duncan, Allen Ginsberg, Amiri Baraka (then LeRoy Jones) and Jack Spicer. Compared to the "closed verse" poets featured in the rival anthology, Donald Hall's *New Poets of England and America* (1957), the "New Americans" were indeed a breath of fresh air. But from the hindsight of the twenty-first century, their fabled "opening of the field" was less revolution than restoration: a carrying-on, in somewhat diluted form, of the avant-garde project that had been at the very heart of early modernism. Indeed, what strikes us when we reread the poetries of the early twentieth century is that the real fate of first-stage modernism was one of deferral, its radical and utopian aspirations being cut off by the catastrophe, first of the Great War, and then of the series of crises produced by the two great totalitarianisms that dominated the first half of the century and culminated in World War II and the subsequent Cold War.

We often forget just how short-lived the avant-garde phase of modernism really was. In textbooks and university courses, as in museum classifications and architectural surveys, "modernism" is a catch-all term that refers to the literature and art produced up to the war years of the 1940s. The Reina Sophia in Madrid, for example, is the national Museum of Modern Art but its collection, largely from the Fascist 1930s, has little in common with avant-garde attempts to transform the very nature of the art work. On the contrary, such self-declared avant-gardists as Robert Delaunay or Futurists as Giacomo Balla and Carlo Carrà are here represented as conventional realists, producing landscapes, still lifes, and cautious portraits in muted colors. The same phenomenon occurs, of course, in the former Soviet Union, but it also occurs, if less dramatically, in American poetry. A poet like Delmore Schwartz, I shall suggest in my final chapter, may have thought of himself as the heir of Eliot, but between the initiatory force of Eliot's "awful daring of a moment's surrender" and Schwartz's "Eliotic" style, something pivotal has given way. Indeed between the two world wars (and well beyond the second one) it almost seems as if poems and art works made a conscious effort to repress the technological and formal inventions of modernism at its origins.

Now that the long twentieth century is finally behind us, perhaps we can begin to see this embryonic phase with new eyes. Far from being irrelevant and obsolete, the aesthetic of early modernism has provided the seeds of the materialist poetic which is increasingly our own – a poetic that seems much more attuned to the ready-mades, the "delays" in glass and verbal enigmas of Marcel Duchamp, to the non-generic, non-representational texts of Gertrude Stein, and to the sound and visual poems, the poem-manifestos and artist's books of Velimir Khlebnikov than to the authenticity model – the "true voice of feeling" or "natural speech" paradigm – so dominant in the 1960s and 1970s.

Indeed, as I shall want to suggest in chapter 1, the "artifice of absorption" (Charles Bernstein's term) of language poetry has less in common with Allen Ginsberg's "First thought, best thought" paradigm or even with Frank O'Hara's brilliant and witty "Lucky Pierre" Personism, than with the early poetic experiments of that seemingly most august High Modernist, T. S. Eliot. For the Eliot of 1911, who composed "The Love Song of J. Alfred Prufrock" and "Portrait of a Lady," was probably the first poet writing in English who understood Flaubert's radical doctrine of the *mot juste* and the Mallarmean precept that poetry is "language charged with meaning" – a language as intense and multi-vocal as possible – a precept picked up some eighty years later by poets as diverse as the Harryette Mullen of *Muse and Drudge* and the Karen Mac Cormack of *Quirks and Quillets*.

Those who denigrate Language poetry and related avant-garde practices invariably claim that these are aberrations from the true lyric impulse as it has come down from the Romantics to such figures as the most recent Poet Laureates – Rita Dove, Robert Pinsky, and Stanley Kunitz. But laureate poetry – intimate, anecdotal, and broadly accessible as it must be in order to attract what is posited by its proponents as a potential reading audience – has evidently failed to kindle any real excitement on the part of the public and so decline-and-fall stories have set in with a vengeance. Great poets, we read again and again, are a thing of the past: a "posthumanist" era has no room for their elitist and difficult practices. Accordingly, the main reviewing media from the *Times Literary Supplement* to the *New York Times Book Review* now give "poetry" (of whatever stripe) extremely short shrift.

But what if, despite the predominance of a tepid and unambitious Establishment poetry, there were a powerful avant-garde that

4

takes up, once again, the experimentation of the early twentieth century? This is the subject of the present study. Designed as a manifesto, it makes some of the polemic claims we associate with that short form even as it suffers from its inevitable omissions. Because I am here interested in foundational poetic changes, I shall have little to say about many of the poets who have been most important to me and whom I have written about again and again over the years: Ezra Pound, William Carlos Williams, and Wallace Stevens, Guillaume Apollinaire and Blaise Cendrars, George Oppen and Lorine Niedecker, David Antin and John Cage, John Ashbery and Frank O'Hara. Again, because of space constraints, I have not discussed contemporary poets outside North America. Indeed, the inclusion in the last chapter of a mere handful of contemporary poets – Susan Howe, Charles Bernstein, Lyn Hejinian, and Steve McCaffery – provides no more than a prolegomenon to what I take to be the enormous strength of this second wave of modernism. From A to W – from Bruce Andrews and Rae Armantrout to Rosemarie Waldrop and Mac Wellman (with our Z poet, Louis Zukofsky, occupying a central link between the first wave and the second) – there are dozens of important poets in the US and many more in the UK, Ireland, and Australia, in Europe and Latin America, that belong here and that I have either written about or plan to. Here, however, my attention is devoted to four early modernists (or call them avant-gardists) whose specific inventions have changed the course of poetry as we now know it: Eliot, Stein, Duchamp, and Khlebnikov.

I do not want to imply that modernism, as here presented, is somehow normative, that it is superior to earlier – as to what will be later – poetic movements. Obviously – and study after study has argued the case – there is large-scale continuity between modernism and the Romantic tradition; many of the features I shall be discussing, for that matter, could just as easily be found in the poetry of George Herbert as in that of Eliot or Pound. But what interests me is the unfulfilled promise of the revolutionary poetic impulse in so much of what passes for poetry today – a poetry singularly unambitious in its attitude to the materiality of the text, to what Khlebnikov described as the recognition that "the roots of words are only phantoms behind which stand the strings of the alphabet." It is this particular legacy of early modernism that the new poetics has sought to recover.

"To imagine a language," said Wittgenstein, "is to imagine a form of life." This book studies such key poetic "imaginings" both at the beginning of the twentieth century and at the millennium, so as to discover how their respective "forms of life" both converge and cross.

1

Avant-Garde Eliot

This charm of vacant lots!
The helpless fields that lie.
Sinister, sterile and blind –
Entreat the eye and rack the mind,
Demand your pity.
With ashes and tins in piles,
Shattered bricks and tiles
And the débris of a city.
　　　　　T. S. Eliot, "Second Caprice
　　　　　in North Cambridge," 1909

Easing the thing
Into spurts of activity
Before the emptiness of late afternoon
Is a kind of will power
Blaring back its received vision
From a thousand tenement windows
Just before night
Its signal fading
　　　　　John Ashbery, "Tarpaulin"

In *The Poetics of Indeterminacy* (1981) I drew a sharp distinction
between Eliot's symbolist mode and the more "literalist" indeterminacy of John Ashbery. Twenty years later, in the context of recent

poetic developments, I would qualify my earlier reading by noting that the comparison was to the later Eliot, not to the poet, then largely unknown, made familiar by Christopher Ricks's superb edition of the hitherto unpublished poems written between 1909 and 1917. The Eliot of 1909 was still using rhymed stanzas, but the mood of "Second Caprice" certainly paves the way for "Tarpaulin," although Ashbery's referents are more oblique: witness his refusal to spell out what sort of "received vision" or "signal fading" the act of "easing" (lowering) the tarpaulin window canopy might produce. In both poems, at any rate, there is ambivalence to what Eliot calls, in the second stanza of "Caprice," the "unexpected charm" and "unexplained repose" of the blighted urban landscape, Ashbery's "thousand tenement windows" recalling, of course, the "thousand furnished rooms" of Eliot's second "Prelude."

"Tarpaulin" appeared in Ashbery's 1975 collection *Self-Portrait in a Convex Mirror.* What about more recent poets? Here is a set of statements of poetics that come out of the Language movement:

> There are no thoughts except through language. . . . The look of the natural [is] constructed, programmatic – artful . . . there is no natural look or sound to a poem. Every element is intended, chosen. That is what makes a thing a poem. . . . Fundamentally, construction is at the heart of writing. (Charles Bernstein 1986: 49)

> Nothing is given. Everything remains to be constructed. . . . As I begin working, far from having an "epiphany" to express, I have only a vague nucleus of energy running to words. As soon as I start *listening* to the words they reveal their own vectors and affinities, pull the poem into their own field of force, often in unforeseen directions. (Rosmarie Waldrop 1996: 74)

> Unlike most political poetry of the last twenty years, Language writing bases its analysis of authority not on the author's particular politics but in the verbal means by which any statement

claims its status as truth. Moreover, by foregrounding the abstract features of the speech act rather than the authenticity of its expressive moment, the poet acknowledges the contingency of utterances in social interchange. (Michael Davidson 1995: 70)

By emphasizing its writtenness, its literariness, the poem calls attention to the complexity of its constructedness. (Lyn Hejinian 2000: 329)

The key concept for each of these poets is that of *constructivism* – an understanding of poetry in its classical Greek meaning as *poiesis* or *making*, with the specific understanding that language, far from being a *vehicle* or conduit for thoughts and feelings outside and prior to it, is itself the site of meaning-making. When, for example, Bernstein declares that "There are no thoughts except through language," he is echoing Wittgenstein's famous aphorism in the *Tractatus* (5.62): "*The limits of my language* . . . mean the limits of my world," or again, his admonition in *Zettel* (160): "Do not forget that a poem, even though it is composed in the language of information, is not used in the language-game of giving information." But the emphasis on language construction also recalls the following dicta:

It is not the "greatness," the intensity, of the emotions, the components, but the intensity of the artistic process, the pressure, so to speak, under which the fusion takes place, that counts . . . the difference between art and the event is always absolute.

Or again:

The point of view which I am struggling to attack is perhaps related to the metaphysical theory of the substantial unity of the soul: for my meaning is, that the poet has, not a "personality" to express, but a particular medium, which is only a medium.

Or this one:

> When a poet's mind is perfectly equipped for its work, it is constantly amalgamating disparate experience; the ordinary man's experience is chaotic, irregular, fragmentary. The latter falls in love, or reads Spinoza, and these two experiences have nothing to do with each other, or with the noise of the typewriter or the smell of cooking; in the mind of the poet these experiences are always forming new wholes.

These citations will be readily recognized as drawn from the critical writings of Eliot: the first two (SE: 19–20) come from "Tradition and the Individual Talent" (1919), the third (ibid.: 287) from "The Metaphysical Poets" (1921). The new poetics of suspicion would no doubt balk at the notion of "forming new wholes," but otherwise there is nothing Eliot says here that is at odds with the statements cited above by Bernstein and Davidson, Waldrop and Hejinian. For them, as for Eliot, art is inherently a form of *transformation*, which means that, in his words, *the difference between art and the event is always absolute.* Indeed, what Steve McCaffery has called a "concern with the incidentality of the signifier rather than the transcendality of the referent" (McCaffery 1986: 19) has less affinity with the expressivist paradigm of the 1960s – a model still dominant today – than with the poetics of Eliot or Pound or James Joyce. Like the poems of Waldrop and Hejinian, Davidson and Bernstein, whose critical statements are cited above, such McCaffery poems as "Teachable Texts" and "Critique of Cynical Poesis" (both of them in *The Cheat of Words*) are surely closer to *Finnegans Wake* than to Elizabeth Bishop's "Crusoe in England" or even Allen Ginsberg's "Sun Flower Sutra."

Any consideration of the deferral of modernism, which has produced this curious poetic lag (*Lag* happens to be one of McCaffery's most interesting long poems), will have to come to terms with the still-vexed case of T. S. Eliot, the American avant-gardist of 1910–11, who had, by the late 1920s, transformed himself into the self-proclaimed "classical," Anglo-Catholic, Royalist poet and the conservative critic and editor of the *Criterion* we know from the textbooks. It is this "figure" that Cynthia Ozick (1989), in a well-known essay for the *New Yorker*, declared to be a dead duck – a poet nearly forgotten and, in her eyes, deservedly so. "It may be embarrassing," Ozick wrote, "for us now to look back at [the] nearly universal obeisance to an autocratic, inhibited, depressed, rather narrow-minded, and considerably bigoted fake Englishman. . . . In his person, if not in his poetry, Eliot was, after all, false coinage" (ibid.: 121). And Ozick concludes:

> Whether postmodernism is genuinely a successor or merely an updated variant of modernism remains unresolved. Yet whichever it turns out to be, *we do know for certain that we no longer live in the literary shadow of T. S. Eliot.* . . . High art is dead. The passion for inheritance is dead. Tradition is equated with obscurantism. The wall that divided serious high culture from the popular arts is breached. . . . The newest generation in the line of descent from Williams, though hardly aware of its own ancestry, follows Williams in repudiating Eliot. . . . As Eliot in his time spurned Milton's exalted epic line as too sublime for his need, so now Eliot's elegiac fragments appear too arcane, too aristocratic, and too difficult for contemporary ambition. (Ibid.: 152, 154; my emphasis)

I recall reading these words when they first appeared and finding them harsh but not entirely inaccurate. Who, in those post-1960s liberationist times, could readily admire an overtly anti-Semitic, politically reactionary poet, who seemed to be obsessed with original sin, feared his own sexuality, and displayed an obvious contempt for women? "Lord! spare us from any more Fisher Kings!" quipped Frank O'Hara (1977: 163); indeed, for O'Hara's generation Eliot was a sort of joke – the prim and proper Englishman with bowler hat and umbrella, who referred to himself in "Ash Wednesday," written when he was just over forty, as "the agèd eagle," no longer willing to "stretch its wings." And – yes – in 1989, "advanced" American poetry did seem to be firmly in the Williams camp: Williams, after all, was democratic, colloquial, populist, his short "verbal snap-shots" accessible, unassertive, anti-closural, and, in the words of Blaise Cendrars (1919: 146), "wide open onto the boulevards." As for Eliot, even Donald Davie, hardly an admirer of the poet known in Britain as Carlos Williams, declared that Eliot had had no lasting influence on English poetry, which was, Davie claimed, written under the sign of Thomas Hardy (Davie 1972: 3). Davie thus joined forces with his otherwise antithetical critic Harold Bloom, who had gone on record in 1970 to say that "Eliot and Pound might prove to be the Cowley and Cleveland of this age" (Bloom 1970: v–vi). In *The Poetics of Indeterminacy*, as I noted above, I myself subordinated Eliot's *Symboliste* modernism to what I called, citing a John Ashbery title, "the Other Tradition" (Perloff 1999b: 11–19). And in his important reap-praisal called *Modernisms*, Peter Nicholls writes that in Eliot's early Laforguean poems, "allusion and pastiche work to create a curiously empty poetic voice for which irony is a constant reminder of the self's instability" (Nicholls 1995: 181).

"When we think of the world's future, we always mean the des-tination it will reach if it keeps going in the direction we can see it going in now," wrote Wittgenstein on one of the note cards col-lected in *Culture and Value*; "it does not occur to us that its path is not a straight line but a curve, constantly changing direction" (Wittgenstein 1980: 3). In the same year (1989) that witnessed Cynthia Ozick's *New Yorker* essay – and of course it was the year the Berlin Wall came down and the Soviet empire ceased to be – Charles Bernstein published a manifesto called "Artifice of Absorp-tion" committed to the notion that indirection, resistance, and *difficulty* must be central to poetry. "The obvious problem," writes Bernstein, with reference to the "natural look" then dominant, "is that the poem said in any other way is not the poem." In this sense, poetry is nothing if not "artifice," demanding a language of "im-permeability," involving, in a purposely Gargantuan and ungram-matical catalogue:

12

exaggeration, attention scattering, distraction,
digression, interruptive, transgressive,
undecorous, anticonventional, unintegrated, fractured,
fragmented, fanciful, ornately stylized, rococo,
baroque, structural, mannered, fanciful, ironic,
iconic, schtick, camp, diffuse, decorative,
repellent, inchoate, programmatic, didactic,
theatrical, background muzak, amusing: skepticism,
doubt, noise, resistance.

(Bernstein 1992: 29–30)

"Artifice of Absorption" takes its exemplars of "resistance" from poets as varied as Gertrude Stein, Michel Leiris, Steve McCaffery, and Clark Coolidge. Eliot, unsurprisingly, is not in evidence. But it is interesting to note that Bernstein's discussion of the "anti-absorptive" is not unlike Eliot's famous account in "The Metaphysical Poets" (1919) of the way Donne and his circle "possessed a mechanism of sensibility which could devour any kind of experience," as well as Eliot's conclusion that "poets in our civilization, as it exists at present, must be *difficult*" (Eliot 1953: 287, 289). And by 1998, in a reevaluation of the career of Allen Ginsberg in the wake of that poet's recent death, Bernstein speculated on the negative impact a poet's public persona can have on audience reaction to that poet's actual work and surprised his audience with the following:

The twentieth-century poet [Ginsberg] ends up most resembling is not Bill Williams of Paterson but Tommy Eliot of St. Louis. Resembles but only in the sense of a reverse or polarized image; for Eliot became the poet as symbol of the closed, the repressed, the xenophobic, the authoritative, in short, of high culture in the worst sense, while Ginsberg became the symbol of the open, the uncloseted, the anti-authoritarian; indeed of low culture in the best sense. Ginsberg's move from ethnically particularized Jewishness (Al from Jersey) to small b buddhism . . . is correlative to Eliot's move from Christian-

13

American to High Church Anglican – both cases an assumption of a new religion as vehicle for universal identification that gets you high or anyway higher. Ginsberg, after all, is an anarchist in politics, a libertine in lifestyle, a buddhist [*sic*] in religion – the virtual inverse of Eliot's monarchist in politics, uptight in lifestyle, Anglican in religion. . . . [Ginsberg's] poetry was obscured by his public stature while that stature provided an important, and relatively rare, platform for an admirable form of liberationist politics. The dynamic is not unrelated to the case of Eliot, for insofar as he became a symbol of poetry as the antithesis of adolescence, the greatest achievements of his own poems were also obscured; indeed, this is the central obscurity of Eliot's poetry . . . after all "Prufrock" is also a great work of the adolescent sublime. . . .

So today I call [Ginsberg and Eliot] back from the nether world of cultural representatives to the practice, their practice, still largely obscured, of the writing and performance of poems. (Bernstein 2000: 271–2)

A surprising statement, this, from a poet who, according to the usual narrative of poetic filiation, should be indifferent, if not hostile, to Eliot. In what follows I want to take up Bernstein's challenge and look at Eliot, not as the cultural representative he has been all too long, but with regard to his actual *practice*, specifically his early practice of which "The Love Song of J. Alfred Prufrock," completed in the summer of 1911,[1] is the key exemplar.

Prufrock Among the Edwardians

In his later years, when asked about his formative influences, Eliot repeatedly insisted that there were no poets, British *or* American, who meant anything to the 22-year-old poet who wrote "Prufrock." For example:

14

Whatever may have been the literary scene in America between the beginning of the century and the year 1914, it remains in my mind a complete blank. I cannot remember the name of a single poet of that period whose work I read: it was only in 1915, after I came to England, that I heard the name of Robert Frost. Undergraduates at Harvard in my time read the English poets of the '90s who were dead: that was as near as we could get to any living tradition. Certainly I cannot remember any English poet then alive who contributed to my own education. Yeats was well known, of course, but to me, at least, Yeats did not appear, until after 1917, to be anything but a minor survivor of the '90s. (Eliot 1996: 388)

And again: "There was no poet, in either country, who could have been of use to a beginner in 1908. The only recourse was to poetry of another age and to poetry of another language" (ibid.).

That language was, of course, French, and the poetry in question was primarily that of Jules Laforgue, whose decisive influence on Eliot has been extensively discussed (see Knowles and Leonard 1991). Ronald Schuchard (1999) argues that, despite his protests to the contrary, the "deepest emotional affinity" of the young Eliot was with the English poets of the Yellow Nineties, especially Lionel Johnson, who paved the way for his reading of Baudelaire and Verlaine, Laforgue and Corbière (ibid.: 3–24, 70–101). "The primary importance of Laforgue to Eliot," writes Schuchard, "was the sudden discovery of his own poetic voice." "But," Schuchard cautions, "[Eliot] turned the ironic technique of deflating the emotional sentimentalism in the poem against Laforgue by further mocking the philosophical sentimentalism underlying Laforgue's lunar symbolism" (ibid.: 77). Indeed, on closer inspection, those would-be Laforguean ironies mask what is a sharp break, not only with the Rhymers' Club, but also with the delicately ironic self-deprecation of Laforgue and Corbière. "The kind of verse which began to be written about 1910," Eliot was to say, "made the same break with tradition that we find in that of Wordsworth and Coleridge" (Eliot 1996: 388). If this claim sounds excessive, we might remind ourselves of what that immediate tradition actually looked like.

In *The New Poetic* C. K. Stead performed a great service to students of literary history by tracking the actual poems popular in England in the decade 1900–10: chiefly "versified Imperialist sentiments, the public school spirit, or patriotic fervour" (Stead 1987: 49). One of the most admired figures was William Watson:

> You in high places; you that drive the steeds
> Of empire; you that say unto your hosts;
> 'Go thither', and they go; and from our coasts
> Bid sail the squadrons, and they sail, their deeds
> Shaking the world . . .
>
> (Ibid.: 52)

Another was the bestselling young Patrick MacGill, whose *Songs of the Dead End* (1912) features "poetry of the people" like the following:

> He is the drainer –
>   Out on the moorland bleak and grey,
> Using his spade in a primitive way, through
> Chilling evening and searing day. Call him a
> Fool and well you may –
>   He is the drainer.
>   (Stead 1987: 64)

The lowest point, according to Stead, was reached in 1909: "The 'aesthetic' movement of the nineties had long since collapsed with the trial of Wilde when, as F. M. Ford puts it, 'Poets died or fled to other climes, publishers also fled'" (ibid.: 53). In April 1909 Swinburne died and in May, George Meredith. That left Yeats and Hardy, but the former wrote almost no poetry during the decade, while the latter, so Eliot told Pound in a letter, was a poet to whose "merits" he himself was utterly "blind" (Eliot 1996: 394–5).[2] Again, I don't think Eliot is merely being coy here: Hardy was a great poet, but no one, I think, would argue that a poem like "The Convergence of the Twain: Lines on the Loss of the Titanic" (1912), which opens with the tercet:

> In a solitude of the sea
> Deep from human vanity
> And the Pride of Life that planned her, stilly couches she . . .

represents a marked break with nineteenth-century poetic tradition.

The situation in the US, at least from the perspective of a rebellious young man in love with French literary culture, was not much better. In 1910–11, when "Prufrock," "Portrait of a Lady," and "Preludes" were written, mainstream American poetry looked like this:

> Buildings above the leafless trees
>   Loom high as castles in a dream,
> While one by one the lamps come out
>   To thread the twilight with a gleam.
>
> There is no sign of leaf or bud,
>   A hush is over everything –
> Silent as women wait for love,
>   The world is waiting for the spring.
>   (Sara Teasdale,
>   "Central Park at Dusk")

And the most distinguished American poet of 1910, Edward Arlington Robinson, couched his ironies in conventionalized language and flowing tetrameter rhyming stanzas, as in "For a Dead Lady':

> No more with overflowing light
> Shall fill the eyes that now are faded,
> Nor shall another's fringe with night
> Their woman-hidden world as they did.

17

> No more shall quiver down the days
> The flowing wonder of her ways,
> Whereof no language may requite
> The shifting and the many shaded.

Here the poet typically uses Pre-Raphaelite locutions ("overflowing light," "eyes that now are faded," "quiver down the days," "flowing wonder of her ways"), as well as the inversions ("No more shall"), and archaisms ("Whereof"). So pervasive were these poetic norms that even the young Ezra Pound, writing in 1910, was producing dramatic monologues like "Paracelsus in Excelcis':

> 'Being no longer human why should I
> Pretend humanity or don the frail attire?
> Men have I known, and men, but never one
> Was grown so free an essence, or become
> So simply elements as what I am
> The mist goes from the mirror and I see!
> Behold! The world of forms is swept beneath –
> Turmoil grown visible beneath our peace,
> And we, that are grown formless, rise above –
> Fluids intangible that have been men,
> We seem as statues round whose high-risen base
> Some overflowing river is run mad,
> In us alone the element of calm!
>
> (Pound 1990: 30)

"*Personae*," quipped David Antin, "is a period piece full of *fin de siècle* language and poses, the work of an Anglicized schoolboy wearing Provençal, French, Roman and Chinese costumes and writing 'verse'" (Antin 1974: 9). Certainly "Paracelsus" is a far cry from the Imagist manifesto produced by Pound just a few years later, with its three famous principles: "Direct treatment of the thing, whether subjective or objective," "Use no word that does not contribute to the presentation," and "Compose in the sequence of the musical phrase,

18

not in sequence of a metronome" (Pound 1954: 3). "Paracelsus" is replete with vague and conventional phrasing, as in "don the frail attire" or "Turmoil grown visible beneath our peace"; the syntax is inverted ("Men have I known"; "never one / Was grown so free an essence"; "Fluids intangible"), and, as is the case in Robinson's "For a Dead Lady" and Teasdale's "Central Park at Dusk," imagery is largely conventional: the mist covering the mirror signifies blindness, and the speaker's inner calm is predictably opposed to the external turmoil of the "overflowing river."

Now let us try to imagine what it must have been like, in the poetic milieu discussed thus far, to read a poem that goes like this:

> Let us go then, you and I
> When the evening is spread out against the sky
> Like a patient etherized upon a table;
> Let us go, through certain half-deserted streets,
> The muttering retreats
> Of restless nights in one-night cheap hotels
> And sawdust restaurants with oyster-shells:
> Streets that follow like a tedious argument
> Of insidious intent
> To lead you to an overwhelming question . . .
> Oh, do not ask, 'What is it?'
> Let us go and make our visit.
>
> (Eliot CP: 3)

What would have struck a reader of 1911 about these lines? First and foremost, I would posit, their *sound*. For the pervasive rhymed stanzas, blank verse, or, on rare occasions, complex Provençal or Renaissance verse forms, as in Pound's "Sestina: Altaforte" of 1909, Eliot substituted a sound structure that, far from being some sort of container for the matter to be conveyed, actually produces that matter.

Lét ûs gó thên ‖ yóu ând Í

19

where the seven monosyllables, each one demanding some stress, and with a caesura after "thên," create a note of torpor, an inability to move, that is further accentuated by its pairing, via rhyme, with a second line, this time eleven syllables long and carrying at least six primary stresses –

> Whên the évenîng ís spreád oút agaínst the ský –

the line dragging along in a catatonic manner that extends into line 3, which is even longer (twelve syllables):

> Líke a pátient étherízed upón a táble

The speaker's frozen state is further emphasized by the awkward shift from falling to rising and back to falling rhythm in "etherized upon a table."

These delicate adjustments are not ones that Eliot could have derived from Laforgue, if for no other reason than that French prosody, dependent as it is on quantity rather than stress, cannot produce such marked shifts in intensity and pitch. We might also note the effect created by the internal rhyme of "th*en*" / "Wh*en*," and "ag*ainst*," and the eye rhyme "then" and "when" have with "ev*en*ing." For the Eliot of "Prufrock," *sound* is never just an accompaniment to something to say. In lines 4–5, for example, "The mútterîng retreáts" (six syllables) literally provides an echo, as in a dark passageway, to the preceding representation, in an eleven-syllable, six-stress line, of the "half-deserted streets" – an echo, incidentally, that is visual as well as aural, the fifth line being a short response to its rhyming partner. The *s*'s and *t*'s coalesce in what seems to be a whispered proposition coming from a doorway: *ssstt!* And now the poem shifts ground and moves into the iambic pentameter couplet:

> Of réstless níght*s* in óne-nîgh*t* cheáp hotéls
> And sáwdû*st* réstaûrán*ts* with óy*s*ter shélls

"The limit of language," wrote Wittgenstein, "is shown by its being impossible to describe the fact which corresponds to (is the translation of) a sentence, without simply repeating the sentence" (C & V: 5). Suppose, in Eliot's couplet, the word "restless" were replaced by "troubled" or "anxious." The loss of the *st* sound, the chiastic chiming of the *le* with the *el* of "hotels" and "shells," of the sound echo of the first syllable of "*rest*less" in "saw*dust*" and "*oys*ter" and especially the loss of the morphemic link between "*rest*less" and "*rest*aurants," would do much to undercut the poem's spell. Then, too, the repetition of the word "night" works both phonemically and semantically. We can hear the echo of footsteps making their way down the "half-deserted streets." And that echo is heightened by the insistent repetition. If the phrasing were, say, "Of restless nights in crummy flophouses," the aural excitement of the passage would be largely undercut.

The lines, in any case, are followed by another, quite uneven couplet:

> Streéts that fóllow lîke a tédious árgumênt
> Of insídious intént

where the first twelve-syllable line is almost syncopated by containing only four strong stresses that produce a heavy falling rhythm, whereas the echo in the second short seven-syllable line has only two. Syntactically, the couplet creates suspension, for "streets" is grammatically in apposition to the "streets" of line 4 rather than the nouns that immediately precede it. Again the *s*'s and *t*'s coalesce to produce an unpleasant hiss – a hiss that paves the way for the non-rhyming and non-chiming line "To lead you to an overwhelming question . . . ," where the "question" is drawn out by the extra syllable in an otherwise iambic pentameter line and the three spaced dots. And then comes the incongruously jingling couplet,

> Oh, do not ask, 'What is it?'
> Let us go and make our visit.

21

A standard tetrameter couplet? Even here, it seems something is wrong, for the first line is a syllable short, thus demanding a stress, so to speak, on the question mark. The look of the stanza contributes to this impression: the juxtaposition of long and short lines creates a diagonal crossing, as in "streets"–"retreats"–"hotels" or "argument"–"intent"–"question." The diagonals, in turn, contradict what should be the circular movement from the first "Let us go" to the second.

Now consider the figural construction of the passage. We are so used to the famous metaphysical conceit in which the evening sky is seen as an etherized patient, that we tend to forget how strange these lines actually are. For to take an abstraction like "the evening" and have it be "spread out against the sky" gives the surreal sense that time can actually occupy space – a proto-Einsteinian notion – and also a notion that becomes a central motif in this poem in which time has such powerful agency. As for "etherized," it was Stephen Spender who noted that the adjective connotes not only anaesthetic (ether) but also "ethereal," a favorite adjective in Romantic and Pre-Raphaelite poetry. "The combination of the clinical and the romantic connotations," writes Spender, "suggests the state of suspended consciousness of the 'patient' and the head of the dreamer full of the night sky and stars" (Spender 1975: 41–2). The resonance of the line would thus be lost if it read, say, "Like a patient anaesthetized upon a table," or "numb upon a table."

Eliot's insistence on finding precisely the right word can be traced back to Flaubert's *mot juste*, whose role in literature both Eliot and Pound may well have first come across in Walter Pater's seminal essay on "Style" (1889), which ecstatically defines *le mot juste* as "the one word for the one thing, the one thought, amid the multitude of words, terms, that might just do: the problem of style was there! – the unique word, phrase, sentence, paragraph, essay or song" (Pater 1925: 29). Pound, as Richard Sieburth points out, construed the *mot juste* as an ethical rather than a merely aesthetic precept; for him, the "just word . . . was merely an aspect of that larger ethic of precise definition which Pound would later define politically as Confucian *chêng ming*" (Sieburth 1978: 102). The potential identity of word and thing, which is the basis of Pound's understanding of the ideogram, has been shown to be fallacious by poststructuralist theorists, as by Wittgenstein before them; an excellent critique of the Pound–Fenollosa doctrine of the ideogram has also been made by the Brazilian Concrete poet Haroldo de Campos in his book *Ideograma*. But for all practical purposes what matters here is that the language of "Prufrock" epitomizes, in Pound's words, "language charged with meaning to the utmost possible degree" (LE: 3). Consciously or not, Eliot recognized early in his career that the words and phrases making up a given poem must function relationally within the verbal construct. Thus *restless* points, in quasi-Oulipean form, not only to its referent outside the poem, but also to the *restaurants* of the next line.

Flaubert is apposite to "Prufrock" in another way. In a discussion of character in *L'Education sentimentale* Eliot comments:

> Frédéric Moreau . . . is constructed partly by negative defini-
> tion, built up by a great number of observations. We cannot
> isolate him from the environment in which we find him; it
> may be an environment which is or can be universalized:
> nevertheless it, and the figure in it, consist of very many
> observed particular facts, the actual world. Without the world
> the figure dissolves. (SE: 152)

This is, as Spender (1975: 36) notes, a perfect description of "Prufrock" itself. For, as has often been observed, Eliot's is the most curious of dramatic monologues. It is spoken by an identifiable "persona," as we used to call the dramatized subject, and yet its affect is hardly that of an aging man ("I grow old . . . I grow old"), and whenever the reader thinks she/he can attribute a statement to a prissy and prudish man of a certain age named J. Alfred Prufrock, a passage intervenes that sounds like the voice of the poet himself, a poet who was 23 in 1911. For example:

Shall I say, I have gone at dusk through narrow streets
And watched the smoke that rises from the pipes
Of lonely men in shirt-sleeves, leaning out of windows?
(CP: 5)

Charles Altieri has put the matter well in an essay on Eliot's "Symboliste subject": "There is far too much of the author in the character to sustain the distance, yet far too much of the fool in the character for the author to be content with the identification." Thus, "we find ourselves entering a sensibility so fluid and evasive that it makes classical distance necessary, but at the same time renders it impotent" (Altieri 1989: 149). Here is the "negative definition, built up by a great number of observations" Eliot speaks of with regard to *L'Education sentimentale*. Prufrock cannot be separated from the poet who has invented him, nor from his environment, from those "Streets that follow like a tedious argument / Of insidious intent." The pronouns "you and I," in this scheme of things, are not just self and mask, id and ego, or whatever other binaries have been proposed over the years as central to the poem. For the poem's perspective, like the Cubist paintings Eliot later claimed not to like, is always unstable, repeatedly shifting, giving us multiple and conflicting views of the subject. Even without the epigraph from *Inferno* XXVII,[3] the mode of "Prufrock" is one of instability and dislocation – an instability as notable on the aural and visual as on the semantic level – and yet not, strictly speaking, free verse either. In Eliot's own words, "The ghost of some simple metre [in this case, iambic pentameter] lurks behind the arras in even the 'freest' verse; to advance menacingly as we doze, and withdraw as we rouse" (Eliot 1965: 187).

The syntax of "Prufrock," as we can see immediately from its opening, is as distinctive as its sound structure. For if "Prufrock" is not a psychologically coherent Browningesque monologue, neither is it a collage like *The Waste Land*, in which radical parataxis governs the structure. Nor again does the poem's language represent its speaker's "stream of consciousness," for that term, like its alternate

24

name "interior monologue," can only refer to the free associations made by someone specific – think of Joyce's Stephen Dedalus or Leopold Bloom – whereas Prufrock is no more than what Hugh Kenner called a "zone of consciousness'" (Kenner 1959: 40), and even this term doesn't quite convey the illogic whereby the neurotic questions "Shall I part my hair behind? Do I dare to eat a peach?" give way to the profoundly ironic insight of the final tercet, "We have lingered in the chambers of the sea / By sea-girls wreathed with sea-weed red and brown / Till human voices wake us, and we drown." The closural effect of this ending is marked, but since, in the poem itself, human voices never do "wake us," since the "chambers of the sea" point back metonymically to those rooms where "the women come and go" as well as to the "music from a farther room" that muffles the "voices dying with a dying fall," the act of "drowning" is curiously suspended.

The syntax of "Prufrock" is characterized by what Brian Reed, writing about Hart Crane's syntax, aptly calls "attenuated hypotaxis," that is a sequence of "tenuously interconnected" clauses and phrases "possessing some relation of subordination to another element," but with the connections blurred, "inhibit[ing] the formation of clear, neat, larger units" (Reed 2000: 387). Such *faux*-hypotaxis, Reed argues, was to become, in its more extreme forms, the characteristic mode of John Ashbery and Robert Creeley, Tom Raworth and Lyn Hejinian – none of whom, we might add, has claimed Eliot as a precursor. "The Love Song of J. Alfred Prufrock" thus emerges as a curious anomaly. Its complex perspectivism has more in common with Cubism and Surrealism than with the ironic, still essentially naturalist poetic mode of Hardy or Robinson that precedes it; then again, it has little in common with the more orderly sequential–associative mode of late modernist poets like Randall Jarrell or Elizabeth Bishop. What J. C. Mays aptly calls the poem's "counterpointed pronouns" – *I, you, we* – coupled with "the tendency of images, such as the fog, imaged as a cat, to balloon away from their referents and assume an uncontrollable life of their own" (Mays 1994: 111), the abrupt tense and mood shifts, the juxtapositions of ordinary speech rhythms with passages in foreign languages, and especially the foregrounding of sounds and silences (represented by the poem's visual layout), relate "Prufrock" to Constructivist notions of "laying bare the device," of using material form – in this case, language – as an active compositional agent, impelling the reader to participate in the process of construction.

Finally, there is Eliot's particular brand of urbanism, an awareness of proletarian life, derived, no doubt, at least in part from Baudelaire, but quite new on the Anglo–American scene. "Will I have to explain to young readers," George Oppen asked his daughter in a letter of 1962, "that the first shock of Eliot's 'damp souls of housemaids' and similar lines was not the rather perfunctory dismissal of housemaids as people, *but the fact that he saw them at all?*" (Oppen 1992: 58). The reference is to Eliot's "Morning at the Window" (CP: 19): what Oppen means is that the dismissal, at least on the part of his own left-wing circle, of Eliot's metaphor as a snobbish putdown of the lower classes, ignores the fact that the very act of writing about the "damp souls of housemaids / Sprouting despondently at area gates" was something of a revolution in his time and place. And since Oppen (b. 1908) would not have read "Prufrock" much before the later 1920s, think of how startling the metaphor must have been when the poem was fist published.

Oppen, in any case, reminds us that Eliot's precise but surreal urban images look ahead to the poetic cityscapes of Frank O'Hara and Ron Silliman, as well as to Oppen's own great poem of 1968, "Of Being Numerous." "Sawdust restaurants with oyster-shells," for example, is nothing if not graphic, and yet the reduction of the sexually charged oyster to mere shell is complicated by the paragram on "sawdust," "saw" raising issues of sight and rupture that permeate this poem where even a "smile" is figured as an act of *biting* the other. As is the case with Oppen's dislocated city-dweller, the Prufrock poet never stands *outside* the poetic discourse itself. Unlike the unnamed woman who, "settling a pillow by her head," insists "That is not what I meant at all. That is not it, at all" (CP: 6), Prufrock seems unable to assert anything or to generalize as to what he "means." The poet cannot, in other words, *interpret* the situations he portrays so graphically. "To come to self-consciousness," Altieri notes, "is to find oneself irreducibly in dialogue with one's projections of an other, equally part of one's subjective life, and equally destabilized" (Altieri 1994: 196). "Are these ideas right or wrong?" asks the young man in "Portrait of a Lady," having just noted "the smell of hyacinths across the garden / Recalling things that other people have desired" (CP: 11). And in this radically modernist lyric, the question, like its follow-up, "And should I have the right to smile?" is left hanging.

Eliot was to invent the term *objective correlative* to describe the poetic containment of the contradictory questions and vocal registers that come into play in a poem like "Prufrock." But in his early work these dialogic units remain in suspension in ways that mark a clear-cut break with the dominant poetics of Eliot's day. Indeed, when, in the spring of 1914, Conrad Aiken took "Prufrock" to a "poetry squash" in London, Harold Monro, the editor of the "advanced" journal *Poetry and Drama*, pronounced it "absolutely insane" (Gordon 1999: 68), and when "Prufrock" finally appeared in book form in 1917, the anonymous *Times Literary Supplement* reviewer declared: "Mr. Eliot's notion of poetry – he calls the "observations" poems – seems to be a purely analytic treatment . . . uninspired by any glimpse beyond them and untouched by any genuine rush of feeling. As, even on this basis, he remains frequently inarticulate, his 'poems' will hardly be read by many with enjoyment" (Dalton 1917: 73). Even Harriet Monroe, the editor of *Poetry* in the early war years, stalled for fifteen months before running "Prufrock" in 1915 – this despite Pound's constant badgering (Pound 1950: 40–1, 66–7).

Of course "Prufrock" was soon to become a celebrated modern poem, but the New Critical classic of the 1950s, when "Prufrock" was studied in college classrooms across the country, is not ours. What was once praised as a searing self-portrait of an over-refined young man, prudish, self-conscious, and impotent in the face of his hidden desires, is now more admired for its verbal than its psychological configurations, underscoring the faith of our own moment that, in Bernstein's words, "the poem said in any other way is not the poem," that " 'artifice' is the contradiction of 'realism,' with its insistence on presenting an unmediated (immediate) experience of facts, either of the 'external' world of nature or the 'internal' world of the mind" (Bernstein 1992: 16, 9), and that "the unre-flected reliance on the conceit of the sincerity of the personal voice of the poet" must be rejected (Bernstein 2000: 65). This recalls Eliot's famous pronouncement that "The poet has not a 'personal-ity' to express, but a particular medium, which is only a medium and not a personality, in which impressions and experiences combine in peculiar and unexpected ways."

But – and this is the conundrum that has so clouded the issue – how did the poet of "Prufrock" and "Tradition and the Individual Talent" become, in just a few short years, the conservative editor of the *Criterion*, and then the Elder Statesman of the Eliot legend? Here we must take up that still neglected issue: the role the Great War played (and didn't play) in the poet's consciousness.

"Looking into the Heart of Light, the Silence"

In October 1910, following his graduation from Harvard, Eliot went to Paris for the academic year. He planned to attend the Sorbonne and hear Henri Bergson's weekly philosophical lectures at the Collège de France. At his *pension*, 151 bis rue St. Jacques, he met a young medical student who wrote poetry named Jean Verdenal and they became close friends. By November, Eliot had written Part I of "Portrait of a Lady." The following April he paid his first short visit to London. In July he left for a holiday in Munich and north-ern Italy; here he completed the third "Prelude" and the final version of "Prufrock." By mid-September he had returned to America, planning to work for his Ph.D. in philosophy at Harvard (L: xx–xxi).

This chronology is familiar but its subtext has been largely ignored. The edition of Eliot's correspondence includes no more than seven letters from this period: four, with witty cartoons, from the poet to his nieces (Theodora Eliot Smith and Eleanor Hinkley), three in French from Jean Verdenal, and one from Alain-Fournier. It is thus difficult to describe Eliot's state of mind in this *annus mirabilis*, but nearly fifty years later he recalled, "I had at that time the idea of giving up English and trying to settle down and scrape along in Paris and gradually write French" (L: 15). And indeed it seems to have been an unusually happy time for the poet, despite his mother's misgivings. "I can not bear," she wrote a few months before his departure, "to think of you being alone in Paris, the very words give me a chill. English speaking countries seem so different from foreign. I do not admire the French nation, and have less confidence in individuals of that race than in English" (L: 13).

Eliot obviously felt otherwise about "that race." Here is a snatch from a letter written to Eleanor, then 20 years old, on his return from his first trip (two weeks) to London:

I just came back from London last night, and found a pile of letters waiting for me, with yours sitting on the top. I mounted to my room to read them; then my friend the *femme de chambre* burst in to see me. . . . She tells me I am getting fat. Also she had a store of news about everyone else in the house. Monsieur Dana has gone to the école Normale, where he has to rise every day at seven. This is a prime joke, and lasted for ten or twelve minutes. Monsieur Verdenal has taken his room, because it is bigger than M. Verdenal's room, and gives upon the garden. Had I been out into the garden to see how the trees *poussent*? So then I had to go into M. Verdenal's room to see how the garden did. Byplay at this point, because M. Verdenal was in the garden, and because I threw a lump of sugar at him. And a Monsieur *américain* named Ladd has taken M. Verdenal's room. He does not speak French very well yet.

He speaks as Monsieur spoke in November. (And I shortly heard Monsieur Ladd bawling through the hall "A-vous monté mes trunks à l'attique?" – I settle the affair by crying out "les malles au grenier!". (L: 17–18)

Even if we take into account that Eliot is trying to amuse his niece, this is a very exuberant letter, the poet comically imitating the chambermaid's speech patterns. In contrast to Prufrock, reproached for his thin arms and legs, Eliot is told he's getting fat. He has fun correcting the new American boarder. And most surprisingly, he playfully throws a lump of sugar at his friend Verdenal. One cannot quite imagine the poet of *The Waste Land* doing this.

Paris, he goes on to tell Eleanor,

has burst out, during my absence, into full spring; and it is such a revelation that I feel that I ought to make it one. At London, one pretended that it was spring . . . but one continued to hibernate among the bricks. And one looked through the windows, and the waiter brought in eggs and coffee, and the *Graphic* (which I conscientiously tried to read, to please them) . . . and all was very wintry and sedate. But here! – . . . (L: 18)

When the "prim but nice English lady at the *pension* asks him what famous sites he has visited, he tries to one-up her with the names of obscure churches and the Camberwell Work House. "She knew none of these. 'I have it on you!' I cried (for I know her well enough for that). But she does not understand the American dialect" (L: 19).

That last comment reminds us that Eliot was not, when he wrote "Prufrock," the self-conscious Englishman we know from various recordings, a poet who even speaks French with what he takes to be the proper accent. Indeed, at this stage he is hardly enthusiastic about anything English, Paris being the poetic center of his universe. And here the important relationship with Jean Verdenal comes in. There is no evidence that Verdenal and Eliot were lovers: Verdenal's letters make no allusion to any sexual relationship and Eliot's own letters were destroyed.[4] What is clear, however, is that the two were close and fond friends, that they shared an interest in music, theater, philosophy, poetry – and Paris street life. Both disliked positivism and materialism, searching for some kind of spiritual truth. "My dear friend," writes Verdenal in February 1912 to Eliot back at Harvard, "we are not very far, you and I from the point beyond which people lose that indefinable influence and emotive power over each other, which is reborn when they come together again. It is not only time which causes forgetfulness – distance (space) is an important factor" (L: 32). But the assumption is always that once distance is erased, their friendship will inevitably be what it was.

Between 1912 and 1914 Eliot was working on his philosophy degree and wrote almost no poetry.[5] In July 1914 he returned to Europe, but this time to Marburg to improve his German and read German philosophy; in the fall he was to take up residence at Merton College, Oxford, to continue his studies. On the Atlantic crossing Eliot wrote one of his witty letters to Eleanor, this time mimicking the speech patterns and foibles of his fellow travellers: "Well I never should have said you came from St. Louis. . . . When I look at the water, heven, it 'eaves my stomach 'orrible. . . . My but you do have *grand* thoughts! . . . why aren't you dancing?" (L: 39). The poet seems to be in high spirits: on July 19 he writes Conrad Aiken an amusing letter describing his new life in Marburg, enclosing caricatures of various Herr Professors and Marburg ladies, a few of his scatological Bolo poems, and a draft of "St. Sebastian." "I think," he remarks, "that this will be a very pleasant exile (L: 41)."

Eliot's "very pleasant exile" lasted no more than a few weeks: it was abruptly cut off by the outbreak of World War I. At first the poet accepted what his hosts and new friends evidently told him, declaring that Germany was "quite right" in its claim on Belgium (L: 52); he was soon to take the other side, but not without regretting his having to leave Marburg and move on, prematurely, to London. When, a month later in London, he made the acquaintance of Ezra Pound, he expressed his concern to Aiken: "Pound wants me to bring out a Vol. after the War. The devil of it is that I have done nothing good since J. A[lfred] P[rufrock] and writhe in impotence. . . . Sometimes I think – if I could only get back to Paris. But I know I never will for long. I must learn to talk English" (L: 58).

If I could only get back to Paris. The motif runs through the early letters, coupled with the sense of resignation that it won't happen. On the contrary, the war has created a new arena of "petty worries":

> In America we worry all the time. That, in fact, is I think the great use of suffering, if it's *tragic* suffering – it takes you away from yourself – and petty suffering does exactly the reverse, and kills your inspiration. *I think now that all my good stuff was done before I had begun to worry – three years ago.* (L: 58; my emphasis)

The candor of the young Eliot is remarkable. But what does he mean about "petty suffering" and having "begun to worry?" The sexual problem (Eliot admits to Aiken, around this time, that he is still a virgin!) is acute; it was never, of course, resolved in a satisfactory way, Eliot never seeming to have had a satisfying sexual relationship with a woman and, so far as we know, never daring to have one with a man. "Nervous sexual attacks," as Eliot refers to them (L: 75), are, in any case, exacerbated by the constraints of war and the guilt, later expressed in "Gerontion," of having fought, neither at the "hot gates" (a reference to Thermopylae) nor "in the warm rain." There follows one of Eliot's most brilliant jagged couplets, its accents, underscored by heavy alliteration and assonance, and concluding with the harsh fricative, dipthong and voiceless stop of "fought":

> Nor knée déep in the sált mársh, héaving a cútlass,
> Bítten by fliés, ‖ fóught

(CP: 29)

What has never been quite understood, I think, is to what degree the war transformed, not only the lives of the so-called "war poets," but those that stayed home as well. The war meant that Eliot did not go to the Continent for five years; more important, once submarine warfare posed problems for Atlantic crossings, Eliot couldn't travel to the US either. Thus, as in the case of other avant-gardists like Pound and Marinetti, Stravinsky and Kandinsky, the cosmopolitanism of the *avant guerre* gave way to an imposed nationalism, cutting off, literally in midstream, the revolutionary possibilities that the early century had seemed to offer (see Perloff 1986: 2–43). True, there was the Dada interregnum at the Cabaret Voltaire in Zurich. But this couldn't (and didn't) last, and in the postwar period "avant-garde" came to mean something rather different.

Eliot, in any case, spent the war years in a curious form of exile. "I don't think," Tom writes Eleanor from Oxford, a town he detested, "that I should ever feel at home in England, as I do for instance in France. Perhaps I admire the English more in some ways but find the French more congenial. I should always, I think, be aware of a certain sense of confinement in England, and repression; one puts up with it in one's native land, and is simply more conscious of it in a country in which one does not *have* to live" (L: 61). The poet's avant-garde writing is thus understood to stem from a time "before I had begun to worry" – his more carefree French time. And even after he moved to London, a city he found much more congenial than Oxford, he repeatedly refers to himself as "very foreign" (L: 65) – indeed, a *metic*, as he was to put it as late as 1919 in a letter to Mary Hutchinson (L: 318). The term *metic*, Jean-Michel Rabaté notes in an important essay on Eliot's "in-between" status, "designates not a total foreigner, but a stranger who is admitted to the city (originally Athens) because of his utility: he pays certain taxes . . . and is granted rights and franchises although rarely admitted fully into the communal mysteries" (Rabaté 1994: 212).

This describes Eliot perfectly. In the Paris of 1910 – or, for that matter, the Marburg of 1914 – he had not expected to be "admitted to the city," and could hence enjoy it as a student of a challenging alien culture; but the forced exile of war – a war at once meaningless and one in which he couldn't himself participate, not being an English citizen – was quite different. "The War suffocates me," he writes Aiken, again from Oxford in February 1915, "and I do not think that I should ever come to like England – a people which is satisfied with such disgusting food is *not* civilized" (L: 88). Just three months later, on May 2, Jean Verdenal, sent with his infantry regiment to the Dardanelles as a medical orderly, was killed while attending a wounded soldier on the battlefield (see L: 20).

Eliot's first book, *Prufrock and Other Observations* (1917), has the dedication "To Jean Verdenal 1889–1915." Eliot later enlarged this epigraph as follows:

FOR
JEAN VERDENAL
1889–1915
MORT AUX DARDANELLES

... LA QUANTITATE
COMPRENDER DEL AMOR C'A TE MI SCALDA
QUANDO DISMENTO NOSTRA VANITATE
TRATTANDO L'OMBRE COME COSA SALDA.

These words are spoken by Statius at the climax of *Purgatorio* XXI, when Dante reveals to the Roman poet that the figure he is addressing is none other than his beloved Virgil and that Virgil too is dead: "[Now you may] comprehend the measure of the love that burns in me for you, when I forget our vanity and treat a shade as a solid thing."[6]

For a poet as reserved, oblique, and self-protective as was the poet of *The Waste Land*, this is a remarkable declaration of love. No doubt, Eliot could not talk about the extent of his pain to his relatives or even his friends. A month later, in any case, he married Vivienne

Haigh-Wood, whom he had met at a dance a few months earlier, with the disastrous consequences that are well known. "Everyone's individual lives are so swallowed up in the one great tragedy," Eliot writes his father in 1917 (after the US entered the war and after he had tried −and failed − to enlist), "that one almost ceases to have personal experiences or emotions, and such as one has seem so unimportant!" (L: 214).

The distancing use of "one" here is revealing, as is Eliot's increasing use, even in letters to good friends like Richard Aldington and Wyndham Lewis, of the signature TSE rather than "Tom." Publication, never uppermost in the mind of the prewar poet, who let "Prufrock" and "Portrait of a Lady" languish in his drawer for years, now becomes paramount. "You see," he writes to John Quinn, "I settled over here in the face of strong family opposition, on the claim that I found the environment more favourable to the production of literature. This book [the forthcoming *Poems 1920*] is all I have to show for my claim" (L: 266). This "show," it turns out, couldn't be made because a week after Eliot wrote Quinn, his father, who had never forgiven him, was dead.

Now we begin to notice a gradual but decisive change in Eliot's outlook. By 1921 the poet who felt he had to get back to France if he were to be a real poet, who mourned "Jean Verdenal, mort aux Dardanelles" with the words of Dante's Statius, is writing to Wyndham Lewis: "Now as to Paris. I can't feel that there is a great deal of hope in your going there permanently. Painting being so much more important in Paris, there are a great many more clever second-rate men there . . . to distinguish oneself from. Then you know what ruthless and indefatigable sharpers Frenchmen are" (L: 446).

"Gerontion" (1920) and *The Waste Land* (1922) testify to Eliot's turn away from a Paris that was the proud capital of the avant-garde, with the concomitant move, conscious or otherwise, toward suppressing his status as *metic*, as the foreigner of the *avant guerre*, who could never feel quite at home in London. If the Prufrock poet longs to make contact with "lonely men in shirt-sleeves, leaning out of windows," if he admits to having "lingered in the chambers of the sea / By sea-girls wreathed with seaweed red and brown," Gerontion has thoroughly internalized sexual references, the threat now coming overtly from those Others who don't "belong," beginning with the Jew who "squats on the window sill, the owner / Spawned in some estaminet of Antwerp." In this poem, "Christ the tiger" comes "In depraved May, dogwood and chestnut, flowering judas" to be treated to a kind of Black Mass:

> To be eaten, to be divided, to be drunk
> Among whispers; by Mr. Silvero
> With caressing hands, at Limoges
> Who walked all night in the next room;
> By Hakagawa bowing among the Titians;
> By Madame de Tornquist, in the dark room
> Shifting the candles; Fräulein von Kulp
> Who turned in the hall, one hand on the door.
>
> (CP: 29–30)

This passage is justly celebrated for its mysterious resonance: who are these sinister art collectors with their mongrelized names (Portuguese? Japanese? German?), their "caressing hands" and secret movements? For the quasi-Cubist perspective of "Prufrock" Eliot has now substituted a Gothic *frisson*: the precision here is no longer the paragrammatic language of "sawdust restaurants with oyster shells," but a nightmare vision in which those undesirable Others with composite names like De Bailhache, Fresca, and Mrs. Cammel (the double *m* pointing to suspicious Jewish origin) are "whirled / Beyond the circuit of the shuddering Bear / in fractured atoms." The poet, now standing outside this "circuit" as benumbed observer, can do no more than witness their destruction.

Originally intended to be a prologue to *The Waste Land* (see L: 504–5), "Gerontion" is Eliot's first exercise with Jacobean blank verse, although the iambic pentameter is only the base rhythm (as in "Excíte the mémbrane, whén the sénse has coóled") and there is brilliant variation throughout, as in the fifteen-syllable broken line, "The tíger spríngs in the néw yeár. ‖ Ús he devoúrs. ‖ Thínk at lást." But as that "Us he devours" testifies, the curious directness of "Do I dare? Do I dare?" now gives way to a ritualized discourse: the Jacobean imitation, one might say, is almost too good. Then, too, "Gerontion" is visually more conservative than the early work, the blank verse, however varied, forming, in places, a neat verse column.

"Gerontion," with its stark meditation on the "great refusal" of the Word ("After such knowledge, what forgiveness?") and the resultant inability to escape the "cunning passages" and "contrived corridors" which is the labyrinth of history, is a great modernist poem but not a poem, I think, anyone has claimed for the avant-garde. For if, in 1911, "Prufrock" created a new poetic field, by 1920, after all, Gertrude Stein had already published *Tender Buttons* and composed such major portraits as "Marry Nettie," Blaise Cendrars had taken the implications of Prufrockian monologue to the extremes of *Le Panama ou les aventures de mes sept oncles*, Mina Loy had written her outrageous "Songs for Johannes," and Duchamp had produced his first readymades. In this context, Gerontion's emphasis on the need for *knowledge* marks an interesting departure from Eliot's early poetry. "Are these ideas right or wrong?" asks the poet of "Portrait of a Lady," unable to formulate an answer. Gerontion, by contrast, knows what's wrong, knows that "I that was near your heart was removed therefrom."

The addressee of these lines is evidently Christ – both as the infant Jesus ("The word within a word, unable to speak a word") and Christ the Tiger, the "sign" of whose "coming" Gerontion has rejected. But what is especially interesting here is that "you and I" are no longer interchangeable pronouns, that "you" is now *outside* the poet's own circle of fragments, the poem's technique thus looking ahead to Eliot's famous "mythic method" in *The Waste Land*, which, despite its distinct dramatis personae – Marie, Ezekiel, the Hyacinth Girl, Madame Sosostris, the society woman in "The Game of Chess," Tiresias – is by no means a "dialogic" poem in the

Bakhtinian sense, the narrator's final question, "Shall I at least set my lands in order?" moving him somewhere outside and above the fray those others are caught in, into the realm of the final refrain "Shantih. Shantih. Shantih." The appeal, however oblique, to an outside source of authority makes for more authorial control (the third item in the Sanskrit triad, "Da, Dayadhvam, Damyata," "Give, sympathize, control") than the fragmentation, parataxis, and collage structure of *The Waste Land* would suggest — a structure, that as the poem's consecutive drafts reveal (see Eliot 1971), is largely the product of Pound's severe cuts. The deference to traditional and external authority ("your heart would have responded / Gaily, when invited, beating obedient / To controlling hands"), in any case, goes against the iconoclasm we associate with an oppositional poetics.

There is a passage in *The Waste Land* that is highly revealing in this connection, namely the episode in the Hyacinth Garden, which is framed by the promise and then tragedy of the Tristan and Isolde story, as told by Wagner:

> You gave me hyacinths first a year ago;
> 'They called me the hyacinth girl.'
> — Yet when we came back, late, from the hyacinth garden,
> Your arms full, and your hair wet, I could not
> Speak, and my eyes failed, I was neither
> Living nor dead, and I knew nothing,
> Looking into the heart of light, the silence.
>
> (CP: 54)

Much ink has been expended in deciphering these lines, with their transformation of the slain fertility god Hyacinthus into the Hyacinth girl as bearer of the sexually charged spiked blossoms.[7] The moment described is one of being taken wholly out of oneself ("neither / Living nor dead"), most probably a moment after intense love-making ("your arms full and your hair wet"), beyond speech and clearly beyond the poet's usual corrosive irony.

In a 1934 issue of the *Criterion* Eliot reviewed a book about the prewar Paris of 1910–11. "I am willing to admit," he wrote, "that my own retrospect is touched by a sentimental sunset, the memory of a friend coming across the Luxembourg Gardens in the late afternoon, waving a branch of lilac, a friend who was later (so far as I could find out) to be mixed with the mud of Gallipoli" (see Miller 1990: 222). That friend was of course Jean Verdenal and although the hyacinth is here replaced by the Whitmanian lilac, it is hard not to read the Hyacinth Garden episode in the light of Eliot's "retrospect" as "The awful daring of a moment's surrender / Which an age of prudence can never retract." "By this, and this only," says the poet, "we have existed" (CP: 68).

I do not want to suggest anything as vulgar or simplistic as that Eliot's own avant-garde writing died in Gallipoli with Jean Verdenal; obviously, there are many other factors, including the daily trauma of the poet's marriage, his financial difficulties, his new literary affiliations, and his increasing alienation from the public sphere and the political life of Europe. I am merely suggesting that between Eliot's radical poetry of the *avant guerre* and its postwar reincarnation, a decisive change had taken place. *The Waste Land*, in this scheme of things, emerges as the brilliant culmination of the poetic revolution that began with "Prufrock" in 1911 rather than as itself a revolutionary breakthrough or rupture. Indeed, after *The Waste Land*, what we know as modernism was to lose its utopian edge and become much darker, its face no longer turned toward the "new" in the same way. And here Eliot's editorship of the *Criterion*, which began with the October 1922 issue in which *The Waste Land* itself was published,[8] is emblematic.

Volume 1, no. 1 (October 1922) opens with a curious throwback: George Saintsbury's essay called "Dullness," discussing such writers as Thomas Carlyle, who presumably avoided it. And *The Waste Land* itself is placed between T. Sturge Moore's essay "The Story of Tristram and Iseult in Modern Poetry," with its focus on Swinburne and Laurence Binyon, and a fairly conventional short story by May Sinclair called "The Victim," which concerns a chauffeur, haunted by a phantom, who finally married his sweetheart. More significant is the "foreign" material included. The issue features Dostoievsky's "Plan of a Novel" ("The Great Sinner"), translated by S. S. Koteliansky and Virginia Woolf – nice literary material but hardly news by this date. And the review essay on recent German poetry is written by Herman Hesse, who describes "Dadaism" as a literary group that "wants at least to have a little fun at the expense of the philistines and to laugh a while and to make merry before the ground collapses beneath them" (p. 90). The fatuousness of this statement cannot be redeemed by the genteel essay on *Ulysses* by Valery Larbaud, which argues – nicely but not very interestingly – that Leopold Bloom cannot simply be equated with his creator.

Ezra Pound makes his appearance in no. 2 with a feisty piece called "On Criticism in General, *Et qu'on me laisse tranquille.*" After the Napoleonic wars, Pound announces, "England fell back into the tenebrosities of the counterreformation, and has remained there ever since" (p. 143). But Pound, when included at all, as he is with the Malatesta Cantos in July 1923, seems to be there for friendship's sake rather than for any significant relationship with the other poets included or, for that matter, with Eliot himself.

The third issue (April 1923) introduces such emerging conservatives as Julien Benda and François Mauriac. The foreign periodicals reviewed are hardly the Dada or new Surrealist little magazines but the *Nouvelle Revue Française* (which was featuring the work of the future Fascist Drieu La Rochelle) and *Die Neue Rundschau*. Eliot himself contributes a eulogy for Sarah Bernhardt. The death of the great actress, mourns Eliot, represents the "decay of theatre, the chaos of the modern stage." "In the cinema," he notes, "which has perpetuated and exaggerated the most threadbare devices of stage expression, the failure is most apparent" (p. 306). So much for the art form generally held – for example, by Walter Benjamin – to constitute the new cutting edge.

Indeed, it is interesting to consider what is *not* included in the *Criterion's* first year of publication: no Dada, no Surrealism, no discussion of the visual arts, no Gertrude Stein or William Carlos Williams, no Picasso or Picabia. Indeed, 1922, the year of Joyce's *Ulysses*, Wittgenstein's *Tractatus*, and Duchamp's *Large Glass*, becomes the year (at best) of Paul Valéry and Virginia Woolf, and at worst of Stefan Zweig and Charles Whibley. The contrast to the earlier *Egoist* (1914–17), whose editor Dora Marsden deferred (at least at the beginning) to Pound, is telling. The *Egoist* contained the serialization of Joyce's *Portrait of the Artist* and Pound's own *Gaudier Brzeska*, poems by H. D., William Carlos Williams, and D. H. Lawrence, an essay by Remy de Gourmont on Lautréamont and another essay on Pratella and Futurist music. The very last issue of the *Egoist* (June 1917) contains Pound's spirited defense of Eliot, "Drunken Helots and Mr. Eliot" (pp. 72–5), as well as a portion of Eliot's own "Tradition and the Individual Talent."

Between the demise of the *Egoist* and the birth of the *Criterion*, five years passed. The new journal gives little hint that there had been, on both sides of the Channel and in Dada New York, a vibrant utopian avant-garde. In the context of the *Criterion* it is all too easy to overlook the revolutionary force of Eliot's early poetry, its uncompromising drive to break the vessels, to jumpstart and recharge poetic idiom. *Prufrock and Other Observations* (1917), declared Ezra Pound (LE: 422), "is the best thing in poetry since . . . (for the sake of peace I will leave that date to the imagination)." And indeed the imagination continues to be startled by the sheer inventiveness of the early poems, in which metonymy, pun, paragram, and the semantic possibilities of sound structure are exploited to create verbal artifacts, characterized by a curious mix of immediacy and complexity, of colloquial idiom and found text in the form of foreign borrowings. Not linearity or consistency of speaking voice or spatial realism, but a force-field of resonating words – this is the key to Eliot's early poetic. Thus the "sea-girls" of Prufrock's final tercet, are described as singing their siren song "in the chambers of the sea." Why "chambers," not caves or depths or coral reefs? Because the mermaids are no more than the fantasy version of those women "in the room," who "come and

41

go / Talking of Michelangelo." Such juxtapositions produce what is the poem's *aura*.

Some eighty years later, in his witty essay in criticism "The Marginalization of Poetry," written in mock-Popean couplets (with six words to a line), Bob Perelman notes:

> Strikingly original language
>
> is not the point; the degree
> to which a phrase or sentence
>
> fits into a multiplicity of contexts
> determines how influential it will be.
> (Perelman 1999: 140)

Not much of the poetry published in the *Criterion* could claim such multiplicity of contexts for its "phrases or sentences"; indeed, in Eliot's own later poetry, context would appreciably narrow. But "Prufrock" itself, with its mysterious "Arms . . . braceleted and white and bare / (But in the lamplight, downed with light brown hair)" looks ahead to the "language charged with meaning" of our own moment. I close with Karen Mac Cormack's 1997 poem intriguingly called "French Tom":

> it is often in the nineteenth despair export alone
> has been famine its youth said of
> the enormity
> including vivid to many
> in late blur and who came sad fleeing
> to be almost forgotten went where more is
> the fact found still
> close ties since unbroken arrival
> always established trading
> prominent but by formidable says among others
> even so in once kept ancient

in another ahead of advancing persuaded into neutral
here survives between neither owns

(Mac Cormack 1997: 45)

Here radical ellipsis takes the "Prufrock" mode to its extreme. But
the "nineteenth despair export alone," whose "enormity" is pro-
cessed only as a "late blur . . . to be almost forgotten," is one that
that other French Tom would have understood only too well.

2

Gertrude Stein's Differential Syntax

What is the difference between a thing seen and what do you mean.

Gertrude Stein, Mrs Reynolds

Successions of words are so agreeable.

A sentence means that there is a future.

Gertrude Stein, "Arthur a Grammar"

The first and only meeting between T. S. Eliot and Gertrude Stein took place on November 15, 1924 in her Paris salon at 27, rue de Fleurus. In the *Autobiography of Alice B. Toklas* Stein remembers it with some malice:

> Eliot and Gertrude Stein had a solemn conversation, mostly about split infinitives and other grammatical solecisms and why Gertrude Stein used them. Finally Lady Rothermere and Eliot rose to go and Eliot said that if he printed anything of Gertrude Stein's in the Criterion it would have to be her very latest thing. They left and Gertrude Stein . . . began to write a portrait of T. S. Eliot and called it the fifteenth of November, that being this day and so there could be no doubt but that it was her latest thing. It was all about wool is wool and silk is silk or wool is woollen and silk is silken. She sent it on to

T. S. Eliot and he accepted but naturally he did not print it.
(Stein 1998 I: 857)

This turns out to be untrue since, after much procrastination, "The
Fifteenth of November" did appear in the January 1926 issue of
the *Criterion* (pp. 71–5). "Fortunately," as Stein puts it delicately in
"The Fifteenth of November," "replacing takes the place of their
sending and fortunately as they are sending in this instance if three
are there and one has returned and one is gone and one is going
need there be overtaking." Eliot, she knew only too well, had no
use for her writing. He had, after all, politely declined to publish
her Cambridge lecture "Composition as Explanation" (1926), soon
dismissing it in print as the work of a person who is "going to make
trouble for us," indeed "one of the barbarians" (Eliot 1927: 595).
"Gertrude Stein was delighted," we read in the *Autobiography*, "when
later she was told that Eliot had said in Cambridge that the work
of Gertrude Stein was very fine but not for us" (Stein 1998 I: 858).

But not for us. For most of the century this view of the irrecon-
cilable difference between Eliot and Stein has prevailed. And yet it
may be more accurate to think of their poetics as two sides of the
same coin. I shall deal with those two sides in a moment, but first
it might be useful to examine that coin itself, which is the modernist aesthetic, shared by Eliot and Stein, even as it was shared by
Pound and Joyce, and the other central figures of the period.

First, consider the material conditions in which Eliot and Stein
produced their work. Both were exile poets – a situation that made
their awareness of their native American English all the more acute.
Like Eliot's "Prufrock," Stein's "Miss Furr and Miss Skeene," which
I shall discuss below, was written in Paris in 1911; indeed, Miss Ethel
Mars and Miss Maud Hunt Squire, the midwestern American ladies
who came to Paris to take up art work and who provided the
model for Stein's Helen Furr and Georgine Skeene, could well have
emerged from the very drawing rooms frequented by J. Alfred
Prufrock and Eliot's other leisured Bostonians. As in the case of
"Prufrock," the publication of "Miss Furr and Miss Skeene" was

delayed by the war – in Stein's case until 1922, when it appeared in *Geography and Plays*. As with Eliot, therefore, a form of avant-garde writing came to be associated with the 1920s even though it was conceived before the great rupture of the war years.

Second – and here Stein has often been misunderstood – both poets took the difference between "art" and "life" as axiomatic. In her late essay "What are Master-pieces" (1935), for example, Stein begins by distinguishing between talking and writing – a distinction that Derrida has made the cornerstone of poststructuralist theory, reversing the traditional order which gave "talking" priority. Stein herself gives neither talking nor writing pride of place, maintaining that each has its function. "I talk a lot I like to talk and I talk even more than that I may say I talk most of the time and I listen a fair amount too and as I have said the essence of being a genius is to be able to talk and listen to listen while talking and talk while listening" (Stein 1998 II: 355). Here is the preoccupation with "genius" that Bob Perelman (1994: 129–69) has discussed so interestingly, but note that her particular kind of "genius" – talking and listening at the same time – is qualified in the conclusion of the sentence: "this is very important very important indeed *talking has nothing to do with creation*" (Stein 1998 II: 355; my emphasis).

Why not? For one thing, as Stein puts it in *Everybody's Autobiography*, "everybody talks as the newspapers and movies and radios tell them to talk the spoken language is no longer interesting and so gradually the written language says something and says it differently than the spoken language" (Stein 1964: 13). More important, "talking" is related to "identity," "writing" to "creation" or art. "The thing one gradually comes to find out," we read in "Master-Pieces," "is that one has no identity that is when one is in the act of doing anything. Identity is recognition, you know who you are because you and others remember anything about yourself but essentially you are not that when you are doing anything" (Stein 1998 II: 355). And now comes the famous, "I am I because my little dog knows me," followed by an enigmatic and important disclaimer: "but, creatively speaking the little dog knowing that you are you and your recognizing that he knows, that is what destroys creation. That is what makes school" (ibid.). What Stein implies here is that self-consciousness – "your recognizing that he knows" – a strong awareness of oneself, of *identity*, is the enemy of artistic creation, which depends precisely upon an emptying-out of such selfhood. "At any moment when you are you you are you without the memory of yourself because if you remember yourself while you are you you are not for purposes of creating you" (ibid.: 356). This formulation, purposely childlike and "basic" as it is, recalls those famous sentences in "Tradition and the Individual Talent": "The progress of an artist is a continual self-sacrifice, a continual extinction of personality," and "Poetry is not a turning loose of emotion, but an escape from emotion; it is not the expression of personality, but an escape from personality" (Eliot 1953: 17, 21).

"That," says Stein, referring to her little dog's recognition of herself, "is what makes school." And she adds: "Picasso once remarked I do not care who it is that has or does influence me as long as it is not myself." Here one is reminded of the "Picasso" portrait of 1911, with its distinction between *working* and *following*: "One whom some were certainly following was one who was completely charming"; "One whom some were certainly following was one working" (Stein 1998 I: 282). The distinction between the "one" and those who are "following" (the "school") is made throughout "Picasso," even as Isadora Duncan, in the 1912 portrait "Orta, or One Dancing," is repeatedly called "one being one," or "one being the one," or "being that one the one she was being" (ibid.: 285–303). The distinction between the one and the many, between the one who is working and the ones who are following, is one Stein never repudiated. Followers, disseminators, those who belong to the "school," have identity, personality, something specific to say; Picasso, by contrast, is "one having something coming out of him."

"The difference between art and the event," as Eliot put it, "is always absolute" (Eliot 1953: 17). Stein and Eliot also agree that poetic composition is not a question of *what* but of *how*. "There is a great deal of nonsense talked," Stein declares in "Master-pieces," "about the subject of anything":

> After all there is always the same subject there are the things you see and there are human beings and animal beings and everybody you might say since the beginning of time knows practically commencing at the beginning and going to the end everything about these things . . . it is not this knowledge that makes master-pieces. Not at all not at all at all. (Stein 1998 II: 356)

Art, for Stein, has nothing to do with subject matter or psychology. How Hamlet reacts to his father's ghost, for instance, has nothing to do with the nature or value of *Hamlet* the play. "That would be something anyone in any village would know they could talk about it talk about it endlessly but that would not make a master-piece and that brings us once more back to the subject of identity" (ibid.). Indeed, identity, thriving as it does on memory and psychology, stands in the way of creation. The would-be artist becomes self-conscious, watching the impression she or he is making on others, and "that is the reason that oratory is practically never a master-piece very rarely and very rarely history" (ibid.). "It is very interesting," Stein adds, "that letter writing has the same difficulty, the letter writes what the other person is to hear and so entity does not exist there are two present instead of one and so once again creation breaks down." And Stein corrects her earlier formulation *vis-à-vis The Making of Americans* that "I wrote for myself and strangers." "If I did write for myself and strangers," she insists, "if I did I would not really be writing because already then identity would take the place of entity" (Stein 1998 II: 357).

A concern for *identity* is thus seen to be at odds with the very process of artistic creation. Although her own writings cannot be pigeonholed as belonging to this or that genre, Stein does maintain the modernist distinction between poetic and rhetoric, between aesthetic and instrumental value:

In writing about painting I said a picture exists for and in itself and the painter has to use objects landscapes and people as a way the only way that he is able to get the picture to exist. That is every one's trouble and particularly the trouble just now when every one who writes or paints has gotten to be abnormally conscious of the things he uses that is the events the people the objects and the landscapes. (Ibid.)

The demand for autonomy – what Stein calls *entity* – is here made forcibly; entity is defined as "a thing in itself [the Kantian *Ding-an-sich*] and not in relation" (ibid.: 358). "Identity is not what any one can have as a thing to be but as a thing to see" (ibid.: 363). Subject matter, the world outside the text or the picture frame, matters only with respect to what the artist *does with it*. "Nowadays everybody all day long knows what is happening and so what is happening is not really interesting, one knows it by radios cinemas newspapers biographies autobiographies until what is happening does not really thrill any one" (ibid.: 357).

The master-piece, the work that lasts, is, then, never characterized by its identity, by what it "remembers." "It is an end in itself and in that respect it is opposed to the business of living which is relation and necessity" (ibid.: 358). Here Stein is closer than she realized to the youthful aesthetic of her sometime rival James Joyce. "In order to see that basket," Stephen Dedalus explains to Lynch in the *Portrait of the Artist as a Young Man*, "your mind first of all separates the basket from the rest of the visible universe which is not the basket. . . . You apprehend it as *one* thing." Then, "you pass from point to point, led by its formal lines . . . you feel the rhythm of its structure. . . . Having first felt that it is *one* thing you feel now that it is a *thing*." And finally, "You see that it is that thing which it is and no other thing" (Joyce 1982: 230–1). It doesn't matter that Joyce refers to these three aspects of art as *integritas*, *consonantia*, and *quidditas* – terms that Stein would no doubt have found pretentious; the fact remains that, as we know from the Picasso portrait, "working" (as opposed to "living" or being "charming") produces that "something" which is art, a something perceived as "a solid thing, a charming thing, a lovely thing, a perplexing thing, a disconcerting thing, a simple thing, a clear thing, a complicated thing, an interesting thing, a disturbing thing, a repellant thing, a very pretty thing" (Stein 1998 I: 283).

"The artist, like the God of the creation," says Stephen Dedalus, "remains within or behind or beyond or above his handiwork, invisible, refined out of existence, indifferent, paring his fingernails" (Joyce 1982: 233). Despite the adolescent bravado of this famous formulation, it is not unlike Stein's distinction, cited above, between "a thing to see" and "a thing to be," between *identity* and *entity*. "If you write the way it has already been written," we read in the lecture "What is English Literature," "the way writing has already been written then you are serving mammon, because you are living by something some one has already been earning or has earned. If you write as you are to be writing then you are serving as a writer god because you are not earning anything" (Stein 1998 II: 223).

Art is by definition not earning anything, which is to say, *disinterested*. From Baudelaire and Mallarmé to Pound and Joyce, the rejection of instrumental value is a cornerstone of modernism. It has two corollaries that Stein also observes: the purity of medium and the insistence on Making It New. In *Everybody's Autobiography* Stein recounts her famous fight with Picasso on the occasion of his taking up poetry:

> When I first heard that he was writing poetry I had a funny feeling. It was Henry Kahnweiler the dealer who first told me about it. What kind of poetry is it I said, why just poetry he said you know poetry like everybody writes. Oh I said.
>
> Well as I say when I first heard he was writing I had a funny feeling one does you know. Things belong to you and writing belonged to me, there is no doubt about it writing belonged to me. (Stein 1964: 15)

Stein's sense of ownership and entitlement has often been lampooned: in the Larry Rivers/Frank O'Hara collaborative lithographs called *Stones*, for example, there is a cartoon version of Gertrude telling Pablo: "Poetry belongs to me and painting to you!" (see Perloff 1997: 102–3). But Stein's indignation that Picasso should think he could write poetry is based on the modernist faith in technique as something to be learned and worked at. "You know perfectly well the miracle never does happen the one that cannot do a thing does not do it but it always gives you a funny feeling" (Stein 1964: 15–16). When Stein went to Picasso's studio and he read her his poems in French and Spanish, "I drew a long breath and I said it is very interesting." And again, "I had a funny feeling the miracle had not come the poetry was not poetry it was well Thornton [Wilder] said like the school of Jean Cocteau" (ibid.: 18). This is indeed a put-down.

> You see I said continuing to Pablo you can't stand looking at Jean Cocteau's drawings, it does something to you, they are more offensive than drawings that are just bad drawings now that's the way it is with your poetry it is more offensive than just bad poetry . . . somebody who can really do something very well when he does something else which he cannot do and in which he cannot live it is particularly repellent. (Ibid.: 17)

Indeed, as Stein explained it to Picasso a few days later, "the egotism of a painter is an entirely different egotism than the egotism of a writer" (ibid.: 18).

Picasso, whose egotism was quite big enough to encompass both roles, was furious at Stein. He didn't speak to her for years. But Stein stood her ground: in *Everybody's Autobiography* she takes pains to explain the distinction between writing and painting. "The writer can include a great deal into that present thing and make it all present but the painter can only include what he sees and he has so to speak only one surface and that is a flat surface which he has to see and so whether he will or not he must see it that way" (ibid.: 34–5). This distinction may well have prompted Frank O'Hara to write his brilliant parody-poem "Why I am not a Painter" (1957).

Stein, in any case, made a similar distinction between painting and photography: "photography is different from painting, painting looks like something and photography does not. And Cézanne and Picasso have nothing to do with photography but Picabia has. Well." (Stein 1964: 58). As for Surrealism, with its drive to exceed its chosen medium, Stein was unimpressed. "The surréalistes," she remarks in *Alice B. Toklas*, "are the vulgarization of Picabia as Delaunay and his followers and the futurists were the vulgarization of Picasso" (Stein 1998 I: 865). In *Everybody's Autobiography* she is even more severe: André Breton, she declares, "admires anything to which he can sign his name and you know as well as I do that a hundred years hence nobody will remember his name you know that perfectly well" (Stein 1964: 36).

Such statements of dismissal seem to anticipate the purist aesthetic of a Clement Greenberg. But – and here the picture becomes complicated – despite her objection to Picasso's poetry, Cocteau's drawing, or Breton's manifestos and poem-paintings, Stein found congenial the work of the most radical avant-gardist of all, Marcel Duchamp. How and why this is the case is the subject of the next chapter; here let me just say that Duchamp, being neither a bona fide painter *nor* a self-designated poet, could be admired as a maker of the readymades, which were not so much intermedia as other-media and hence represented the ability – highly valued by modernism – to "Make It New!" Indeed, Pound's "No good poetry is ever written in a manner twenty years old" might have been Stein's own credo, as might Pound's dismissal of the nineteenth century as "a rather blurry, messy sort of a period, a rather sentimentalistic, mannerish sort of a period" (Pound 1993: 11), which is echoed in Stein's assertion, in "What is English Literature," that in nineteenth-century English literature "explaining" became predominant, "And with explaining went emotional sentimental feeling" (Stein 1998 II: 214). In the nineteenth century, she adds dismissively, "words no longer lived . . . phrases became the thing" (ibid.: 215).

One of Stein's key statements in this regard is cited by Thornton Wilder in his introduction to *Four in America*. Wilder recalls that when Stein lectured at the University of Chicago, a student asked her for an explanation of "A rose is a rose is a rose." She answered:

> Now listen! Can't you see that when the language was new –
> as it was with Chaucer and Homer – the poet could use the
> name of a thing and the thing was really there? He could say
> "O Moon," "O sea," "O love" and the moon and the sea and
> love were really there. . . . Now the poet has to work in the
> excitingness of pure being: he has to get back that intensity
> into language. I think that in that line the rose is red for the
> first time in English poetry for a hundred years.

And Wilder further recalls:

> Miss Stein once said: Every masterpiece came into the world
> with a measure of ugliness in it. That ugliness is the sign of
> the creator's struggle to say a new thing in a new way, for an
> artist can never repeat yesterday's success. And after every great
> creator there follows a second man who shows how it can be
> done easily. Picasso struggled and made this new thing and
> then Braque came along and showed how it could be done
> without pain. (Wilder 1947: vi–vii)

Stein's distinction between Picasso's "struggle" and Braque's "painless" recreation recalls Pound's distinction in "How to Read" between the "inventors" and the "diluters" – between the "discoverers of a particular process or of more than one mode and process" and those "who do more or less good work in the more or less good style of a period" (Pound LE: 23–4). Again, Stein's is a thoroughly modernist endorsement of genius theory, as is her contention that the "new" is so difficult to absorb that it is first perceived as "ugly," a notion that will be picked up, later in the century, in such texts as Charles Bernstein's "Artifice of Absorption." As for the literary "inventor" Stein looked to as a model, like Eliot and Pound, she repeatedly singled out Flaubert.

53

For Eliot, as I suggested in chapter 1, Flaubert is the progenitor of the *mot juste*, the inevitability and economy of poetic language as well as its necessary detachment from its creator. But Stein's take is somewhat different. In the "Transatlantic Interview 1946" she declares:

> Everything I have done has been influenced by Flaubert and Cézanne, and this gave me a new feeling about composition. Up to that time composition had consisted of a central idea, to which everything else was an accompaniment and separate but was not an end in itself, and Cézanne conceived the idea that in composition one thing was as important as another thing. Each part is as important as the whole. . . .
>
> After all, to me one human being is as important as another human being . . . the realism of the people who did realism before was a realism of trying to make people real. I was not interested in making the people real but in the essence or, as a painter would call it, value. . . . I got it largely from Cézanne. Flaubert was there as a theme. He, too, had a little of the feeling about this thing. (Hass 1976: 15–16)

The Cézanne reference sheds light on Stein's proto-Cubist compositions, in which the figure–ground contrast is dissolved and one thing is indeed as important as another thing (see Perloff 1999b: 67–108). But the Flaubert connection is harder to understand. Stein's Flaubert is not the purveyor of clear, visual images or resonating nouns; nor is it enough to read Stein's *Three Lives* as an update of Flaubert's *Trois Contes*. Rather, as Lyn Hejinian, whose poetry is perhaps the most "Steinian" of our own time, points out in a brilliant essay on *Three Lives* (Hejinian 2000: 82–8), Flaubert seems to have given Stein the license to stress *composition* rather than *representation*, the play of signifiers rather than the pointing relation of signifier to signified. "Nothing changes from generation to generation except the thing seen and that makes a composition" (Stein 1998 I: 520).

"What seems beautiful to me," Flaubert wrote in a famous letter to Louise Colet that Hejinian cites in her "Two Stein Talks," "what I should like to write, is a book about nothing, a book dependent on nothing external, which would be held together by the internal strength of its style . . . a book which would have practically no subject, or at least one in which the subject would be almost invisible, if that is possible." Again,

> The closer expression comes to thought, the *closer language comes to coinciding and merging with it*, the finer the result. . . . It is for this reason that there are no noble subjects or ignoble subjects; from the standpoint of pure Art one might almost establish the axiom that there is no such thing as subject – style in itself being an absolute manner of seeing things.

And a third statement that must have delighted Stein: "A good prose sentence should be like a good line of poetry – *unchangeable*, just as rhythmic, just as sonorous" (Flaubert 1980: 154, 166; my emphasis).

Not the word or noun phrase (the naming function) but, in Flaubert's words, "clear, sharp sentences, sentences which stand erect, erect while running" (ibid.: 160), becomes central. "Erect while running" because the "new sentence," as Ron Silliman (1987: 63–93) was to call it half a century later, allows for no distinction between something called "language" and something else called "thought" – only, in Flaubert's words, a "coinciding and merging." One begins, not with an idea to represent in words, words that are then arranged in sentences, but with those sentences themselves. "I really do not know that anything has ever been more exciting than diagramming sentences," Stein declares in "Poetry and Grammar" (Stein 1998 II: 314). Grammar, by this account, is never arbitrary: part of speech, tense, case, and especially syntax have their own connotative power. For Eliot's emphasis on *naming* ("Madame Sosostris, wicked clairvoyante"), on getting the noun phrase just right, as in "patient etherized upon a table" or "Unreal city," Stein substitutes *word order* – an order so expressive that there would be no need for most punctuation:

A question is a question, anybody can know that a question is a question and so why add to it the question mark when it is already there when the question is already there in the writing. Therefore I could never bring myself to use a question mark, I always found it positively revolting, and now very few do use it. Exclamation marks have the same difficulty and also quotation marks, they are unnecessary, they are ugly, they spoil the line of the writing or the printing. (Stein 1998 II: 317)

Only the period remains, for "as long as human beings continue to exist and have a vocabulary, sentences and paragraphs will be with us and therefore inevitably and really periods will be with us" (ibid.: 321–2).

The difference between Eliot and Stein can thus be understood as epistemological rather than aesthetic. Using the distinction drawn at the opening of the *Philosophical Investigations*, we might say that Eliot is an Augustinian, Stein a Wittgensteinian. Eliot – and this would also be true of Pound or Stevens – believes that words have a naming function, that they *mean* individually, whereas Stein believes that meaning is only conveyed by *use*, and hence by the larger context of the sentence. To see how this difference operates, we might begin with Stein's 1911 "story," "Miss Furr and Miss Skeene."

Regularly Gay There

"Sentences," we read in "Poetry and Grammar," "are not emotional but paragraphs are" (Stein 1998 II: 322). Whimsical as this statement sounds, it makes good sense: like a line in poetry (e.g., "Let us go then, you and I"), which is not fully meaningful until it is followed by another line and another, until it has become part of a stanza or verse paragraph or even a page, the sentence is only a building block in the larger unit which is the paragraph. As Ron Silliman was to put it, "linguistic units integrate only up to the level of the sentence, but higher orders of meaning – such as emotion – integrate at higher levels than the sentence" (Silliman 1987: 87).

Consider the opening paragraph of "Miss Furr and Miss Skeene":

Helen Furr had quite a pleasant home. Mrs. Furr was quite a pleasant woman. Mr. Furr was quite a pleasant man. Helen Furr had quite a pleasant voice, a voice quite worth cultivating. She did not mind working. She worked to cultivate her voice. She did not find it gay living in the same place where she had always been living. She went to a place where some were cultivating something, voices and other things needing cultivating. She met Georgine Skeene there who was cultivating her voice which some thought was quite a pleasant one. Helen Furr and Georgine Skeene lived together then. Georgine Skeene liked travelling. Helen Furr did not care about travelling, she liked to stay in one place and be gay there. They were together then and travelled to another place and stayed there and were gay there. (Stein 1998 I: 307)

Stein's use of repetition here, far from being excessive and boring as new readers of her work often assume, is characterized by its mathematical precision. A sentence is placed before us and then repeated with slight variation, each instance making us revise our sense of the one preceding it so that gradually meaning accrues. Thus, the seeming innocence of what sounds like a First-Grade Reader ("See Spot. See Spot run.") becomes something quite other. Consider what happens to the phrases *quite a pleasant* (used five times), *cultivating* (five), *voice* (five), *gay* (three), and *there* (four) against the background of the repetition of the comically synonymous, sexually charged names *Furr* and *Skeene* and the rhyme *Georgine Skeene*.

"Helen Furr had quite a pleasant home." It sounds neutral enough, "pleasant" being one of those noncommittal adjectives that vary according to their context and the intonation of the speaker's voice, especially when the adjective is qualified by "quite a." The shift from *having* to *being* in the next two sentences and the substitution "Mrs. Furr" and then "Mr. Furr" for Helen Furr, have a subtle effect. First, "quite a pleasant" suggests comfort and ordinary pleasures when applied to a "home," but by the third repetition it all begins to sound boringly bourgeois – a shade stifling for the Helen who is presumably Mr. and Mrs. Furr's daughter. However, so the fourth sentence suggests, Helen Furr may have something of her own: "quite a pleasant voice, a voice quite worth cultivating." The substitution of "voice" for "home" in what is otherwise a sentence whose main clause is identical to the first sentence, as well as the introduction of the new information contained in "a voice well worth cultivating," raises interesting expectations. Perhaps Helen Furr's "quite pleasant voice" is no more significant than the rest of the "pleasant" family apparatus. But "worth cultivating" suggests that something is about to change for Helen, although it's not clear what it means to "cultivate" a voice or what it is that makes a voice worth "cultivating."

The seventh sentence introduces the story's key word, "gay" (quite possibly used for the very first time in Stein's story in its contemporary sense of homosexual, but here only as an undertone).[1] It also introduces the word "living." We can now surmise that whatever "living" is like in the "quite a pleasant" Furr home, it is not sufficiently "gay" for Helen. And now comes the complex sentence, "She went to a place where some were cultivating something, voices and other things needing cultivating." The place is as unspecified as are the adjectives "pleasant" and "gay" and the participle "cultivating." And just what are those "other things needing cultivating"? We can read a variety of stories, sexual or merely social, into these curiously neutral words. By the end of the paragraph we only know that Helen Furr and Georgine Skeene were "together then" (when?) and "stayed there and were gay there" (where?), but that there is also an area of difference between them: "Georgine Skeene liked travelling. Helen Furr did not care about travelling, she liked to stay in one place and be gay there." Just as fur and skin are synonymous nouns that can also have very different meanings, so the two women are separated by their attitude toward "travel," a word that again can have numerous – and, for that matter, contradictory – implications.

Having set up her network of sentences in which "pleasant," "voice," "living," "cultivating," "travelling," and "gay' – those non-specific and wonderfully suggestive words – circulate, the rest of the narrative follows. Being "regularly gay every day" gradually begins to change, although the reader cannot specify where and when. For one thing, "cultivating" proceeds at a different pace, Georgine Skeene's voice being "some said, a better one" and "a quite richly enough cultivated one," whereas Helen Furr's "quite pleasant" voice is no more than a "pleasant enough" one. In any case, Georgine Skeene "would have liked to do more travelling," and does travel to "a place where her brother had quite some distinction." She goes there alone – a prefiguring of things to come – whereas the two women visit Helen Furr's "pleasant home" together. The first climax, if we can speak of climaxes in this verbal ballet, comes in Helen's reaction to one of these visits, rhyme producing meaning even more insistently than Eliot's refrain "In the room the women come and go / Talking of Michelangelo":

Certainly Helen Furr would not find it gay to stay, she did not find it gay, she said she would not stay, she said she did not find it gay, she said she would not stay, where she did not find it gay, she said she found it gay where she did stay and she did stay there where very many were cultivating something. She did stay there. She always did find it gay there. (Stein 1988 I: 308)

Notice the mathematical neatness of the permutative process. The opposition between "she would not stay where she did not find it gay" and "she found it gay where she did stay" provides us with what John Ashbery has called, in a discussion of *Stanzas in Meditation*, "a general, all purpose model which each reader can adapt to fit his own set of particulars" – not an account of what happened but "a way of happening" (Ashbery 1990: 109). Why did Helen Furr break with her "quite pleasant" parents? Because they disapproved of Georgine Skeene? Of her way of life? Or because she wanted to devote herself to her "voice"? Or had found her place in the sun where "some" were "cultivating" "other things needing cultivating"? Or none of the above?

This break, in any case, is now followed by the introduction of a new complicating motif: the factor of men. "There were some dark and heavy men there then. There were some who were not so heavy and some who were not so dark. Helen Furr and Georgine Skeene sat regularly with them" (Stein 1988 I: 309). What transpires between the two women and these men is never specified. "Dark and heavy" connotes masculinity – men who are really men – but then Helen Furr and Georgine Skeene also "went" (a wonderfully neutral word that has become part of our vocabulary like "seeing someone") with those who were "not so dark" and "not so heavy." Is Miss Furr and Miss Skeene's "gay" liaison now compromised by heterosexual relationships? Or what? How are their "voices" affected? We only know that Miss Furr and Miss Skeene "went with them, went somewhere with them, went with some of them."

And now "living" and "cultivating" give way to a new participle: learning. Learning "little things, gay little things," learning ways to be "gay every day," "using these little things they were learning to have to be gay." And "gay" becomes more and more obsessive an adjective, as "regular" begins to give way to a particular moment in time: "Georgine Skeene went away to stay two months with her brother. Helen Furr did not go then to stay with her father and her mother." The affair is evidently over; Helen Furr is now able to be "gay longer every day than when the two of them had been being gay" (ibid.: 310). And the final page defines what being "gay" without Georgine Skeene is like. Helen Furr's voice is now a "quite completely well enough cultivated one" and "she did not use it very often." She no longer needs her "voice" – at least not a "cultivated" voice – in order to be gay. "Very many were telling about using other ways in being gay." *Telling* is the new word here and we now find Helen "telling others how to be gay." The final sentence reads:

"She was living very well, she was gay then, she went on living then, she was regular in being gay, she always was living very well and was gay very well and was telling about little ways one could be learning to use in being gay, and later was telling them quite often, telling them again and again" (ibid.: 311–12).

Telling has thus replaced *pleasant, cultivating*, and *travelling*. But note that *voice*, originally, one assumes, a singing voice that needs "cultivating," remains central to the "telling," and that Helen Furr is now "regular in being gay." The story's ending is thus equivocal. Ulla Dydo sees it as dark: "Without a lover, without an echo [Helen Furr's] stories lose life, her manner rigidifies, and the voice that the two had so carefully cultivated speaks in shrill hysterical repetitions, alone" (Dydo 1993: 254). But one could just as well make the opposite case: now that Helen Furr has learned her way around, has become, so to speak, street-smart in the gay community in which she travels, she becomes the mentor, the teller of tales. No longer dependent upon her "pleasant enough" parents, she is now in the thick of the action, "living where many were cultivating something" and teaching "very many then little ways they could use in being gay" (Stein 1988 I: 312).

There is no way to decide between these two and other possible readings. All we can say for certain is that something has changed, that the coming together of Helen Furr and Georgine Skeene has transformed Helen's life. But the specifics remain elusive. As in a Zen koan, repetition produces enlightenment for the reader, but enlightenment is not equivalent to knowledge. What does it mean to travel? What happens when the ladies *sit* with "some" men who are "dark and heavy"? What, for that matter, does it mean to "sit" with someone?

For Eliot, Flaubert was the master of precision, of finding exactly the right word or phrase – the objective correlative – to embody a particular emotion or situation. Stein's Flaubert, by contrast, is the shaper of economical and carefully formed sentences. Eliot's words resonate with metaphoric and symbolic implication; Stein's are just ordinary words – pleasant, voice, working, travelling, gay, regularly, learning, telling, there, then – and they are used quite literally. But what is the literal meaning of "pleasant"? Of "regularly"? Of "telling"? We can give synonyms for "pleasant" such as "nice," "agreeable," or "likable," but finally the meaning of a sentence like "Helen Furr had quite a pleasant voice, a voice quite worth culti- vating" remains equivocal, its import changing even as we read the sentence that follows: "She did not mind working." "Miss Furr and Miss Skeene" is not so much *about* a love affair as it is about the paradigmatic process of union and dissolution. Not psychology (we never really know what either character is thinking), not ethical or political import (Stein neither takes sides nor does she use the lesbian affair to make a particular point); rather, in the words of Stein's later title "Sentences," of how a given situation changes. "A sentence expresses that they continue when they start that is the left and right and also the place is chosen" (Stein 1995: 145).

Like Eliot, then, Stein foregrounds the constructedness of the poetic text, but for her, constructedness is not a question of metaphor or symbol, allusion or citation, and certainly not of collage. Rather, her characteristic constructions depend on the placement of ordinary words in what are usually simple declarative sentences that combine in a tightly interlocking paragraph (and set of paragraphs) in which the verbal, visual, and aural are one, the conundrum being that whereas Eliot's poetry looks like poetry, Stein's often (as here) looks at first glance like ordinary prose.

But how ordinary is it? Consider again the passage quoted above:

> Certainly Helen Furr would not find it gay to stay, she did not find it gay, she said she would not stay, she said she did not find it gay, she said she would not stay, where she did not find it gay, she said she found it gay where she did stay and she did stay there where very many were cultivating something. She did stay there. She always did find it gay there.

This sounds like a chant or nursery rhyme: both aurally and visu- ally, the hallmark of the passage is its extreme artifice. The rhyming of the stressed monosyllables "gay" and "stay," "there" and "where," and the repetition of units of monosyllables, as in "she did not" and "she would not," puts into sharp relief the disyllabic and trisyllabic words not caught in the network of aural and visual chiming: in this case, "Certainly Helen Furr" and "cultivating something." Certainly Helen Furr wants to be of the party of cultivating something and the paragraph enacts her decision in what is, to use James Joyce's term, a *verbivocovisual* complex.

A Room of One's Own

Despite its systemic patterning and its large-scale indeterminacy, "Miss Furr and Miss Skeene" does not violate the continuity of "normal" narrative: first x, then y, then z. But within a year of producing this piece, Stein had moved on to the more radical mode of writing we find in *Tender Buttons* (published privately in 1914 by Donald Evans's Claire Marie Press). It was this mode that made Stein a favorite laughing stock. "The words in [*Tender Buttons*]," wrote an anonymous reviewer for the *Louisville Courier-Journal*, "are English words, but the sentences are not English sentences according to the grammatical definition. The sentences indicated by punctuation do not make complete sense, partial sense, nor any other sense, but nonsense" (White 1984: 9). It is a view still held by many critics: reviewing the Library of America two-volume *American Poetry: The Twentieth Century* (2000), for the *New York Times Book Review*, William H. Pritchard complains: "Stein thought her effusions in "Tender Buttons" were poems, but almost 15 pages of them didn't convince me" (Pritchard 2000: 10).

Tender Buttons was begun in pre-World War I Spain. Alice recalls its gestation as follows:

These were the days in which [Gertrude] wrote Susie Asado and Preciosilla and Gypsies in Spain. She experimented with everything in trying to describe. She tried a bit inventing

63

words but she soon gave that up. The english language was her medium and with the english language the task was to be achieved, the problem solved. The use of fabricated words offended her. It was an escape into imitative emotionalism.

No, she stayed with her task, although after the return to Paris she described objects, she described rooms and objects, which joined with her first experiments done in Spain, made the volume Tender Buttons. (Stein 1998 I: 782)

This is an important statement, distinguishing Stein's practice not only from the collage-making of Eliot and Pound, both of whom incorporated any number of foreign-language citations and allusions into their texts, but also from Duchamp's playful neologisms and Khlebnikov's etymological sound play – "fabricated words" if ever there were any, which I shall take up in subsequent chapters.

In postmodern poetics these modernist practices often intersect with the "ordinary language" paradigm of Stein. But it is important to remember that Stein herself was a language purist even as she was a purist *vis-à-vis* her chosen medium. "With the english language the task was to be achieved, the problem solved," and the English language in question was, as I have argued elsewhere (Perloff 1996b), ordinary language, especially the connectives George Oppen was to call, some fifty years later, the "little words I love so much" – articles, conjunctions, prepositions, pronouns (Power 1978). Whereas the noun or noun phrase was obviously central to Eliot:

> The winter evening settles down
> With smell of steaks in passageways.
> Six o'clock.
> The burnt-out ends of smoky days.
> (CP: 12)

and even more so to Pound:

> Palace in smoky light,
> Troy but a heap of smouldering boundary stones,

Anaxiforminges! Aurunculeia!
Hear me. Cadmus of Golden Prows!

(Pound 1993: 13)

Stein regularly dismissed the noun as the least interesting part of speech. In "Poetry and Grammar" we read: "A noun is a name of anything, why after a thing is named write about it. A name is adequate or it is not. . . . Nouns are the name of anything and just naming names is alright when you want to call a roll but is it any good for anything else (Stein 1998 II: 313–14). Adjectives are not much better: "Adjectives effect nouns and as nouns are not really interesting the thing that effects a not too interesting thing is of necessity not interesting" (ibid.: 314). Verbs and adverbs are better because "they can be mistaken": "verbs can change to look like themselves or to look like something else they are, so to speak, on the move and adverbs move with them." And "then comes the thing that can of all things be most mistaken and they are prepositions." "I like prepositions the best of all" (ibid.: 315). They, as well as articles and conjunctions, "have a greater possibility of being something" (ibid.: 316).

When, later in "Poetry and Grammar," Stein famously distinguishes "poetry" from "prose" by declaring that "Poetry is concerned with using with abusing, with losing with wanting, with denying, with avoiding with adoring with replacing the noun," whereas "prose is essentially and determinately and vigorously not based on the noun" (ibid.: 327), she is thinking, of course, of conventional poetry. To Make It New, one must, as she found out in writing *Tender Buttons*, make "a thing that could be named without using its name." "Was there not," she asks, "a way of naming things that would not invent names, but mean names without naming them" (ibid.: 330)? "And so in Tender Buttons and then on and on I struggled with the ridding myself of nouns" (ibid.: 334).

The "ridding myself of nouns" was central to a process that is still largely misunderstood. It is common to read, in current Stein criticism, that the title of her individual "Tender Buttons" – "Glazed

Glitter," "Sugar," "A Box," "Mildred's Umbrella," "Cranberries," "Milk," "Eggs" – are purposely misleading, that they have nothing to do with the descriptions that follow. After all, this line of reasoning goes, what relationship can there be between "A blind agitation is manly and uttermost" and the title "A Cutlet"? But, of course, as in any text, once the title, centered on the page and italicized, is given, there is no ignoring its referent. As we read the sentence or paragraph beneath a given title, we inevitably have that title at the back of our minds and try to see how title and text might relate.

Another common misconception about *Tender Buttons* is that Stein's focus on what Nicola Pitchford calls "the gendered realm of consumer culture and domestic space" was designed as an "attack on patriarchal representation" and that this subversive element is the book's novelty (Pitchford 1999: 650). Such a reading ignores the simple fact that Stein's carafes and cups, her cushions and shawls, her boxes and umbrellas, were the verbal equivalents of Picasso's, Braque's, and Gris's similarly "domestic" still-life – still-life that, like hers, featured fractured and dismembered carafes and tablecloths, playing cards and wine goblets, fruit knives and buttons. Indeed the term "consumerism" imposes an odd spin on Stein's "objects," "food," and "rooms" – items which are neither more nor less than the stuff of her everyday domestic life. Just as William Carlos Williams wrote poems about parsley in a glass on the kitchen sink or an old woman eating plums that "taste good to her," so Stein's *donnée* was that poetry begins at home.

And here again Stein is and is not like Eliot. The "cups, the marmalade, the tea," "cakes and ices" and "coffeespoons" of "Prufrock" have their counterpart in *Tender Buttons*, but whereas Eliot's eating and drinking rituals are always associated with the futility and false consciousness of modern social life, Stein's are regularly associated with pleasure, especially the sexual pleasure of women. Prufrock's question "Do I dare to eat a peach?" has no place in the world of *Tender Buttons*, where indeed one dares to eat a peach but where,

66

in any case, the issue is not conformity to this or that social norm, but the nature of *peachness* itself. Potatoes and cranberries, eggs and milk, carafes and boxes – to meditate on these ordinary things is to refigure one's own place in the world of objects. Here is Stein's account in "Portraits and Repetition" of the impetus of *Tender Buttons*:

> I began to wonder . . . just what one saw when one looked at anything really looked at anything. Did one see sound, and what was the relation between color and sound, did it make itself by description by a word that meant it or did it make itself by a word in itself. All this time I was of course not interested in emotion or that anything happened. I was less interested then in these things than I ever had been. I lived my life with emotion and with things happening but I was creating in my writing by simply looking. I was as I say at that time reducing as far as it was possible for me to reduce them, talking and listening. . . .
>
> And the thing that excited me so very much at that time and still does is that the words or words that make what I looked at be itself were always words that to me very exactly related themselves to that thing the thing at which I was looking, but as often as not had as I say nothing whatever to do with what any words would do that described that thing. (Stein 1998 II: 303)

Note here again the distinction Stein makes between poetry and life: "I lived my life with emotion and with things happening but I was creating in my writing by simply looking." "Poetry," Stein might say with Eliot, is not the "turning-loose of emotion but an escape from emotion," although, as in his case, her words are themselves bristling with emotional, and especially sexual, reference.

Consider the second poem in the "Objects" section of *Tender Buttons*:

Glazed Glitter

Nickel, what is nickel, it is originally rid of a cover.

The change in that is that red weakens an hour. The change has come. There is no search. But there is, there is that hope and that interpretation and sometime, surely any is unwelcome, sometime there is breath and there will be sinecure and charming very charming is that clean and cleansing. Certainly glittering is handsome and convincing.

There is no gratitude in mercy and in medicine. There can be breakages in Japanese. That is no programme. That is no color chosen. It was chosen yesterday, that showed spitting and perhaps washing and polishing. It certainly showed no obligation and perhaps if borrowing is not natural there is some use in giving.

(Stein 1998 I: 313)

This, like all the pieces in *Tender Buttons*, is often labeled "abstract" or "non-representational" in that it provides the reader neither with a coherent train of thought about something recognizable nor a coherent image of a coin or nickel object; indeed, there is no one object represented, although there are certainly references to a nickel jar or carafe (in keeping with the first poem, "A carafe, that is a blind glass"), or, say, a nickel spittoon. But what is it that is "charming very charming" and what is the relationship of nickel receptacle to such gerunds as "borrowing" and "giving"?

Stein, I remarked earlier, avoided the explicit allusion and citation that is characteristic of Eliot, and she had no use for neologisms. But etymology, the source of punning and riddling in such fellow artists as Duchamp and Khlebnikov, was very much her thing. According to the OED, nickel is "a hard silvery-white lustrous mineral, usually occurring in combination with arsenic or sulphur and associated with cobalt; it is both malleable and ductile, and is now largely employed for various purposes, especially in alloys." Its secondary meaning is, of course, a coin (in the US, dating from 1858, a one-cent piece). Nickel, the OED tells us, was named by

the Swedish mineralogist Axel F. von Cronstedt in 1754, by abbre-
viation of the German *kupfernickel*, (*coppernickel*), "the mining name
of the copper-colored ore (niccolite) from which the metal was first
obtained by Cronstedt in 1751." In German, the *nickel* of *kupfernickel* means "dwarf, rascal, mysterious demon, the name being given
to the ore because it actually yielded no copper in spite of its
appearance."

Did Stein know this particular etymology? Not necessarily, but
she would have known the German connotations of *nickel*, which
in this case, together with her familiarity with nickel and its uses as
well as the sound of the word with its hard *k*, is quite enough. Thus
her title immediately alludes to the inferiority of nickel among
metals: all that glitters, she suggests slyly, is not gold, and besides the
metal is glazed, coated with a glossy surface. Indeed, the alliterative
"Glazed Glitter" connotes an artificial sparkle, a "cover" designed, it
seems, to make the ordinary mineral more attractive. The poet
acknowledges this condition in her opening sentence "Nickel, what
is nickel, it is originally rid of a cover." Then, too, the "cover" in
question points back to the carafe ("A kind in glass") in the previous poem and forward to the next piece, "A substance in a cushion,"
where we read "A cushion has that cover." Indeed, throughout
Tender Buttons Stein is concerned with containers, whether bottles
or boxes, little closets or even rooms – with things that can be
opened and closed and that have an inside and an outside. But
unlike its "cousins," Stein's nickel receptacle doesn't seem to have
anything very interesting inside it and doesn't come wrapped like a
present. So "there is no search."

Stein's composition cannot be paraphrased: "There is," as she says
herself a few sentences later, "no programme." All the same, hers
is, like Pound's or Eliot's, language charged with meaning. For one
thing, nickel is a hard substance not a tender button (with its French
double entendre as *bouton tendre* or nipple). The very sound of the
word "nickel" conveys that hardness, and the velar stop *k* is repeated
throughout Stein's poem, in "cover," "come," "sinecure," "dean,"
"cleansing," "convincing," "color." And *nickel* is also a paragram on

the word *nick*, whose meaning as a noun – "notch," "groove," "slit," or "incision" – intensifies the sense of *hardness* of the metal: a soft object cannot really have a nick in it. Then, too, the poem puns on "nick" as in "nick of time," and, in keeping with the time theme, "Glazed Glitter" records some sort of "change" – appropriate since a nickel is itself small change – from its natural hardness, a getting rid, so to speak, of nickel's metallic quality. "The change in that is that red weakens an hour" – that red fades in time. "Red" versus "nickel," soft versus hard, weakening versus strength. And why not, since the hard mineral which is nickel (that rascal or demon) *glitters* when *glazed*? The contemplation of its motion is "charming very charming."

The second paragraph may well play on the definition of nickel as "usually occurring in combination with arsenic or sulphur" and "both malleable and ductile." Nickel receptacles were familiar paraphernalia in Stein's medical school days as, for that matter, in the kitchens and bathrooms of Paris; they were more practical than glass or porcelain containers: "There can be breakages in Japanese." "There is no color chosen" because the color is always the same, but when a nickel object is first bought or acquired ("It was chosen yesterday") its glaze has not worn off and it is shiny and attractive, as it will be again after "washing and polishing." So, however ordinary and uninteresting nickel is, "there is some use in giving." A glazed nickel cannister or box would make a nice gift.

But what makes this oblique description a meaningful poem? If the text neither allows us to visualize the object of Stein's contemplation nor invites us to participate in the poet's meditation on this modest little counterpart of Keats's Grecian urn, if it neither seems to express the poet's emotions nor to make a statement about truth or beauty, what is "Glazed Glitter" – or for that matter, what are any of these "Tender Buttons" – for?

Here the syntax provides a clue. Stein's main verb is the copula, used in the present tense (fourteen times), primarily in the constructions, "what is," "that is," "there is," together with their negation, as in "There is no gratitude in mercy and in medicine"; "That is no programme." The mode is therefore one of definition, specifically the form of definition found in the riddle. Conventionally, writes Andrew Welch (1978: 30), "riddle takes the form of a question and answer, i.e., a deceptive question and a 'right' answer which pierces some central ambiguity in the question," for example: "What runs but never walks?" (a river) or "What goes out without putting its coat on?" (a fire). By this token, Stein's are of course *faux*-riddles; in her case, riddling questions (appropriately without question marks) have no "answers," ambiguous or otherwise. What they do is expose the mysterious uses of language and hence the difficulties in communication.

"Glazed Glitter" is one of a series of poems that meditate on the appearance and function of containers, from the "Carafe that is a blind glass" (see Hejinian 2000: 99–103) to the two poems, each bearing the title "A Box" (Stein 1998 I: 314, 316–17). If these texts recall Cubism in their mode of decomposition and reconstruction of disparate verbal elements (Perloff 1995: 190–2; 1996a: 83–114), they are also, to use Eliot's term, objective correlatives for a particular set of emotions. When nickel is "originally rid of a cover," "red" that "weakens an hour" shows through – red, which relates back to the "single hurt color" of the carafe in the previous poem. In the second "A Box" red literally "shows" beneath the "sick color that is grey"; indeed, in these poems about objects and foods, there are soft things inside or underneath covers – sometimes an oyster, as in "A substance in a cushion" (Stein 1998 I: 313) and again in "Cups" (ibid.: 338), where we are told that cups "need a pet oyster," and in "Orange" (ibid.: 343), where the punning riddle begins "Why is a feel oyster and egg stir" – sometimes "potatoes cut in between" (ibid.: 339), sometimes "the dark red" that is "bitten, really bitten" (ibid.: 336). In the course of the sequence, that which is inside the "cover" is increasingly exposed, in an array of references to the female sex organs and to love-making. "Glitter," for that matter, can easily refer, as it does for a poet like Robert Herrick in "Upon Julia's Clothes," to the "brave vibration, each way free" of the naked body: "O, how that glittering taketh me!" but then Stein's "glitter" is "glazed" – covered and protected – so that even here artifice or artfulness reigns.

In the course of *Tender Buttons* the eroticism, still carefully masked in "Objects," becomes more marked. "Custard," for example, is described as having "aches when"; "Asparagus" as "a lean to hot," "Butter" as "a need that a state rubber is sweet and sight and a swelled stretch" (ibid.: 338–9). One cannot, then, dismiss these poems as "nonsense" or accuse their author of failing to display emotion. As Stein herself puts it in "A carafe that is a blind glass," hers is a sequence that is "not unordered in not resembling." *Tender Buttons* concludes with a long prose poem called "Rooms" that begins with a sentence that might be the epigraph of the whole sequence – "Act so that there is no use in a center" – and concludes with the following paragraph:

A light in the moon the only light is on Sunday. What was the sensible decision. The sensible decision was that notwithstanding many declarations and more music, not even notwithstanding the choice and a torch and a collection, notwithstanding the celebrating hat and a vacation and even more noise than cutting, notwithstanding Europe and Asia and being overbearing, not even withstanding an elephant and a strict occasion, not even withstanding more cultivation and some seasoning, not even with not drowning and with the ocean being encircling, not even with more likeness and any cloud, not even with terrible sacrifice of pedestrianism and a special resolution, not even more likely to be pleasing. The care with which the rain is wrong and the green is wrong and the white is wrong, the care with which there is a chair and plenty of breathing. The care with which there is incredible justice and likeness, all this makes a magnificent asparagus, and also a fountain. (Ibid.: 355)

This is a delicate parody of the Romantic tradition. As in such famous poems as Keats's "Eve of St. Agnes" and Coleridge's "Frost at Midnight," the moonlit night is the scene of imagination and erotic longing. But Stein playfully inverts the Romantic topos, giving in to a "sensible decision," a decision that involves a long-winded argument that "notwithstanding" any number of eventualities – the word "notwithstanding" is used five times, followed by "not even withstanding (once) and "not even" (four times) – "all this" (all what?) "makes a magnificent asparagus, and also a fountain."

The "notwithstandings" in the passage are worth examining. To begin with, "declarations" and "music," the trappings of romantic love, are discarded. Next, we read "notwithstanding the choice and a torch and a collection," three nouns that seem not to be parallel but which make perfect sense when we stop to consider that traditional romantic love stories invariably involve choices, that they take place (*pace* Shakespeare and the mock-heroic Byron) by torchlight or perhaps in church when someone is taking up the collection. Notwithstanding, furthermore, "the celebrating hat and a vacation" – trappings, this time, of romance as it is rendered in Impressionist painting as well as, for that matter, in Cézanne's Provençal landscapes and Picasso's portraits of Fernande wearing a large hat. The Big Picture – Europe, Asia, the world of elephants, of "the ocean being encircling" and tales of drowning – is not for Stein. "Not even with terrific sacrifice of pedestrianism and a special resolution, not even more likely to be pleasing." What is rejected here is the literary drive to say something important, to make manifestos, and finally, to write so as to *please* an audience still accustomed, in these *avant guerre* years, to the jingly poems of Sara Teasdale or John Masefield. One must, in short, be *pedestrian* in both senses of the word, a poetic footsoldier rather than a general or admiral.

To turn one's back on poetic conventions, Stein implies, is to enter what is best described as a room of one's own. But she goes much further than Virginia Woolf in making a clean sweep of the old rooms. "The rain is wrong and the white is wrong": once the "lovely" Romantic imagery has been discarded, even rhyme becomes a new possibility: "the care with which there is a chair and plenty of breathing." In the end, *Tender Buttons* offers its readers "incredible justice and likeness" in the orgiastic form of "a magnificent asparagus, and also a fountain." "Asparagus" is the title of one of the poems in the *Food* section – "Asparagus in a lean in a lean to hot. This makes it art and it is wet wet weather wet weather wet" – where the ambiguous grammar evokes an image of "lean" "hot" stalks, juicy and tender. But how is "asparagus" related to "fountain"? Not logically or spatially, surely; we would not find the two together in a still-life by Gris or Braque, much less Cézanne. But Stein's focus on the *wet* and erectile property of asparagus allows her to make a fanciful leap to her final word "fountain" – with its traditional sexual connotations, connotations soon to be played upon in that famous readymade not unlike Stein's own objects – namely Duchamp's *Fountain*. Not the moon or the green and white of nature is requested, but "a chair and plenty of breathing."

Like "Prufrock," *Tender Buttons* was a coterie work until after World War I, but whereas Eliot's poem became, by the 1920s, a celebrated work, Stein's "prose" sequence didn't come into its own until after World War II, and even today it remains largely unread – an "eccentric" text that presumably cannot be deciphered. Yet once we understand Stein's way of writing sentences, her use of sound play and pun, her particular use of ellipsis and asyntacticality, metonymy and synecdoche rather than metaphor and symbol, her penchant for parody rather than irony, and especially her curious use of repetition, not of key nouns, but of "colorless" connectives like "notwithstanding," she emerges as not so different, after all, from the early Eliot. "Prufrock," let's remember, is also a pedestrian, a walker in the city, and although Stein's allusions, like her reference to Picasso's portrait of Fernande in her "celebrating hat," are more oblique than Eliot's allusions to Lazarus or John the Baptist or Hamlet – and, as I noted earlier, she scrupulously avoids citation – she shares Eliot's Mallarmean conviction that the poet begins, not with ideas to be embodied in words, but with the words themselves. Both poets may be said to follow the Flaubertian dictum that: "the *closer language comes to coinciding and merging with [thought]*, the finer the result . . . from the standpoint of pure Art one might almost establish the axiom that there is no such thing as subject – style in itself being an absolute manner of seeing things [my emphasis]."

Form, in *Tender Buttons* as in "Prufrock," is meaning. But by the time Eliot reluctantly published Stein's "The Fifteenth of November" in *Criterion*, things had changed. As she puts it in that text:

> Entirely a different thing. Entirely a different thing when all of i has been awfully well chosen and thoughtfully corrected.
> He said we, and we.
> We said he.
> He said we.
> We said he, and he.
> He said.
> We said.
> We said it. As we said it.

(Stein 1998 I: 72)

Whereas Stein moved further away from "subject" toward language-game, producing certain texts that even her staunchest admirers have found trying in their unreadability, Eliot began to poeticize specific topoi, as in the litany to the Virgin Mary in Part II of "Ash Wednesday," where a particular understanding of the central Christian paradox seems to precede the poet's actual word choice:

> Lady of Silences
> Calm and distressed
> Torn and most whole
> Rose of memory
> Rose of forgetfulness
> Exhausted and life-giving . . .

(CP: 62)

How does this difference play out in the twenty-first century? Let me conclude by citing the opening of an intriguing little book by Darren Wershler-Henry:

> Jetsam in the laminar flow andor find the threads in redhats andor litter a keyboard with milletseed so that exotic song-birds might tap out their odes to a nightingale andor transcribe the letters pressed onto the platen when stalactites drip on the homerow keys andor reconstruct the ruins of a bombedout capital I andor reinvent the canonic works of western art as a series of roadsign glyphs andor commission an artist to paint the large ass of marcel duchamp andor use a dotmatrix printer to sound out a poem in which each line is a series of pauses whose length is determined by formatting codes. (Wershler-Henry 2000: 1)

Wershler-Henry's prose — one long sentence that goes on for fifty pages like some mad version of a computer program — markedly recalls the locutions and rhythms of Steinian prose. Again, his "andor's" function very much like the "notwithstanding" of *Tender Buttons* — "andor" suggests, as Michael Turner notes in his blurb, "a variable state of inclusion and choice or exclusion." But interestingly, Wershler-Henry's parodic "roadside glyphs" are primarily loaded and allusive nouns, more fully in the Eliot than the Stein tradition: for example, "exotic songbirds," "odes to a nightingale," "stalactites," and the "ruins of a bombedout capital."

Then, too, Wershler-Henry refers to "the large ass of marcel duchamp" — a playful allusion to Duchamp's *Large Glass* as well as his moustached and goateed Mona Lisa, with its punning title *L.H.O.O.Q.* ("Elle a chaud au cul"; "She has a hot ass"). That link — and there are many others in *the tapeworm foundry* — suggest that neither the Stein nor the Eliot strains retain their pure forms when they become prominent, as they do at the end of the century. One of the complicating factors — the "escape from a paragraph by elop-ing along bottomless discourses," as Wershler-Henry puts it — is precisely the Duchamp input. And that brings me to my next chapter.

3

The Conceptual Poetics of Marcel Duchamp

> The river bears no empty bottles, sandwich papers,
> Silk handkerchiefs, cardboard boxes, cigarette ends
> Or other testimony of summer nights.
>   T. S. Eliot, "The Fire Sermon," *The Waste Land*

> *Duchamp:* I had no position. I've been a little like Gertrude
> Stein. To a certain group, she was considered an interesting
> writer, with very original things . . .
> *Cabanne:* I admit I never would have thought of comparing
> you to Gertrude Stein . . .
> *Duchamp:* It's a form of comparison between people of that
> period. By that, I mean that there are people in every period
> who aren't "in."
>   Pierre Cabanne, *Dialogues with Marcel Duchamp*

Empty bottles and cardboard boxes: for the Eliot of *The Waste Land*
these are the very emblem of twentieth-century refuse, the detritus
of an Age of Mechanical Reproduction antithetical to the individual talent and, in Pound's stinging words about Usury, "CONTRA
NATURAM." In *Tender Buttons*, by contrast, those expendable
bottles and boxes become the object of intense concentration: consider the first of two prose poems entitled "A Box":

Out of kindness comes redness and out of rudeness comes rapid same question, out of an eye comes research, out of selection comes painful cattle. So then the order is that a white way of being round is something suggesting a pin and is it disappointing, it is not, it is so rudimentary to be analyzed and see a fine substance strangely, it is so earnest to have a green point not to red but to point again. (Stein 1998 I: 314)

Unlike Eliot's cardboard box, Stein's cannot be visualized. Is it small or large, made of wood or enamel, lined with cardboard or velvet? We cannot say, any more than we can determine whether this is a jewelry box or sewing box, a large carton in which to keep papers or a small pill box. Yet *boxness* is immediately established, not just by the title, but by the fourfold repetition of the words "out of." Qualities are defined as emerging *out of* something, the items related by sound and visual appearance rather than direct reference. As in "Glazed Glitter," discussed in chapter 2, Stein's meanings here are extremely oblique. "Out of kindness comes redness" – out of the giver's kindness, perhaps, comes the "redness" of the gift, a valentine, or some other token of love – whereas "out of rudeness" comes "rapid same question": the interruption that is unnecessary because the question has been asked before. "Out of an eye comes research": the beauty of this phrase is that a specific physical organ, the eye, is now set over against those abstract nouns, kindness and rudeness. Perhaps, Stein implies, we better leave such abstractions aside and trust the "research" that "comes" from the eye, and the "selection" or discrimination that characterizes art even if the process involves "painful cattle" (rhymes with "tattle," and hence part of Stein's everyday life).

But what is the principle of selection, of producing "order" in this elusive passage? In the second sentence, the repeated "out of" is replaced by the copula – "the order is," a "white way of being round is," "it is not," "it is so rudimentary," "it is so earnest" – these assertions being balanced by the question "is it disappointing." The box, it seems, is a kind of mental box of tools: a "white way of being round" that suggests a "pin," a "green point not to red" (with puns on "too" and "read"), "but to point again." As in "A Carafe, that is a Blind Glass," the focus is on "an arrangement in a system of pointing." "Is it disappointing," we read, knowing it can't be since "pointing" is still there, but now amalgamated into a larger word that shifts its meaning. Hence, "it is not, it is so rudimentary to be analyzed."

Stein's deconstruction of *boxness* is thus very different from Eliot's images of cardboard boxes washed up on the banks of the Thames. But suppose one doesn't create verbal equivalents of boxes or bottles but exhibits these very things as works of art? In the same year that Stein published *Tender Buttons*, Marcel Duchamp produced his first "readymade," the *Bottle Rack*,[1] as well as the first of the remarkable boxes in which he was to reproduce, in limited editions, his random notes for future projects as well as reproductions of his already existing work, usually in miniature versions.[2] The *Box of 1914* contains sixteen notes and the drawing *To Have the Apprentice in the Sun*, all of them pertaining to the major project which Duchamp had not yet begun to execute and which would not be finished – or, as he insisted, "unfinished" – until 1922; namely, the *Large Glass* (*The Bride Stripped Bare by her Bachelors, Even*). Originally, as he later explained it, Duchamp planned to assemble his notes in a book on the order of the Sears, Roebuck catalogue, where every detail of the *Large Glass* (plate 3.1) might be explained and catalogued (see Jouffroy 1964: 115; Kuh 1962: 81). But bookmaking inevitably involves linear sequence, and Duchamp much preferred the indeterminacy and arbitrariness afforded by the box in which the scraps of paper, sometimes torn from larger sheets, sometimes written on the backs of gas bills, could be read in whatever sequence the viewer/reader might choose.

The situation is further complicated by the issue of facsimile: the notes included in the box were not the originals but contact prints made to size; each reproduction was trimmed and glued onto thick

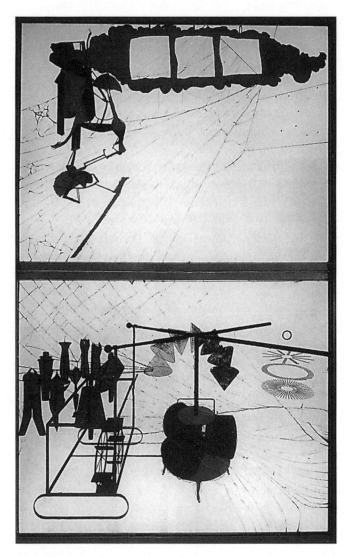

Plate 3.1 Marcel Duchamp, *The Bride Stripped Bare by her Bachelors, Even* or *The Large Glass*, 1915–23. Oil, varnish, lead foil and wire, and dust on glass mounted between two glass panels. 9 ft × 1¼ ins × 5 ft 9¼> ins. Philadelphia Museum of Art, Katherine S. Dreier Bequest. © Succession Marcel Duchamp/ADAGP, Paris and DACS, London, 2001.

mat board and placed in a standard 18 × 24 cm box (see plate 3.2) used for photographic plates (Naumann 1999: 56; Bonk 1998: 97–8). As executed, the *Box of 1914*, produced in an edition of five (thus insuring that there would be no unique art work), curiously joins "impersonal" mechanism and individual artisanship. The secondhand readymade boxes bear almost no hint of their altered contents. "There is," writes Ecke Bonk, "no signature, no date, not even a dedication in or on any of the known boxes" (ibid.: 98). At the same time, the notes themselves are, of course, in Duchamp's own handwriting. Indeed, says Bonk, "Handwriting, the scribbled note with all its corrections, rewriting, and underlining – the visualization of a thought process – became in his hands, a refined, precise instrument. The casual, fragile quality of these random notes was recharged and transformed into a new artistic concept, a kind of reference manual" (ibid.: 97). Linda Dalrymple Henderson further relates this "reference manual" to Leonardo da Vinci's *Notebooks*, an elaborate facsimile edition of which had appeared in the 1890s, and characterizes the *Box of 1914* as "a miniature library or museum of the ideas of a modern artist–engineer."[3]

But what, one may well ask, does all this have to do with poetry? The so-called *White Box* of 1966 (*À L'Infinitif*), contains a note dated 1913 in which Duchamp asks: "Can one make works which are not works of 'art'?"[4] The implications of that question, which Duchamp asked in so many varied ways throughout his career, have resounded through the century and have permanently changed our thinking about art boundaries. In the visual arts, intermedia and multimedia (or, in the case of the readymades and boxes, *other*media) works are no longer a novelty. But in the case of poetry, the conventions die hard. As we saw in chapter 2, even as radical a poet as Gertrude Stein was quite unwilling to concede that "poetry" and "painting" or "poetry" and "photography" might coexist in the same work. For that particular crossing, as well as for the notion that a replica of one's earlier work, miniaturized and rearranged, could itself be a new art work, a new aesthetic had to come into play – the aesthetic we now know as conceptualism.

81

Plate 3.2 Marcel Duchamp, *Box of 1914*, 1913–14. Interior. Philadelphia Museum of Art. Gift of Mme Marcel Duchamp. © Succession Marcel Duchamp/ADAGP, Paris and DACS, London, 2001.

From Morphology to Function

"The function of art, as a question," writes the conceptual artist Joseph Kosuth (1969), "was first raised by Marcel Duchamp. In fact it is Marcel Duchamp whom we can credit with giving art its own identity." And he explains:

> The event that made conceivable the realization that it was possible to "speak another language" and still make sense in art was Marcel Duchamp's first unassisted readymade. With the unassisted readymade, art changed its focus from the form of the language to what was being said. Which means that it changed the nature of art from a *question of morphology to a question of function*. This change – one from "appearance" to "conception" – was the beginning of "modern" art and the beginning of "conceptual" art.
>
> The "value" of particular artists after Duchamp can be weighed according to how much they questioned the nature of art. . . . And to do this one cannot concern oneself with the handed-down "language" of traditional art. (Ibid.: 18)

Yair Guttman (1998) concurs with Kosuth's assessment. "For the conceptualists," he remarks, "the aim of Duchamp's readymade was an investigation of the conditions that make art possible. According to this interpretation, Duchamp asked the following question: Let us take an arbitrary object with no particular aesthetic qualities. Under which conditions can this object be presented as an art object?" (ibid.: 422). In Duchamp's own words cited above: "Can one make works which are not works of 'art'?"

Marxist criticism has construed this question as part of the larger Dada negation of the modern capitalist art market. As Peter Bürger (1984) famously put it:

> When Duchamp signs mass-produced objects . . . and sends them to art exhibits, he negates the category of individual

83

production. The signature is inscribed on an arbitrarily chosen mass product because all claims to individual creativity are to be mocked. Duchamp's provocation not only unmasks the art market . . . it radically questions the very principle of art in bourgeois society according to which the individual is considered the creator of the work of art. Duchamp's Ready-Mades are not works of art but manifestations. (Ibid.: 51)

But the fact is that Duchamp has emerged as nothing if not an "individual" creator and that, Bürger to the contrary, he was, from the beginning, quite content to exhibit his "things" in museums and galleries and then to replicate them, again and again, in the boxes and *boîtes en valise*, now themselves precious museum pieces. Individual inscription on what is paradoxically the "impersonal" ready-made is, as we shall see, central to Duchamp's project, which, far from negating art as a category, directs itself quite specifically at *retinal* art, as it was understood in the turn-of-the-century Paris art milieu in which he came of age. "Since Courbet," Duchamp tells Pierre Cabanne (1971: 43), "it's been believed that painting is addressed to the retina. That was everyone's error. The retinal shudder! Before painting had other functions: it could be religious, philosophical, moral." Thierry de Duve sums it up as follows:

[Duchamp] never wanted to burn down the museums as did Marinetti or to break completely with art as did the Cabaret Voltaire. His "Dadaism" was never made up of social condemnations of art, but only of personal secessions. He never wanted to engage in a tabula rasa of tradition, nor did he believe it was possible to do so. (de Duve 1991: 106)

Indeed, Duchamp's conceptualism is best understood, not as the negation of "art" as such, but as the drive to render unto art the things that are art – which is to say, the realm of the mind as well as the eye, the realm of ideas and intellect as well as visual image. The resulting revolution has transformed both visual and verbal language and is therefore central to poetics in the twentieth century.

84

Stein's relation to this aesthetic is complex. *The Autobiography of Alice B. Toklas* treats Duchamp as a figure of minor importance. Not only is he largely eclipsed by Picasso, but his *Nude Descending a Staircase*, Stein suggests, was largely influenced by François Picabia, who understood "that a line should have the vibration of a musical sound" and knew how to "induce such vibration" (Stein 1998 I: 865). Visual art, in Stein's lexicon, is equivalent to painting, which is, of course, equivalent to retinal imagery. But she shared Duchamp's interest in the questions of non-Euclidean geometry and its implications for literary as well as painterly realism; his predilection for ordinary machine-made objects as readymades is paralleled by her interest in the everyday items being sold by the new department stores like the Bon Marché and Galeries Lafayette. Indeed, Stein's "portrait" "Aux Galeries Lafayette" appeared in the New York Dada periodical *Rogue* in 1915, as did Duchamp's *"The"*, of which more later.[5] And his 1921 readymade *Why Not Sneeze Rrose Sélavy?* – the playfully erotic birdcage filled with marble sugar cubes, cuttlebone, and thermometer – can be linked to Stein's "Lifting Belly" (1917), with its modulation of the following phrases:

> Lifting belly is no joke. Not after all . . . Sneeze. This is the way to say it. . . .
> I do love roses and carnations . . . You know I prefer a bird. What bird?
> Why a yellow bird . . . Lifting belly is so kind. And so cold.
>
> Lifting belly marry . . . Lifting belly is sugar.
>
> Rose is a rose is a rose is a rose.
> In print on top. (Stein 1998 II 417–25, 438–9; cf. Mink 2000: 7–8)

Indeed, it has been suggested that the name of Duchamp's female *alter ego* Rrose Sélavy alludes to Stein and her predilection for what was, in Duchamp's day, an uninteresting, bourgeois female name. As he tells Cabanne:

I wanted to change my identity and first I had the idea of taking on a Jewish name. . . . But I didn't find any Jewish name that I liked or that caught my fancy, and suddenly I had the idea: why not change my sex? That was much easier! (Cabanne 1971: 64)

Here the Jewish lesbian Gertrude, who was to pronounce famously that "A rose is a rose is a rose," provides a nice model.

"Can one make works which are not works of 'art'?" It is on this issue that Duchamp and Stein part company. True, both take their inspiration from the everyday, the ordinary, but for Duchamp, the art work (readymade? box? set of notes? painting on glass?) is neither purely verbal nor purely visual (or musical), nor is it an intermedia composition, combining poetry and painting or poetry and music, etc. The paradox of the Duchampian readymade, as of the *Large Glass*, is that although Duchamp used what seemed to be found objects – an upside-down urinal called *Fountain*, a glass ampule, broken and resealed, called *Air de Paris*, the machine-drawing of an ordinary chocolate grinder – and although he claimed repeatedly that his "choice of readymades [was] based on visual indifference and, at the same time, on the total absence of good or bad taste" (Cabanne 1971: 48; cf. Duchamp 1975: 141–2), the works in his repertoire are now understood to be completely unique. Not, of course, literally unique in the sense of one of a kind; in almost every case, the original has been lost and there are a number of replicas. Rather, their uniqueness, their *aura* is conceptual: the idea, for example, of taking a snow shovel, hanging it by its handle in a glass case – which is hardly the way we normally see shovels – and giving it the witty title *In Advance of the Broken Arm*.

The individual readymades, moreover, display marked family resemblances: the *Chocolate Grinder* and *Water Wheel* in the *Large Glass*, for example, echo the circular movement of going nowhere of the *Bicycle Wheel*, while the erotically suggestive forms of the *Nine Malic Molds* recall *The Bride* painting of 1912 and the moustached and goateed Mona Lisa known as *L.H.O.O.Q.* The notes and

86

sketches made for the *Large Glass* and preserved in the *boîtes en valise* provide a kind of *raison d'être* for these relationships, their *modus operandi* being what Duchamp himself called, no doubt alluding to Alfred Jarry's pataphysics, a "playful physics," "a *reality which would be possible by slightly distending* the laws of physics and chemistry" (Duchamp 1975).[6]

Our own experimental poetries, as we shall see in chapter 5, are unimaginable without the example of Duchamp. John Cage's and Jackson Mac Low's change-generated texts, the procedural poems and fictions of Oulipo, Robert Smithson's site-specific "sculptures," Steve McCaffery's *Carnival* or *Theory of Sediment*, Susan Howe's *Hinge Picture* (a title taken straight from Duchamp's *A L'Infinitif*), Tom Phillips's *A Humument*, Johanna Drucker's *History of The [My] World*, Christian Bök's *Crystallography*, and Kenneth Goldsmith's *Fidget* – all these could be read as under the rubric of what Duchamp termed *delays*. The *Large Glass*, as he put it, in a 1912 note found in the *Green Box* of 1934, was such a *delay*:

Kind of Subtitle
   Delay in glass
Use "delay" instead of picture or painting; picture on glass becomes delay in glass – but delay in glass does not mean picture on glass –
   It's merely a way of succeeding in no longer thinking that the thing in question is a picture – to make a delay of it in the most general way possible, not so much in the different meanings in which delay can be taken, but rather in their indecisive reunion "delay" – / a delay in glass as you would say a poem in prose or a spittoon in silver.[7]

Linda Henderson points out that the term *delay* has perfectly good scientific credentials:

Such a delay is precisely what occurs when a wave of visible light (or any other electromagnetic wave) intersects a pane of glass: it is refracted, or slowed, and thus bent by the encounter. Such effects of refraction, featured in sources on the optics of visible light, had been central to the early investigations of X-rays and to Hertz's experiments with electrical radiations. Distancing himself from the tradition of painting pictures on canvas, Duchamp would create a glass "delay" in an impersonal, mechanically exact style free of touch, which like his ready-mades, also challenged his fellow artists' Bergsonian emphasis on profound self-expression. (Henderson 1998: 120)

Delay, deferment – another favorite Duchamp term, used in the *1914 Box* (see Duchamp 1975: 23, where it is defined as "against compulsory military service: a *deferment* of each limb, of the heart") – *distance*. "I wanted," Duchamp tells Pierre Cabanne (1971: 40), "to give 'delay' a poetic sense that I couldn't even explain. It was to avoid saying, 'a glass painting,' 'a glass drawing,' 'a thing drawn on glass,' you understand? The word 'delay' pleased me at that point, like a phrase one discovers. It was really poetic, in the most Mallarméan sense of the word."

Duchamp's desire to produce art works "free of touch" as well as free of "the retinal aspect" or "retinal shudder" that, as he tells Cabanne, has posed problems for painting ever since Courbet, recalls, improbably enough, Eliot's theory of impersonality. Indeed, in a piece called "The Creative Act," written for a roundtable held at the 1957 meeting of the American Federation of the Arts (where he shared the podium with Gregory Bateson, Rudolf Arnheim, and William C. Seitz), Duchamp declared:

If we give the attributes of a medium to the artist, we must then deny him the state of consciousness on the esthetic plane about what he is doing or why he is doing it. All his decisions in the artistic execution of the work rest with pure intuition and cannot be translated into a self-analysis, spoken or written, or even thought out.

T. S. Eliot, in his essay on "Tradition and the Individual Talent," writes: "The more perfect the artist, the more completely separate in him will be the man who suffers and the mind which creates; the more perfectly will the mind digest and transmute the passions which are its material." . . .

Consequently, in the chain of reactions accompanying the creative act, a link is missing. This gap which represents the inability of the artist to express fully his intention; this difference between what he intended to realize and did realize, is the personal "art coefficient" contained in the work. (Duchamp 1975: 138–9)

"This," notes Eric Cameron (1992: 1) in a lecture that touches on the Duchamp–Eliot relationship, "is the only time Duchamp ever quoted the opinion of a critic word for word. In the spirited debate that follows Cameron's lecture (see de Duve 1992: 31–8), Rosalind Krauss objects strenuously that "Eliot's conception of tradition, his idea of high culture, his notion that art is redemptive, seems to me to be . . . far from my understanding of Duchamp," and that it is a "betrayal of Duchamp" to relate his work "to larger systems of knowledge." But Cameron (1992: 32) reminds her that the juxtaposition of fragments in *The Waste Land* can be seen as "the equivalent of drawing a moustache on the Mona Lisa."

Indeed, Duchamp's desire to produce works in which neither the eye nor the hand would count any longer is not unlike Eliot's insistence, in "Tradition and the Individual Talent," that "poetry is not the expression of emotion but an escape from emotion," that indeed, "the difference between art and the event is always absolute." For once the "event' – say, Duchamp's payment to Daniel Tzanck, on December 3, 1919, for dental work performed – becomes the now famous *Tzanck Check*, drawn on an account at the Teeth's Loan & Trust Company Consolidated, 2 Wall Street, New York for the amount of $115.00, whose line of payment is bisected by the word "ORIGINAL," printed in large block letters (plate 3.3), the

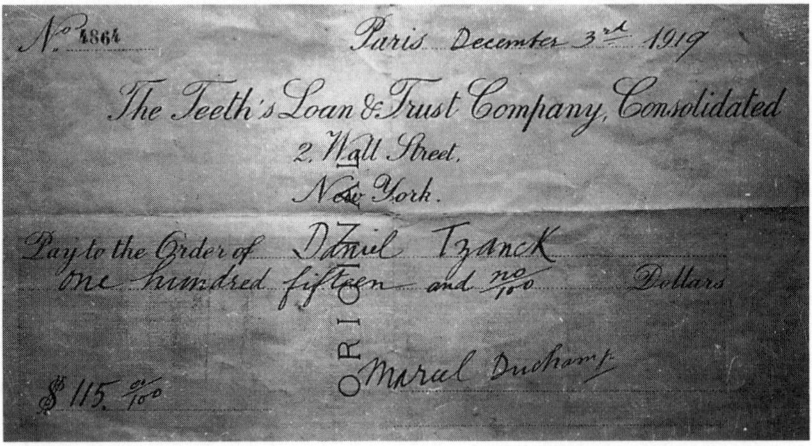

Plate 3.3 Marcel Duchamp, *Tzanck Check*, 1919. Imitated rectified ready-made: enlarged manuscript version of a check. 8¼ × 15⅛ ins. Galleria Schwarz, Milan. Courtesy of Arturo Schwarz. © Succession Marcel Duchamp/ADAGP, Paris and DACS, London, 2001.

temporality of the "event" gives way to the stasis of the art work exhibited in the Philadelphia Museum of Art.

Memory Imprint

Whatever the *Tzanck Check* is or is not, its verbal dimension is surely more prominent than its visual one. Indeed, in classifying Duchamp as belonging to the visual arts (the normal procedure), we overlook, not only the verbal dimension of the readymades themselves (their titles, captions, inscriptions, verbal context), and not only the well-known puns like *La Bagarre d'Austerlitz* and *Ovaire toute la nuit*,[8] but also the series of proto-language poems Duchamp was producing in the mid-teens. In the *Green Box* we find the following note:

Identifying
To lose the possibility of recognizing 2 similar objects – 2 colors, 2 laces, 2 hats, 2 forms whatsoever to reach the Impossibility of

90

sufficient *visual* memory, to transfer from one like object to another the *memory* imprint.

– Same possibility with sounds; with brain facts. (Duchamp 1975: 31)

To remake the verbal world, in Duchamp's lexicon, is to rule out the axis of similarity which is, of course, the axis of metaphor. Conventionally, poetry is based on "recognizing 2 similar objects," in establishing *likeness.* But what if the "*memory* imprint" were erased, forcing the reader/viewer to focus on the *thisness*, the nominalism of each thing? On another slip of paper in *The Green Box* Duchamp develops this notion:

Conditions of a language:
The search for "*prime words*" (divisible only by themselves and by unity).
Take a Larousse dict. and copy all the so-called "abstract" words, i.e. those which have no concrete reference.
   Compose a schematic sign designating each of these words (this sign can be composed with the standard stops).
   These signs must be thought of as the letters of the new alphabet.
   A grouping of several signs will determine
(utilize colors – in order to differentiate what would correspond in this [literature] to the substantive, verb, adverb declensions, conjugations etc.) (Ibid.)

And in a 1914 note in *À L'Infinitif* Duchamp poses the question:

"Grammar" – i.e. How to connect the elementary signs (like words), then the *groups* of signs one to the other; what *will become of the ideas* of action or of being (verbs), of modulation (adverbs) – etc.? (Ibid.: 77)

Here the "solution" is again related to dictionaries: "Look through a dictionary and scratch out all the 'undesirable' words" (ibid.: 78).

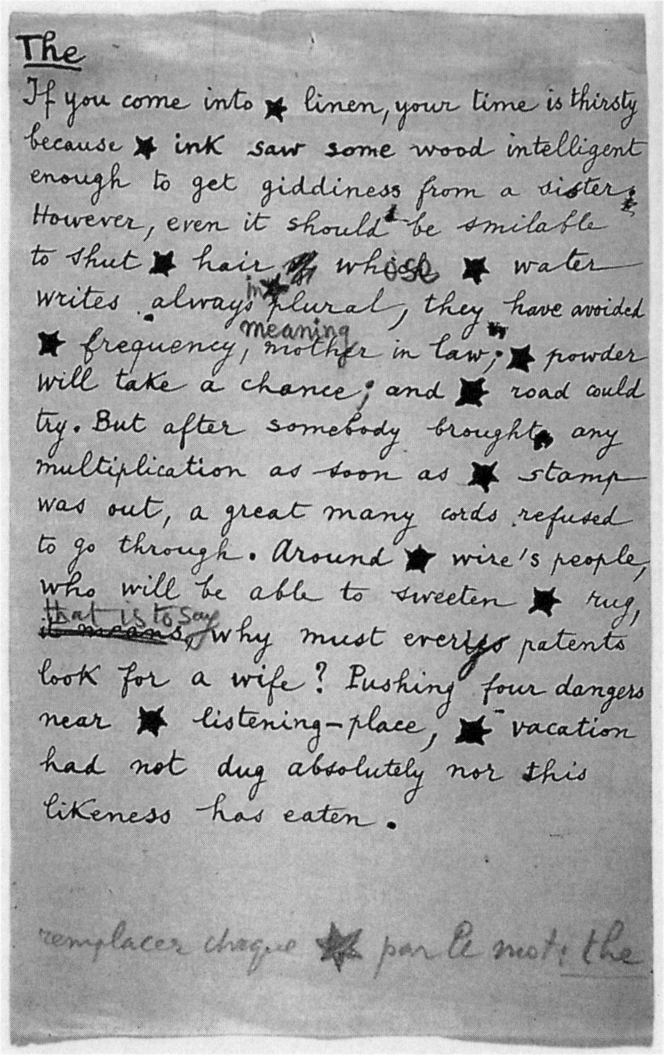

The

If you come into ✦ linen, your time is thirsty because ✦ ink saw ~~some~~ wood intelligent enough to get giddiness from a sister; However, even it should be smilable to shut ✦ hair ✦ whose ✦ water writes always plural, they have avoided ✦ frequency, mother in law; ✦ powder will take a chance; and ✦ road could try. But after somebody brought any multiplication as ~~soon~~ as ✦ stamp was out, a great many cords refused to go through. Around ✦ wire's people, who will be able to sweeten ✦ rug, ~~that is to say~~ ~~means~~ why must every patents look for a wife? Pushing four dangers near ✦ listening-place, ✦ vacation had not dug absolutely nor this likeness has eaten.

remplacer chaque ✦ par le mot: the

Plate 3.4 Marcel Duchamp, *The*, 1915. Ink on paper. 22.2 × 14.3 cms. Philadelphia Museum of Art, the Louise and Walter Arensberg Collection. © Succession Marcel Duchamp/ADAGP, Paris and DACS, London, 2001.

These exercises, so central, a half-century later, to the experiments of John Cage and Jackson Mac Low, as well as the *Oulipo* writers, stands behind a little-known Duchamp text called *"The"* (plate 3.4), written in English shortly after Duchamp arrived in New York and published in *Rogue* in October 1915 under the title "*THE*, Eye Test, Not a 'Nude Descending a Staircase'" (see Naumann 1999: 70, fig. 3.13). Not, in other words, a retinal image representing something *seen*, this "Eye Test" takes, as its visual material, letters, words, and sentences. Perhaps Duchamp has in mind the conundrum he posed a year earlier in a note for the *1914 Box*:

> [see]
> One can look at seeing;
> one can't hear hearing.
> (Duchamp 1975: 23)

The "directions" at the bottom of the handwritten page tell the reader in French to "replace each ★ by the word: 'the.'" Duchamp's sentences are perfectly grammatical – "If you come into ★ linen, your time is thirsty because ★ ink saw some wood intelligent enough to get giddiness from a sister" – and so on. If this sounds like a routine Dada exercise, the distinction is that Duchamp, far from producing random effects, is interested in rule (here the replacement rule) and grammatical relationship. "The verb," he tells Arturo Schwarz (1970: 457), "was meant to be an abstract word acting on a subject that is a material object; in this way the verb would make the sentence look abstract." But what makes the passage look abstract is less noun or verb than the nine giant asterisks which force us to focus on the "the," that invariant, ungendered article, which has no parallel in French or in other inflected languages. Then, too, the presence of the large black asterisks creates a visual configuration on the page that looks ahead to concrete poetry, the words next to an asterisk inevitably receiving pride of place.

"The," in any case, precedes by twelve years the publication of Louis Zukofsky's first major work, "Poem Beginning 'The'," whose

330 numbered lines, divided into six movements, are primarily made up of citations from other texts, for example:

17   By why are our finest always dead?
18   And why, Lord, this time, is it Mauberley's Luini in
      porcelain, why is it Chelifer,
19   Why is it Lovat who killed Kangaroo,
20   Why Stephen Daedalus with the cane of ash,
21   But why les neiges?

(Zukofsky 1991: 9)

Here, citations from Pound's *Hugh Selwyn Mauberley*, Lawrence's *Kangaroo*, Joyce's *Ulysses*, and François Villon's refrain *Ou sont les neiges d'antan?* (which both Pound and Eliot themselves cited repeatedly) are collaged so as to create startling juxtapositions between literary allusions, academic styles, zoological references (the scorpion or May fly, "Chelifer"), and so on. Written when its author was only 21, it is, in some ways, a schoolboy spoof, aimed at the learned allusions of *The Waste Land*. In a trenchant essay, Ming-Qian Ma (1997) argues that "Poem beginning 'The'" anticipates postmodern poetics in its denial of the self as organizing principle, its blurring of text–context (figure–ground) distinctions, and its rendering of information as so much found text. The reference is to the language poets, who have repeatedly expressed a profound debt to Zukofsky's mode here and in "*A*." But I am not sure it is, as Ma suggests, also the case that Zukofsky's verbal texture is a "cluster of words devoid of any qualitative intuition" (ibid.: 145). Surely the poem implies that some citations (e.g., Pound and Joyce above) are more valuable than others. Indeed, Zukofsky's title (and consequent opening lines ("'The' / Voice of Jesus I' . . .") are broadly – and one might say, quite traditionally – satiric and iconoclastic, whereas the earlier "*The*" – minor work that it is in the Duchamp canon – is trying to determine what happens when an invariant one-syllable article, a word that is inescapable in the English language, is embedded in sentences that are grammatically correct but semantically "non-

94

sensical." If Zukofsky's poem is aggressively literary, Duchamp's wants to confront the nature of literary language itself. Can one make works which are not works of "art"?

Consider a second Duchamp text from this period called *Rendezvous 1916* (plate 3.5). To make it, Duchamp took four postcards and taped them together to constitute a rectangular grid; on these he produced a text that has no beginning or end, typing the maximum number of letters across each card and cutting the words at card edge irrespective of the rules of hyphenation. Although the double-spaced typed lines sometimes match, there is no continuity from one card to the next. The postcard set, each bearing an ordinary one-cent stamp on its verso, is addressed to Mr and Mrs Walter Arensberg at 33 West 67th Street, and bears the complete title *Rendezvous de Dimanche 6 Février 1916 (à 1h. 3/4 après midi)*.

Why this specification of time and place? In a note for the *Green Box* Duchamp wrote:

Specifications for "Readymades."
by planning for a moment to come (on such a day, such a date such a minute), "to inscribe a readymade" – The readymade can later be looked for. – (with all kinds of delays).

The *important thing then is just* this matter of timing, this snapshot effect, like a speech delivered on no matter what occasion but *at such and such an hour.* It is a kind of rendezvous.

– Naturally inscribe that date, hour, minute, on the readymade as *information.*

Also the serial characteristic of the readymade. (Duchamp 1975: 32)

Such simulated authenticity was to become a Duchamp trademark. What is presented as a pure moment of inspiration, as improvisation, was actually written, so Duchamp later told an interviewer, "with great pains." "Don't think you can just write pages of it in five minutes – it took me at least two weeks to do it" (Naumann 1999: 66). The self-imposed rule that caused these "great pains" was,

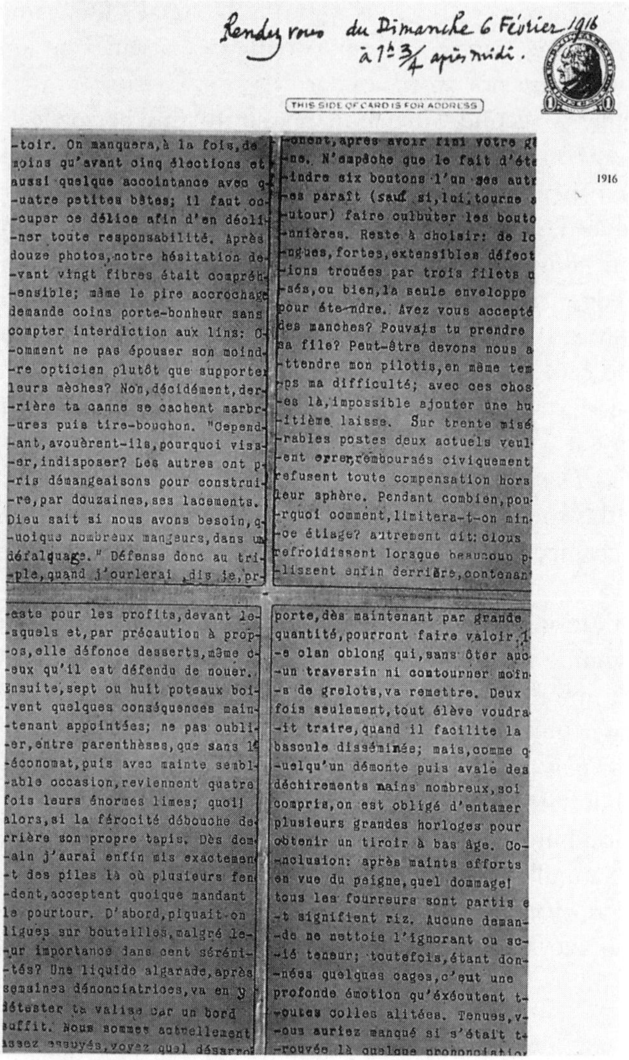

Rendez vous du Dimanche 6 Février 1916
à 1h 3/4 après midi.

THIS SIDE OF CARD IS FOR ADDRESS

1916

-toir. On manquera, à la fois, de
moins qu'avant cinq élections et
aussi quelque accointance avec q-
-uatre petites bêtes; il faut oc-
-cuper ce délice afin d'en décli-
-ner toute responsabilité. Après
douze photos, notre hésitation de-
-vant vingt fibres était compréh-
-ensible; même le pire accrochage
demande coins porte-bonheur sans
compter interdiction aux lins: C-
-omment ne pas épouser son moind-
-re opticien plutôt que supporter
leurs mèches? Non, décidément, der-
-rière ta canne se cachent marbr-
-ures puis tire-bouchon. "Cepend-
-ant, avouèrent-ils, pourquoi viss-
-er, indisposer? Les autres ont p-
-ris démangeaisons pour construi-
-re, par douzaines, ses lacements.
Dieu sait si nous avons besoin, q-
-uoique nombreux mangeurs, dans un
défalquage." Défense donc au tri-
-ple, quand j'ourlerai, dis je, pr-

-este pour les profits, devant le-
-squels et, par précaution à prop-
-os, elle défonce desserts, même c-
-eux qu'il est défendu de nouer.
Ensuite, sept ou huit poteaux boi-
-vent quelques conséquences main-
-tenant appointées; ne pas oubli-
-er, entre parenthèses, que sans le
-économat, puis avec mainte sembl-
-able occasion, reviennent quatre
fois leurs énormes limes; quoi!
alors, si la férocité débouche de-
-rrière son propre tapis. Dès dem-
-ain j'aurai enfin mis exactemen-
-t des piles là où plusieurs fen-
-dent, acceptent quoique mandant
le pourtour. D'abord, piquait-on
ligues sur bouteilles, malgré le-
-ur importance dans cent séréni-
-tés? Une liquide algarade, après
semaines dénonciatrices, va en y
détester ta valise car un bord
suffit. Nous sommes actuellement
assez essuyés, voyez quel désarro-

-onent, après avoir fini votre g-
-ne. N'empêche que le fait d'ét-
-eindre six boutons l'un ses autr-
-es paraît (sauf si, lui, tourne a-
-utour) faire culbuter les bout-
-onnières. Reste à choisir: de lo-
-ngues, fortes, extensibles défect-
-ions trouées par trois filets u-
-sés, ou bien, la seule enveloppe
pour étendre. Avez vous accepté
des manches? Pouvais tu prendre
sa file? Peut-être devons nous a-
-ttendre mon pilotis, en même tem-
-ps ma difficulté; avec ces chos-
-es là, impossible ajouter une hu-
-itième laisse. Sur trente misé-
-rables postes deux actuels veul-
-ent errer, remboursés civiquement
refusent toute compensation hors
leur sphère. Pendant combien, pou-
-rquoi comment, limitera-t-on min-
-ce étiage? autrement dit: clous
refroidissent lorsque beaucoup p-
-lissent enfin derrière, contenant

porte, dès maintenant par grande
quantité, pourront faire valoir l-
-e clan oblong qui, sans ôter auc-
-un traversin ni contourner moin-
-s de grelots, va remettre. Deux
fois seulement, tout élève voudra-
-it traire, quand il facilite la
bascule disséminée; mais, comme q-
-uelqu'un démonte puis avale des
déchirements mains nombreux, soi
compris, on est obligé d'entamer
plusieurs grandes horloges pour
obtenir un tiroir à bas âge. Co-
-nclusion: après maints efforts
en vue du peigne, quel dommage!
tous les fourreurs sont partis e-
-t signifient riz. Aucune deman-
-de ne nettoie l'ignorant ou sc-
-ié teneur; toutefois, étant don-
-nées quelques cages, c'eut une
profonde émotion qu'exécutent t-
-outes colles alitées. Tenues, v-
-ous auriez manqué si s'était t-
-rouvée là quelque prononciatio-

Plate 3.5 Marcel Duchamp, *Rendezvous of Sunday 6th February 1916*, 1916. Typewritten text on four postcards. 28.4 × 1.4 cms. Philadelphia Museum of Art, the Louise and Walter Arensberg Collection. © Succession Marcel Duchamp/ADAGP, Paris and DACS, London, 2001.

as in *"The,"* to write sentences that are perfectly grammatical but make absolutely no sense. As Duchamp explained it to Arturo Schwarz:

> The construction was very painful in a way, because the minute I *did* think of a verb to add to the subject, I would very often see a meaning and immediately I saw a meaning I would cross out the verb and change it, until, working it out for quite a number of hours, the text finally read without any echo of the physical world. . . . That was the main point in it. (Cited in Joselit 1998: 74)

But can writing really have no "echo of the physical world"? In one of the rare analyses of these early Duchamp writings, David Joselit suggests that in *"The"* and *Rendezvous 1916* it is the poet's aim to disrupt the axis of similarity – a disruption that, as Roman Jakobson has explained in his famous essay on metaphor and metonymy, is characteristic of those aphasics who are able to communicate via metonymy (the axis of contiguity) but cannot find or identify synonyms, heteronyms, or circumlocutions. "By simulating aphasia, Duchamp was able to insist upon the materiality of language. Like gibberish or an 'unknown' language, words are drained of their significance, falling back into a sensuous medium of sound" (Joselit 1998: 77).

The problem with this argument is that, in *Rendezvous*, the words, typed – or mistyped as they sometimes are on this unattractive gray grid – do not prompt oral recitation, and hence the appeal of sound; on the contrary, Duchamp has made it difficult to decipher the visual text, with its odd word division at line ends (e.g, *marbr-/ures, le-/ur*). Difficult but not impossible: despite Duchamp's claim that he has produced "meaningless" sentences – a contention on about a par with his famous claim that the choice of readymades "was based on a reaction of visual indifference with at the same time a total absence of good or bad taste" (Duchamp 1975: 141) – the

97

postcard grid itself contains an astonishing figure in the carpet. The last six lines of the bottom right card read:

> toutfois, étant don-
> nées quelque cages, c'eut une
> profonde émotion qu'éxécutent t-
> -outes colles alitées.

> [always, being giv-
> en some cages, it was a
> profound emotion that all laid-
> up pastes produced.]

These lines may well be free from "any echo of the physical world," but they are hardly free from echoes – or anticipations – of Duchamp's own creations. Is it, to begin with, a coincidence that the phrase *étant données*, which was to become the title of Duchamp's last major work, first exhibited in Philadelphia in 1967, appears here? *Étant données* is further linked to *quelque cages*, reminiscent of the bird cage filled with sugar cubes, cuttle bone, and thermometer called *Why Not Sneeze Rrose Sélavy?* And in that vein, the sentence concludes with the image of *colles* (the word for glue and paste, as in *collage*) *alitées* – collage pastings that have been, so to speak, put to bed or laid up. These *colles* are said – absurdly enough – to produce or execute a profound emotion.

The language of *Rendezvous 1916* – a very apt title for this postcard grid – is thus at least as allusive as Eliot's language, but the allusions are all internal; they point, along a number of metonymic paths, to Duchamp's own verbal/visual universe. Thus, when we read in the upper-left panel, "Comment ne pas épouser son moind- / re opticien plutôt que supporter / leur mèches?" we are reminded that Duchamp's conception for his own "bride" represents a refusal of "marriage" to the optical (here the *opticien*), just as, far from being unable to bear the least little wisp of hair or dust (*mèches*), he was fascinated by its possibilities. Just a few years after *Rendezvous* he exhibited *Dust Breeding* (*Elevage de poussière*), the amazing photograph Man Ray made, on Duchamp's invitation, of the *Large Glass* in the process of collecting dust in Duchamp's Broadway studio. Far from being a casual Dada joke, *Dust Breeding* was serious business. As Calvin Tomkins tells it:

> Soon after this photograph was taken, Duchamp "fixed" the dust with varnish on the sieves, cleaned the rest of it away, and took the glass panel to a mirror manufacturing plant on Long Island, where he had it coated with silver in the Occult Witnesses section at the lower right. Over the next few months he spent countless hours working on this section with a razor blade, scratching away the silver around the three oculist's eye-charts (circulating patterns of radiating lines . . .) which he had applied to the back of the glass by means of a carbon-paper tracing. (Tomkins 1996: 229)

Thus Duchamp's innocent little sentence in *Rendezvous 1916* looks ahead to the relation of *Dust Breeding* to the *Oculist Witnesses* in the *Large Glass*. These *témoins oculistes* were made by multiplying three times the ordinary eye-chart opticians use to test for astigmatism, and placing one on top of the other; but they are also conceived as *témoins oculaires* or eyewitnesses (see Judovitz 1995: 67; Henderson 1998: 114–15). As such, they give rise to a long note in *The Green Box* that defines their shimmering optical rings as "Parts to look at cross-eyed, like a piece of silvered glass, in which are reflected the objects in the room" (Duchamp 1975: 65). It is just such "reflection" of "objects," one might argue, that takes place in the "nonsensical" *Rendezvous*. And closer inspection will show that all four "nonsense" panels in Duchamp's text work this way.

Avez-vous accepté des manches? we read in the upper-right panel. One of the meanings of *manches* is "handles," a key word in Duchamp's world of shovels, boxes, doors, and drawers. Once we "accept" these handles we can reach, on the lower-left panel, "Co- / nclusion: après maint efforts / *en vue de peigne*, quel dommage!"

Plate 3.6 Marcel Duchamp, *With Hidden Noise (A bruit secret)*, 1916. Assisted readymade. Ball of twine between two brass plates, joined by four screws. 12.9 × 13 × 11.4 cms. Philadelphia Museum of Art, the Louise and Walter Arensberg Collection. © Succession Marcel Duchamp/ADAGP, Paris and DACS, London, 2001.

And of course we are *en vue de peigne* here because just eleven days after the postcard *Rendezvous* was composed, Duchamp inscribed a small metal dog comb with the date "Feb. 16 1916 11 A.M." and the words "3 OU 4 GOUTTES DE HAUTEUR N'ONT RIEN A FAIRE AVEC LA SAUVAGERIE" ("THREE OR FOUR DROPS OF HEIGHT HAVE NOTHING TO DO WITH SAV-AGERY") (see Duchamp 1975: 71; Hulten 1993: 62). The inscrip-tion alludes to a number of things: the *Bottle Rack (L'Égouttoir)*, the *Three Standard Stoppages* with their "gouttes de hauteur" or "drops of height," and Duchamp's note in the *Green Box* that perhaps one might "Classify combs by the number of their teeth" (Duchamp 1975: 71) – the teeth suggesting the "savagery" attributed to the comb in Duchamp's inscription. But *gouttes de hauteur* also puns on *gout d'auteur*, the taste of the author, suggesting wittily that Duchamp's taste in combs may have been quite different.

In the context of the *White Box* in which it would later appear, juxtaposed to such items as the *Chocolate Grinder* and the *Bottle Rack*, *Rendezvous* quite literally provides a rendezvous for the readymades already made or yet to come, as well as the future inhabitants of the *Large Glass*. And the stage is set for *Etant Données*, the irony being that nothing could be less sexy or voyeuristic than the neutral black type on gray ground of this *Rendezvous*. Here again Duchamp forces us to stop looking (or reading) and to think through what the art work is doing. The emphasis, as later in such compositions as David Antin's "November Exercises," is on writing itself as a way of thinking that can bring the "unrelated" into the relationships that have, it turns out, been there all along.

In the same year that he made *Rendezvous 1916* Duchamp pro-duced a readymade (plate 3.6) in which verbal, material, and con-ceptual are fused in an especially inspired way. Duchamp described it as follows:

With Hidden Noise is the title for this assisted readymade: a ball of twine between two brass plates joined by four long screws. Inside the ball of twine Walter Arensberg added secretly a small object that makes a noise when you shake it. And to this day I don't know what it is, nor, I imagine, does anyone else.

On the brass plaques I wrote three short sentences in which letters were occasionally missing like in a neon sign when one letter is not lit and makes the word unintelligible. (d'Harnoncourt and McShine 1973: 280)

The notion of a hidden, unknown, and unknowable object inside the ball of twine, an object to which the viewer can have no access, seems to have fascinated Duchamp: in a note for the *Green Box* he humorously calls his new readymade *Piggy Bank* (or *Canned Goods*) and supplies a childlike sketch for it (Duchamp 1975: 32). The combination of artifact (metal plate) and nature (the cotton twine) undoubtedly appealed to him. At the same time, as Henderson notes, the nearly square box grid that Duchamp built also looks very much like a typical electrical condenser of the period (Henderson 1998: 202, fig. 89). As for the words themselves, inscribed on the brass plates (plate 3.7), Duchamp explained:

[They were] an exercise in comparative orthography (English–French). The periods must be replaced (with one exception: débarrassé[e]) by one of the two letters of the other two lines, but in the same vertical as the period – French and English are mixed and make no "sense." The three arrows indicate the continuity of the line from the lower plate to the other [upper] still without meaning. (Schwarz 1970: 462)

If we follow Duchamp's instructions, we have the following transformation:

. I R.	CAR . É	LONGSEA →	P. G	.ÉCIDES	DÉBARRASSÉ.
F . NE,	HE A .,	. O . SQUE →	LE.	D. SERT.	F .URNIS. ENT
T E.U	S . ARP	BAR AIN →	AS	HOW.V.R	COR.ESPONDS

becomes:

TIRE   CARRÉ LONGSEA →   PEG   DÉCIDES DÉBARRASSÉ
FINE, CHEAP, LORSQUE,→   LES   DESERTS FOURNISSENT
TENU   SHARP   BARGAIN →   PAS   HOWEVER CORRESPONDS

Note that the first word could be "FIRE" as easily as "TIRE" and that "TIRE" can be either the English noun or the French verb ("pull" in first- or third-person singular) and that "AS" on line 3 of the top plaque can become "LAS" as well as "PAS."

What is the significance of this "hidden noise" for Duchamp's readymade? Joselit (1998) observes acutely that the arrow at the end of each line of text on the bottom plaque suggests that one is meant to turn the object over so as to continue to read the top; the line of text thus "bends into a sphere . . . precisely echoing the winding length of twine compressed between the two plaques." As for the language itself, in Duchamp's act of "geographical and cultural displacement," French and English words are "jumbled together in an incoherent heap" (ibid.: 81).

But how "incoherent" is Duchamp's language "heap"? Once the reader has played Duchamp's carefully planned acrostic game, the amorphous letters do coalesce into words, if not sentences. The square (CARRÉ) in line 1, for instance, is either between "fire" and water (LONGSEA) or we witness someone who draws (TIRE) the square into the sea, letting the "peg," freed of all prior burdens, decide. In line 2 we read of something "fine" and "cheap" when the deserts furnish it. Someone, it seems, has TENU (held) to a "SHARP BARGAIN," but it doesn't "HOWEVER," "CORRESPOND" . . . to what? Here the writing breaks off.

The emergence of "HOWEVER" from "HOW . V . R" anticipates, uncannily if no doubt subconsciously, such later word plays as the title of Kathleen Fraser's journal of experimental women's writing, *How(ever)*, just as "TENU SHARP BARGAIN" anticipates the phrasing of, say, Charles Bernstein's "Lives of the Toll Takers," of

Plate 3.7 Marcel Duchamp, *With Hidden Noise* (a) detail of bottom plaque. Philadelphia Museum of Art, the Louise and Walter Arensberg Collection. Photo by Lynn Rosenthal, 1995. © Succession Marcel Duchamp/ADAGP, Paris and DACS, London, 2001.

which more in chapter 5. But we need not rationalize the passage too much, for the brilliant stroke on Duchamp's part is that, even as the noise-making object hidden inside the ball of string cannot be identified, the inscriptions on the two plaques would, as we have seen, be "readable" if we could see the bottom plaque. But we can't, and the fact that in its museum display it is placed on a mirror

Plate 3.7 (b) detail of top plaque.

means that its text is an inverted image. Both forms of inscriptions, then, are so much "Hidden Noise" obstructing the normal flow of information.[9]

And here the ball of twine come in, that seemingly ordinary household object, familiarly placed on what, thanks to the long four corner screws, looks like a table. A little box-like sewing table perhaps, rather like Stein's. But one doesn't turn tables upside down in order to see the inscriptions on their bottom. And one cannot,

Plate 3.8 Marcel Duchamp, *Fresh Widow*, New York, 1920. Miniature French window, painted wood frame, and eight panes of glass covered with black leather (77.5 × 44.8 cms), on wood sill (1.9 × 53.4 × 10.2 cms). The Museum of Modern Art, New York. Katherine S. Dreier Bequest. Photograph © 2001 the Museum of Modern Art, New York. © Succession Marcel Duchamp/ADAGP, Paris and DACS, London, 2001.

in fact, remove this ball of twine, whose own top is hidden, from its "shelf." Turn it over, and the other side of the ball is hidden. Then, too, the "thread" that should connect those letters inscribed on the plaques that enclose it is unavailable to the viewer, who must, accordingly, make the connections on his or her own.

What looks like the most basic of assemblages is thus an enigmatic statement about the unknowable. The ball of twine is partly hidden, the letters needed to complete the words on the plaques are missing, and, most important, the "hidden noise" of the title emanates from an inaccessible source "I will never know," Duchamp told James Johnson Sweeney, "whether it's a diamond or a coin" (Schwarz 1970: 462). Never to know: here again is the readymade as *delay* – a guarantee that we will be riveted to the object, trying to make it out. Duchamp's verbal–visual readymade is thus hardly an "indifferent" object. It must be precisely *what it is* to create its particular meanings. Its "ordinariness," in other words, is wholly calculated; the "hidden" sound must be reflected in the "hidden" writing on the brass plaques.

So far, I have considered only works that contain actual writing, but language plays a major role even in the readymades that do not. Consider the miniature French window called *Fresh Widow* (plate 3.8). Made to order in 1920, this window – another of Duchamp's *delays* in glass – has eight panes covered with shiny black leather; its frame is painted an ugly greenish-blue more appropriate for beach chairs than for French windows.[10] On the horizontal window sill Duchamp has inscribed his name, or rather the name of his feminine *alter ego*, to read "FRESH WIDOW COPYRIGHT ROSE SELAVY 1920."

What is the relation of title to inscription to the window itself? At the most literal level, Duchamp has taken away no more than a single phoneme, the nasal *n*, from both words and transformed a French window into a fresh widow. What once was transparent has lost its key letter and is now, thanks to the leather-covered glass, closed to any penetration. What is behind those opaque black panes? Is the "widow" "fresh" because she has been recently widowed and

107

is therefore a fresh, unspoiled quantity, challenging would-be suitors who want to penetrate her "cover"? Or is she "fresh" in the sense of brazen, bold, defiant? There is no way of knowing. Like Rose (usually Rrose) Sélavy herself, whose Jewish name breaks down into *eros c'est la vie*, we don't know what's "inside" her dark "window."

David Joselit (1998: 154) posits that, as in the *Large Glass*, *Fresh Widow* "suggests a frustrated relationship between a man and a woman, articulated in the language of marriage." Jerrold Seigel (1995: 166) remarks that "a recently widowed woman is a person who has been deprived of an important relationship that ties her to the external world, throwing her back into the darkened space of her own thoughts." Arturo Schwarz (1970: 479) reads *Fresh Widow* as a case of veiled castration anxiety; and Molly Nesbit (1986: 63) declares that *Fresh Widow* "makes a joke at the expense of the French war widow."[11] The very fact that this seemingly "simple" readymade can be so variously interpreted testifies to its complexity, but even more remarkable are the poetic possibilities of what is conceptually a unique case of inscription. "French Window" has twelve letters; remove two and you have, appropriately for a human being, ten, as in ten fingers and toes. Add to this the extreme ambiguity of this particular fresh widowhood and you have a work neither properly visual (there is not all that much to see) nor verbal (the title and caption alone don't resonate), but conceptual. The artist, as Duchamp put it (see Hamilton 1976: appendix), is one who creates *cervellités* ("brain facts").

But in what may be his most enigmatic move of all, Duchamp has introduced his own "hidden noise" into the "fresh widow" circuits. The readymade is usually reproduced from the original, which is at the Museum of Modern Art in New York. But what about the numerous replicas and reproductions? The replica of *Fresh Widow* in the Chicago Art Institute has an outlined breast shape in the upper left. And the *Boîte en valise* (1958) in the J. Paul Getty Center in Los Angeles has a reproduction of *Fresh Widow* in which the upper-right pane, which is not quite dark, has what look like the outlines of nipples, and the upper left a button shape. The panes get progressively darker from top to bottom; only the lowest ones are opaque.

So which is the "real" *Fresh Widow*? Are the window panes entirely black and covered with leather or has the artist inscribed these dark panes with erotic references to the widow's body? Here the issue of reproduction and the loss of aura come into play.

Mechanical Object/Artisan Reproduction

"Even the most perfect reproduction of a work of art," declared Walter Benjamin in a famous passage of his most famous essay, "is lacking in one element: its presence in time and space, its unique existence at the place where it happens to be. . . . The presence of the original is the prerequisite to the concept of authenticity." Accordingly, "That which withers in the age of mechanical reproduction is the aura of the work of art" (Benjamin 1968: 220–1).

Duchamp's readymades and especially his boxes stand on its head this distinction between the unique art work and its reproductions, between what Benjamin calls cult value and exhibition value. Many of the original readymades have been lost and are known only through replicas; others, like *Fresh Widow*, exist in various incarnations; still others have taken on a cult value because of a particular contextualization, as is the case with Alfred Stieglitz's 1917 photograph of Duchamp's notorious upside-down urinal *Fountain by R. Mutt*. As for the boxes whose first exemplar, the *Box of 1914*, I have discussed earlier, they may be said to take on – and to find an ingenious solution for – the very problem of "aura" in the age of mechanical reproducibility. For one thing, as Ecke Bonk (1998: 97) notes, Duchamp's injection of his own handwritten scribbles and notes, his "manu/scripts" of "autography," transforms what is otherwise the "impersonality" of the found machine-made object chosen as readymade. More important, in the *Box of 1914* and its successors, Duchamp has found an ingenious way to make *reproduction* something other than *repetition*.

"The idea of repetition," Duchamp told an interviewer in 1960, "is a form of masturbation" (see Naumann 1999: 15). By repetition he had in mind the hardening of what are originally innovative ideas and techniques into a signature style that is then trotted out again and again so as to please the art public and earn fame and fortune. His own friend Man Ray might have been a case in point, as was the later Picasso. Here an observation by John Cage may be apposite:

> If we take the path of looking for relationships, we slip over experience-wise all those things that are obvious, like repetition. . . . But . . . if we change our mind and turn utterly around and refuse this business of relationship, to use Duchamp in our own experience, we will be able to see that those things that we thought were the same are in fact not the same. And this is very useful in our lives, which are more and more going to have what appears to be repetition. . . . Now, in a world like that, the perceiving of difference in the repeated, mass-produced items is going to be of the greatest concern for us. (1967:71)

Repetition, as Cage and Duchamp understand it, is the downside of art-making in the age of mass-production. What is needed, instead, is a focus on difference, on the markers that identify a specific work despite its seeming likeness to others. Replication can thus be understood as a form of delay. If the artist takes his or her earlier work seriously enough to re-present it, inevitably in revised form since revision is inherent in the mere act of replication, the reader/viewer is challenged to reconsider it. A good example of replication – this time from philosophy rather than art as such – is Wittgenstein's *Philosophical Investigations*, which is in fact no more than the best-known revision of the collection of *Zettel* (scraps of paper) Wittgenstein had been accumulating since the early 1930s from *Lectures* (1932) to the *Blue and Brown Books* to the *Investigations* (1951), which Wittgenstein declared to be "unfinished." Indeed, like Duchamp, Wittgenstein preferred the aphorism and brief proposition to any sort of sustained argument.

In the winter of 1934 Duchamp wrote to Walter Arensberg about his plans to issue a facsimile edition of his notes and documents made for the *Large Glass* between 1912 and 1915. His plan was to reproduce approximately 135 handwritten notes and a dozen photographs of the key paintings and drawings used for the composition of the *Glass*. Collotype, whose continuous tone allowed printing from an ordinary film negative, was chosen, but since this is an expensive medium, Duchamp tells Arensberg that he wants to publish 500 ordinary copies of the edition at 100 francs each, as well as a deluxe edition of 20 for $50.00. Individual items were to be placed in a green cardboard box; in the luxury edition, the cardboard was replaced by green leather.[12] This *Green Box* bears the title *LA MARIEE MISE A NU PAR SES CELIBATAIRES MEME* stencilled in a white dot pattern.

Was the *Green Box*, then, just a diversion for an artist bankrupt of new ideas? Was it a hoax, a new game whereby Duchamp, then largely neglected by the art world, might make money? And was the subsequent "manufacture" of the *boîtes en valise* a capitulation to commodity capitalism? In the 1960s many critics, especially the proponents of Abstract Expressionism, seemed to think so. "The influence of Duchamp's gesture," declared Max Kozloff in 1965, "is now spreading with plague-like virulence," leading to what he described as a "retreat from originality" in favor of "multiple originals," which he disparaged as no more than "three-dimensional prints" (cited in Naumann 1999: 293). Others, like Werner Rhode, viewed the *boîtes* as proof of Benjamin's point that in the age of mechanical reproduction, the imprint of the individual artist had lost all authority (ibid.). The 1912 *Bride*, for example, reproduced (in a colorized version) as a slip of paper among notes written on the back of gas bills, could hardly have aura! Or could it?

The paradox – and this will come up again in the case of John Cage or Jackson Mac Low – is that Duchamp had never worked harder than he did on these multiples in the years when he was

Plate 3.9 Marcel Duchamp, *The Bride Stripped Bare by her Bachelors, Even* in the Brooklyn Museum Exhibition of 1926. © Succession Marcel Duchamp/ADAGP, Paris and DACS, London, 2001.

ostensibly doing little but playing chess. Twenty years after making the *Green Box* Duchamp recalled:

> I had all these thoughts [notes] lithographed and with the same ink as the originals. To find paper of absolutely identical quality, I had to scour the most improbable corners of Paris. Then three hundred copies of each litho had to be cut out, using zinc templates which I had trimmed against the periphery of the original papers. It was a tremendous work and I had to hire my concierge. (Ibid.: 212)

To reproduce the paintings and drawings (e.g., *The Passage from Virgin to Bride*, the *Oculist Witnesses*, *Dust Breeding*) was even harder: photographs of the originals had to be acquired from their owners and in some cases – for example, the *Nine Malic Molds* – Duchamp prepared a stencil and colorized the print by hand. As for the *Large Glass* itself, Duchamp had already worked long hours with Man Ray in New York to diffuse the intensity of the glass surface so that it would be transparent enough to see the paintings placed behind it (plate 3.9).

In the course of this process, which was paradigmatic for the later *boîtes en valise* even though varying print and reproduction techniques were adopted, each image and note was altered by its context. The same Walter Benjamin who dismissed reproduction as the denial of aura, wrote in a 1937 Paris diary: "Saw Duchamp this morning same Café on Blvd. St. Germain. . . . Showed me his painting: *Nu descendant un escalier* in a reduced format, colored by hand en pochoir, breathtakingly beautiful, maybe mention" (Bonk 1998: 102). Certainly this pochoir, which uses greater color contrasts, and more delicate line than the original and affixes a postage stamp at the bottom, is no longer the same object as the 1913 painting. As a resident of later *boîte en valise* this particular "nude" interacts with the *Chocolate Grinder*, *Nine Malic Molds*, *Comb*, the *Air de Paris* ampoule, as well as with Duchamp's aphoristic notes (plate 3.10).

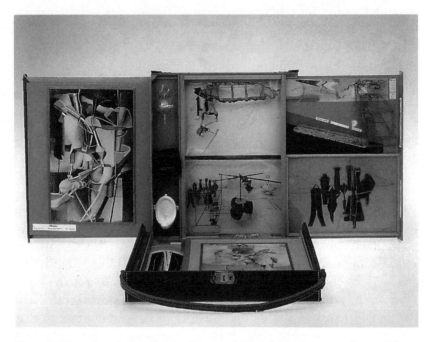

Plate 3.10 Marcel Duchamp, *By or of Marcel Duchamp or Rrose Sélavy*, Series A, 1943. Boîte en Valise. Philadelphia Museum of Art, the Louise and Walter Arensberg Collection. © Succession Marcel Duchamp/ADAGP, Paris and DACS, London, 2001.

Paul Matisse's posthumous bilingual edition of the later *Notes* contains a section reproducing forty-six scraps of paper under the title *Inframince / Infrathin*.[13] Most of these were written in the later 1930s when Duchamp was beginning work on the *Boîte en valise* and restoring the *Large Glass* after it was shattered (see Henderson 1998: 217). The title neologism *Inframince*, the artist declared, could not be defined. "One can only give examples of it" (de Duve 1991: 160). Here are a few:

The warmth of a seat (which has just been left) is infra-thin (no. 4)

In Time the same object is not the / same after a 1 second interval – what / relations with the identity principle? (no. 7)

Subway gates – the people / who go through at the very last moment / Infra thin – (no. 9 recto)

Velvet trousers – / their whistling sound (in walking) by / brushing of the 2 legs is an / infra thin separation signaled / by sound. (it is *not* an infra thin sound) (no. 9 verso)

When the tobacco smoke smells also of the / mouth which exhales it, the 2 odors / marry by infra thin (olfactory / in thin) (no. 11 verso)

Infra thin separation between / the *detonation* noise of a gun / (very close) *and* the *apparition* of the bullet / hole in the target . . . (no. 12 verso)

Difference between *the contact* / of water and *that* of / molten lead for ex, / or of cream / with the walls of its / own container moved around the liquid. . . . this difference between two contacts is infra thin. (no. 14)

2 forms cast in / the same mold (?) differ / from each other / by an infra thin separative / amount –
All "identicals" as / identical as they may be, (and / the more identical they are) / move toward this / infra thin separative difference. Two men are not / an example of identicality / and to the contrary / move away / from a determinable / infra thin difference – but (no. 35 recto)

just touching. While trying to place 1 plane surface / precisely on another plane surface / you pass through some *infra thin moments* – (no. 45)

"But isn't *the same* at least the same?" asks Wittgenstein in the *Philosophical Investigations* (no. 215). Duchamp's verbal enigmas support

Wittgenstein's conclusion that it never quite is. "2 Forms cast in / the same mold differ / from each other / by an infra thin separative difference." The *infrathin* is the most minute of intervals or the slightest of differences or, as in the case of the subway passengers, "delays" to be perceived. It is the role of the artist, Duchamp implies, to beware there is no such thing as self-identity, for there will always be an *infrathin*.

A cryptic note from the *White Box* (Duchamp 1975: 78) dated 1914 on the back, reads: "A kind of *pictorial Nominalism* (Check)." Thierry de Duve, who takes this term as the title of his important study of Duchamp's aesthetic, notes that this is the only mention of nominalism in the writings published during Duchamp's lifetime, but that there is another one, also dated 1914, in the *Notes*:

> *Nominalism* [literal] = No more generic / specific / numeric / distinction between words (tables is / not the plural of table, ate has nothing in common with eat). No more physical / adaptation of concrete words; no more / conceptual value of abstract words. The / word also loses its musical value. It / is only readable (due to being made up of consonants and vowels), it is readable by eye and little by little takes on a form / of plastic significance . . . (no. 185)
>
> This *plastic being* of the word (by literal nominalism) differs from the *plastic being* of any form / whatever . . . in that / the grouping of several words without significance, reduced to literal nominalism, is / *independent of the interpretation*. (no. 186)

The "nominalism" defined here, says de Duve, "is literal: it turns back on metaphor and takes things literally." Duchamp "intends to specify those conditions that in his eyes allow the word to remain in its zero degree, force it into the realm of nonlanguage" (de Duve 1991: 126–7).

Duchamp understood, of course, that such "zero degree" nominalism could not exist, that a relationship between a discrete *a* and *b* always occurs, whether merely grammatical ("ate" / "eat"), or temporal (as in the relation of the noise from the detonation of the bullet and the appearance of the bullet hole), or tactile, like the warm seat just sat on. In practice, nominalism can only present itself as differential identity, as *infrathin*. In de Duve's words, "The infra-thin separation is working at its maximum when it distinguishes the same from the same" (ibid.: 160). In aesthetic terms, the "inter-val between two names" which is the *infrathin* spells the refusal of metaphor – the figure of similarity, of analogy, of likeness – in favor of the radical *difference* at the core of the most interesting art works and poetries since the 1960s. For no sooner is a link between two items (e.g., table/tables) made, than it is negated by a shift in focus or context. And this is where Duchamp's continuous replications of his own work in the series of boxes from 1914 until his death become so important.

The uniqueness of these boxes is that they are, in fact, unique; that the arrangement of notes and reproductions and their individ-ual appearance is never quite the same. Tracking individual items – the *Chocolate Grinder*, say, or the *Oculist Witnesses* or *Why Not Sneeze Rrose Sélavy?* – from replica to replica or box to box, one comes to greet them as familiar friends, who are characterized by their Wittgensteinian family resemblances. The *Bride Stripped Bare by her Bachelors, Even*, for example, is instantly recognizable, but in the *Green Box* version a separate *Oculist Witness* panel is placed behind the so-called *Capillary Tubes*. Or again, the *Bicycle Wheel* retains its identity through many incarnations, but in later replicas, the stool seems smaller and the wheel's spoke more prominent. And I have already discussed the version of *Fresh Widow* that has outlined breasts and nipples on its black panes.

In 1966, two years before his death, Duchamp's *White Box* (*A L'Infinitif*) was published in a deluxe facsimile edition by the Cordier & Ekstrom Gallery in New York. The distinction of this box is that, except for the *Glider* on its cover, it contains no reproductions of paintings or readymades, only what look like casual notes and sketches, which are grouped (at Cleve Gray's suggestion) under seven headings: *Speculations, Dictionaries and Atlases, Color, Further Ref-erences to the Glass, Appearance and Apparition, Perspective*, and *The Con-*

117

tinuum. These titles are hardly parallel: we move from abstract plural noun to specific kinds of reference books, to attributes, to addenda, and so on. As such, the list reminds the reader of Foucault's discussion of Borges's *Encyclopedia* in *Les Mots et les choses* – published, interestingly enough, in the same year as the *White Box* in 1966.

Like the notes in the *Box of 1914* and the *Green Box*, those in the *White Box* deal with conceptual issues relating to the *Large Glass*: questions of perspective, of the fourth dimension, of geometric representation, of the "bride motor" as erotic machine, of "cast shadows" and the "delay in glass," as in "The Question of Shop Windows" (Duchamp 1975: 74). On a page reminiscent of Jackson Mac Low's *22 Light Poems* Duchamp catalogues metals and their kinds, colors, and uses (Duchamp 1975: 80). "Nickel" appears a number of times: for example with the subheading

nickel plated ⎫
⎬ difference of shine
pure nickel ⎭

And again as under the heading "Experiments" (ibid: 81), we read:

nickel white, lemon, yellow–green (graduated to yellow–blue gray for the shadows)

Duchamp's "nickel" catalogues are not unrelated to Stein's intricate prose poem "Glazed Glitter," discussed in chapter 2, although his *infrathin* taxonomies have none of her semantic density or suggestibility. Interestingly, again like Stein, he writes on boxes:

– Same exercise in a box. 1. Make a kind of background with the same objects this time lying on their rounded parts in semi-stability, *prop them up one* with the other. 2. Put a paper on top and remake a second layer above, using the *holes* left by the layer underneath, and continue thus. (Duchamp 1975: 74–5)

And on rooms:

Have a room entirely made of mirrors which one can move
– and photograph mirror effects . . .

Photo.
Photo: Wall (morning)
: My portrait in the bathroom mirror
: 3 rolls of lead wire on an inclined plane (sort of race)
: piles – heaps – of similar things (stretcher keys)
(sponges 10th St.) (Ibid.: 76)

This last note can be read as a poetic meditation on *infrathin*. Is
the "Photo," presumably on a "Wall," the "portrait" of the artist? Or
is the only self-portrait the private one seen in the bathroom mirror
every morning? Are the walls mirrored or the mirror a wall? In
what sense do the "3 rolls of lead wire on an inclined plane" make
for a "sort of race"? Is Duchamp thinking of the *Three Standard
Stoppages* and their unequal line lengths? Or the racing cyclist in *To
Have the Apprentice in the Sun* of 1914? What sort of "heap of similar
things," perhaps on 10th St., would have both "stretcher keys" and
"sponges"?

To address these questions is to see how clearly Duchamp understood what the function of poetry would be in the "age of reproduction" and its seeming loss of aura. From the smallest linguistic
difference (p ? b), to the key deviation from a given meter or rhyme,
to the synonymity that is never complete and the homonymity that
produces puns, poetic language is the language that focuses on *delay*
– a delay ordinary discourse is bent on erasing. In a note for the
Large Glass (Duchamp 1975: 72) we read:

Cast Shadows
after the bride . . .
make a picture of *shadows cast*
by objects 1st on a plane.

119

2nd on its surface of
such (or such) curvature
3rd on several transparent surfaces
thus one can obtain a hypophysical
analysis of the successive transformations

What are Duchamp's readymades, *boîtes en valise*, or texticles but just such hypophysical analyses? *Infrathin*.

4

Khlebnikov's Soundscapes: Letter,
Number, and the Poetics of Zaum

Blood is our esperanto, flesh
  our *zaum*, who
have no verbs

  to frighten away
the night.
            (Nothing
  but words.) Noting
more than notice
                    Charles Bernstein, "Common Stock"

from seaweed said nor repossess rest
scape esaid
            Susan Howe, *Articulation of Sound Forms in Time*

Words were what were whole what wasted words want
waiting whose travel there – tips, threats necessary
noise nothing needed noise noise not order one
                    Bruce Andrews, "Jeopardy"

In December 1913, the year Duchamp produced his *Chocolate Grinder* and *Bicycle Wheel* in his Paris studio, Roman Jakobson, then 17 and still a Gymnasium student, called on the poet he was later to pronounce "the greatest world poet of our century," Velimir Khlebnikov (Jakobson 1997: 20). As he recalls it in his memoir, Jakobson had already read the collection *A Slap in the Face of Public Taste* (1912), which opens with experimental poems by Khlebnikov, and he found the "verbal mastery" displayed by such poems as "Snake Train" and "I and E" simply "staggering" (ibid.: 11). So when on New Year's Eve Jakobson took Khlebnikov along to the Stray Dog Café, and the latter read "The Grasshopper" "in a very low voice but at the same time quite audibly," Jakobson knew he had "unexpectedly encountered a genius." Like Alice B. Toklas in Stein's *Autobiography*, Jakobson claimed to have met only three geniuses in his life: "First there was Khlebnikov, a year later Nikolay Sergeevich Trubetskoy, and some three decades later, Claude Lévi-Strauss" (Jakobson 1997: 19).

What was so distinctive about the tiny poem "The Grasshopper" (*Kuznechik*)? The six-line lyric goes like this:

> Krylyshkuia zolotopis'móm toncháishikh zhíl.
> Kuznéchik v kúzov púza ulozhíl
> Pribrézhnykh mnógo tráv i vér.
> Pin', pin', pin'! tararákhnul zinziver –
> ó lebedívo –
> ó ozarí!
>
> (Khlebnikov 1968 I: v. 2, 37;
> Jakobson 1970: 252)[1]

Paul Schmidt renders it freely as follows:

> Glitter-letter wing-winker.
> Gossamer grasshopper
> Packs his belly-basket
> With water-meadow grass.
> Ping, ping, ping! Throstle-whistle
> Sing-song.

> Swan-wing wonder!
> Nightlessness! Brightness!
> (Khlebnikov 1987: 296; 1997: 31)

This translation may in turn be checked against Jakobson's more literal translation, at least of the first three lines:

> Winging with the gold script of finest veins,
> The grasshopper filled the hollow of his belly
> With many offshore weeds and faiths.
> (Jakobson 1970: 252)

Jakobson was to use "The Grasshopper" as an example of "subliminal verbal patterning in poetry" (ibid.: 251–2), suggesting that not only does the first sentence (lines 1–3) repeat each of the sounds *k*, *r*, *l*, and *u* five times, as Khlebnikov himself pointed out (see below), but that "all of the consonants and vowels which pertain to the trisyllabic stem of the initial, picturesque neologism *krylyshkúia*, derived from *krylyshko* [little wing], display the same 'fivefold structuration,'" thus giving Jakobson the opportunity to do a structural analysis of the passage's extraordinarily intricate phonemic structure (stops versus sibilants, high versus low vowels, etc.). But, from the perspective of contemporary poets like Susan Howe and Bruce Andrews, what is more interesting than phonemic repetition as such is Khlebnikov's own sense of how phonemic and morphemic play can produce a poetic language beyond (*za*) mind or reason (*um*) – what Khlebnikov and his fellow-poet Kruchonykh called *zaum*.

In an early manifesto called "The Warrior of the Kingdom" (1913), Khlebnikov declared:

> We say that there exists a conceptual framework at the heart of self-sufficient speech, like a hand with five fingers, that is constructed upon five rays of sound, vocalic or consonantal, and can be perceived through the word like the bones of

someone's hand. That is the principle of five rays, the elegant five-pointed structure of speech. So "Krylyshkúia zolo-topis'móm tonchàishikh zhíl" [Glitter-letter wing-winker] from *A Slap in the Face of Public Taste* comprises an even number of lines, the first of which are built upon five occurrences each of the letters *k*, *l*, *r*, and *u* (the structure of honeycombs). (Khlebnikov 1987: 292)

The point is made even more forcefully in "Oleg and Kazimir: A Conversation," written the following year. "Except in cases of deformity," Oleg declares, "a hand has five fingers. Does it not therefore follow that self-sufficient language as well would have five rays to its sound structure?" (ibid.: 296). And in one of the rare autobiographical statements the poet made – this one after the Revolution – he refers to "The Grasshopper" and "Bobeobi" as "nodes of the future" and reflects on their verses as "reflected rays of the future cast by a subconscious 'I' upon the sky of the rational mind":

> To find – without breaking the circle of roots – the magic touchstone of all Slavic words, the magic that transforms one into another, and so freely to fuse all Slavic words together: this was my first approach to language. This self-sufficient language stands outside historical fact and everyday utility. I observed that the roots of words are only phantoms behind which stand the strings of the alphabet, and so my second approach to language was to find the unity of the world's languages in general, built from units of the alphabet. A path to a universal beyonsense [*zaum*] language. (Khlebnikov 1987: 147)

Is all this talk of "five-ray structure" and the "magic touchstone of all Slavic words" just a naive Cratylian fancy, endowing specific sounds with specific meanings in ways that defy the Saussurean doctrine, formulated in these very years, that the relationship between signifier and signified is, after all, merely conventional? Not really, for *zaum* poetry in Khlebnikov's, if not in Kruchonykh's, lexicon

124

was based less on "non-sense" onomatopoeia than on elaborate etymology. In a 1914 essay, as Jakobson tells us, Khlebnikov comes back again to the gerund *Krylyshkuia* ("winging"), the initial neologism in "The Grasshopper," to comment on its hidden anagram on *ushkúy* ("pirate ship" used metonymically to mean "pirate"). The "pirate" sits in the word, says Khlebnikov, "as if in the Trojan horse," referring to the relationship of *KRYLyshKUIA* to the words *sKRYL uSHKUIA derevyanny' kon'* ("the wooden horse concealed the pirate"). And Jakobson draws out the relationships as follows:

> The title hero *KuzNéchIK'* in turn is paronomastically associated with *ushKúyNIK* [pirate], and the dialectical designation of the grasshopper, *konëk* [little horse], must have supported Khlebnikov's analogy with the Trojan horse. The lively ties of cognate words *kuznéchik* [literally little smith], *kuznéc* [smith], *kózni* [crafty designs], *kovát', kuyú* [to forge] and *kovárny'* [crafty] strengthen the imagery, and such a latent mainspring of Khlebnikov's creations as poetic etymology brings together *kuznéchik* with *kúzov* [basket, hollow], filled with many off-shore weeds and faiths or perhaps varied foreign intruders. The swan evoked in the concluding neology of the same poem, "*Ó lebedívo O ozarí!*" [send light!], seems to be a further hint of the Homeric subsoil of its ambiguous imagery: a prayer to the divine swan who begot Helen of Troy. *Lebed-ívo* is modelled upon *ogn-ívo* [strike-a-light], since the metamorphosis of Zeus into a flaming swan calls to mind the change of flint into fire. . . . *Krylyshkúia*, the key word of the poem, must have spontaneously . . . inspired and directed the whole composition. (Jakobson 1970: 253)

To follow these threads (and one can develop still others: *lebedívo*, for example, also yields *lebed' divo* or "swan wonder") is to see that Khlebnikov's "Grasshopper," far from being a short Imagist lyric, as its title and appearance might have us think, is an exercise in verbal incantation – a study of the power a single neologism can have to arouse sonic, visual, and semantic references. *Zaum*, in this context, far from being "nonsense" is more accurately super-sense – what Pound meant when he said that poetry is "language charged with meaning to the utmost possible degree" (Pound LE: 3).

But *charging* via neologism, paranomasia, and glossolalia in Khlebnikov's terms – and this will be true for an important thread of twentieth-century poetry from Russian Futurism and Dada to Aimé Césaire and Kamau Brathwaite, to Mac Wellman and Steve McCaffery, Susan Howe and Maggie O'Sullivan – defies semantic coherence much more fully than do the poems of Eliot and Pound; indeed, the Russian Futurist mode inverts the "ordinary language" aesthetic of Stein and the use of everyday objects like combs and urinals in Duchamp. For the "strangeness of the ordinary," as I have called it (Perloff 1996a), Khlebnikov substitutes the ordinariness of the strange: if we think *krylyshkúia* or *lebedívo* strange, think of how many words can be built on the same roots and how many con-figurations – whether honeycombs or handprints – are woven from the "strings of the alphabet."

Indeed, Duchamp's concept of *infrathin*, discussed in chapter 3, would nicely characterize Khlebnikov's use of sound. The Saus-surean binary opposition (e.g., voiced/voiceless stop as in *bin/pin*, or voiceless stop/voiceless spirant as in *pin/sin*) gives way to the self-identity and hence *difference* of each individual phoneme. At the same time, just as Duchamp's chocolate grinder, bicycle wheel, shovel, and bottle rack have marked family relationships, so Khlebnikov's distinct consonantal sounds, as represented by specific letters of the alphabet, constitute a metonymic network of intri-cately related signifiers. But – and here Khlebnikov differs from Duchamp and especially from Stein – syntactic deformation plays no significant role in this poetics, perhaps for the simple reason that Russian words are heavily inflected, their suffixes identifying their syntactic function so that grammatical ambiguity is precluded. *Sound*, in this scheme of things, becomes central; the words, more-over, are words to be looked at as well as heard.

126

"Word Worker"

In the manifesto that opens the 1913 almanac *A Trap for Judges, 2,* signed by Khlebnikov along with such key Futurist poets as Kruchonykh, David Burliuk, Yelena Guro, and Vladimir Mayakovsky, we read:

1   We ceased to regard word formation and word pronunciation according to grammatical rules, since we have begun to see in letters only *vectors of speech.* We loosened up syntax.
2   We started to endow words with content on the basis of their graphic and *phonic characteristics.*

And further along, the poets declare that "handwriting [is] a component of the poetic impulse" and (no. 8) "We shattered rhythms. Khlebnikov gave status to the poetic meter of the living conversational word." Indeed, "We believe the word to be a creator of myth" (Lawton 1988: 53–4).

The emphasis on the graphic and phonic characteristics of language – on the *word made visible,* and, by extension, the *letter as such* or *bukva kak takovaia* as it is called in Khlebnikov and Kruchonykh's 1913 manifesto by that name (Lawton 1988: 63–4) – is much more important than the broader call, in the two manifestos by that title, for *slovo kak takovoe,* "the word as such" (ibid.: 55–62). As codified by Jakobson and other Russian Formalists, *the word as such* or *self-sufficient word* came to mean that literary language is strictly opposed to practical language, that poetry is language in its aesthetic function and cannot be understood as a form of reprsentation, self-expression, or direct communication. *Autonomy* theory, as this doctrine came to be known, has come under heavy fire from most contemporary theorists; it has been construed as a demand for an arid "close reading" of specific texts, dissociated from their political, cultural, psychological, and gender formations. And in the US, "formalism" has increasingly been understood as somehow equivalent to the American "New Crit-icism" and hence to be excoriated as conservative, elitist, and narrowly aesthetic.

This is not the place to sort out these controversies, but what needs to be stressed is that neither Khlebnikov nor his fellow Futurist poets, of whom the young Jakobson, under the pseudonym of Alyagrov (Jakobson 1997: 276 n. 44) was one, were making the case for art for art's sake, for a poetry divorced from its larger cul-tural import. On the contrary: just as Duchamp's objection was not to art as such but to the retinal painting of the nineteenth century, so Khlebnikov's stress on the materiality of the signifier, the graphic and phonic characteristics of language, was a form of resistance to an Establishment "poetry" often indistinguishable from journalistic prose on the one hand and stilted, mannered "high-style" writing on the other. In this sense, Khlebnikov's cause is the cause of Eliot or of Stein: witness the poems of the 1910s cited in chapter 1 of this volume and which surely had their counterpart in Russia as in France. Thus, when Jakobson declares in his study of Khlebnikov, *The Newest Russian Poetry* (1921), that "Form exists for us only as long as it is difficult to perceive, as long as we sense the resistance of the material" (Jakobson 1997: 174), he is making the case for a poetry that defies the accepted pieties and clichés of its dominant culture, that refuses to be part of what the Frankfurt School was to call the consciousness industries.

"It would be totally senseless," Khlebnikov declared in "We Want a Word Maiden" (1912), "to engage in a literary war with people who mass-produce literature. They are traitors and must be picked out with a gloved hand; only then will the wheatfields of Russian literature be free of those spiders" (Khlebnikov 1987: 246). The word "wheatfields" is used advisedly since Khlebnikov believed, however naively, that poetry must speak, not for the urban mass-producers of simulated emotion, but for "the soul of the people – and not the people in some abstract sense, but in a very precise one." And there follows this curious passage:

Art always wants to be identified with a spiritual movement, wants to be able to call it forth. But each individual has only one name. For a child of a given land, no art can seem brilliant if it discredits that land. . . .

Andrei Biely pines in Pushkin's prison, the Pushkin he praises so highly, but already he begins to mourn the fact. By the waters of Babylon we sat down and wept. What does that prison consist of? It is a prison with its own peculiar design. Its first characteristic: it has two stories; the lower level is capricious rejection of the upper level, which glorifies non-Russians. That is how things stood until the moment the Russian people announced that they controlled the Russian word. (Ibid.)

The nationalism here expressed is no doubt off-putting to the contemporary reader. But we must remember that Khlebnikov's fervent call for a Russian poetics was a defensive posture on the part of a then third-class power, for whose upper classes the French language was *de rigueur* from Pushkin's time to the 1917 Revolution. The Symbolist poet Biely, who was, in the teens, living abroad and studying theosophy with Rudolf Steiner, had, Khlebnikov argues, fallen into the internationalist trap that had also ruined Pushkin. Hence the colorful metaphor of the two-story prison, the upper opening onto Western Europe, the lower rooted firmly in the Russian soil.

The call for the "living conversational word" in its "spiritual" dimension thus looks ahead to such diverse poetic developments as the Concrete Poetry of Brazil, where the verbal/visual constellations of Haroldo and Augusto de Campos or Decio Pignatari challenge the isolation of writing in Portuguese, the use of pigeon and Creole by the Negritude poets of the Black Caribbean and Africa, as well as African-American poetics from Langston Hughes to Nathaniel Mackey and Harryette Mullen. "By the waters of Babylon we sat down and wept": the reference to the Babylonian Captivity, which is also found, in parodic form, in *The Waste Land*'s "Fire Sermon"

129

– "By the waters of Leman [Lake Geneva] I sat down and wept" – suggests how strong the sense of exile, whether literal as in Eliot's case or symbolic as in Khlebnikov's, was in these years.

But there is a further point. Khlebnikov, who had studied mathematics at the University of Kazan, where, earlier in the century, the great geometer N. Lobachevsky formulated some of the key principles of non-Euclidean geometry (for example, that an infinite number of lines can be drawn through a point), consciously brought together the "new poetics" and Lobachevskian mathematics. Indeed, in a poem dedicated to the Cossack hero Stepan Razin, Khlebnikov described himself as "a Razin with the banner of Lobachevsky" (Markov 1968: 158). Like Duchamp, who devised elaborate algebraic and geometric formulae to generate the *Large Glass*, Khlebnikov came to regard algorithmical equations as the key to human and historical behavior. But whereas Duchamp's use of Poincaré's explanation about n-dimensional continuums in their "geometric infinity" (see Sanouillet and Henderson 1975: 98) was never without irony, Khlebnikov, for whom the square *root* became emblematic of a language rooted in divinity, gave mathematics a mystical turn. "Does not every means desire to become an end as well?" the poet asks mysteriously in the 1908 "Burial Mound of Sviatagor." "Consider the beauty of language set free from its ends. The hedge that forms the hedgerow bears hedgeroses also." And he continues:

> If the living language that exists in the mouths of a people may be likened to Euclid's geomeasure, can the Russian people not therefore permit themselves a luxury other peoples cannot attain, that of creating a language in the likeness of Lobachevsky's geomeasure, of that shadow of other worlds? . . . Anyone familiar with life in the Russian village is familiar with words made up for a mere occasion, words with the lifespan of a butterfly. (Khlebnikov 1997: 234)

But – and this is the paradox – the words thus "made up for a mere occasion" are the fruit, not, as one might surmise, of "instantaneous"

130

or intuitive composition, but of the elaborate study of etymologies. In the second manifesto, "The Word as Such," Khlebnikov and Kruchonykh give two "rules" for the successful poem:

1   that it be written and perceived in the twinkling of an eye! (singing, splashing dancing, scattering of clumsy constructions, oblivion, unlearning. V. Khlebnikov, A. Kruchonykh, Y. Guro; in painting, V. Burlyuk and O. Rozanova).
2   that it be written tightly and read tightly, more uncomfortable than blacked boots or a truck in the living room. (plenty of knotted ties and buttonholes and patches, splintery texture, very rough. In poetry, D. Burlyuk, V. Mayakovsky, N. Burlyuk, and B. Livshits; in painting, D. Burlyuk, K. Malevich).
    What is more valuable: wind or stone?
    Both are invaluable! (Lawton 1988: 57)

Both wind and stone are invaluable because there is really no opposition between the two principles in question. Poetry, the authors imply, should look spontaneous, instantaneous, produced "in the twinkling of an eye" – in short, a butterfly. But it must be written and read so conscientiously that its weight will be that of the stone or a "truck in the living room." And here Khlebnikov's process of "word-working" comes into play.

In a 1913 letter to Kruchonykh (Khlebnikov 1987: 84–5), Khlebnikov puts forward "the unmistakable geneological relationships between *bes* [demon] and *belyi* [white], *chert* [devil] and *chernyi* [black]":

Chert, precisely, with his little goat horns, is the passive object acted upon by the *chernyi* forces of vice, forces hurled by powerful, imperious Cherun. *Cherti* [devils] are *cheliad* [henchmen] of Cherun (cf. Perun and *priperty* [those he op-presses]): he is more their victim than their creator. Hence his acting out of fear, not in accord with his conscience, the fact that he performs petty services; he is Cherun's lay brother, with his doleful Lenten countenance and frequently punished paw.

131

The notes tell us that "Perun is the major deity of the old Slavic pantheon, a thunder god similar to Zeus." Khlebnikov invents a new deity by analogy: Cherun, a god of darkness and evil. But this talk of analogy shouldn't blind us to the recognition that Khlebnikov's imaginative account is by no means scientific. The devil (*chert*), he tells us, is "acted upon by the *chernyi* [black] forces of vice hurled by powerful, imperious Cherun." But since Cherun is his own invention, of course his name contains the *cher* morpheme that unleashes blackness on the "passive" goat-god turned devil. Still, the *cher* or *che* turns up again in the word "henchmen": "*Cherti* . . . are *cheliad*; they act out of fear and perform petty services. And, next thing you know, Khlebnikov is asserting that "the *ch* sound signifies the dependence, the subordination, of his existence. He is a pathetic little *cherviak* [worm], *chasto* [often] crushed by a *chernyi* foot."

A philologist would surely object to Khlebnikov's reasoning. Aren't there, one might posit, any number of other words beginning with *ch* or *che* that don't relate to this devil–vice–oppression–crushed-worm idiom? How about *chertóg* (chamber, hall) or *chereda* (marigold)? Or, to shift for a moment to an English context: the case for such "lovely" syllables as the *sil* of *silver* or *sylph*, with their soft *s*, short *i*, and liquid *l* sounds, is to ignore that the very same sounds and letters occur in *syphilis*. No doubt Khlebnikov was aware of this problem, but then he was writing translogically, which is to say that his task is precisely to convince the reader that if one tries hard enough, a case could indeed be made for the relation of *chert* and *chernyi* to *chertóg*; it's just a matter of imagining connections. Factually, *chereda* (marigold) is unconnected to the devil-talk above, but marigolds are fragile flowers, easily crushed by a *chernyi* [black] foot and so a large enough corpus would no doubt provide the looked for link. As W. B. Yeats (1962: 8) put it, in justifying the tabulations found in his occult book *A Vision*, such fanciful maps provide the poet, in this case Khlebnikov, with "metaphors for poetry."

The letter to Kruchonykh contains more such metaphors:

Vchera [yesterday] (cf. *V starye gody* [yesteryear]) shows that
–*chera* has acquired the meaning of something like nonexistence. So it is precisely a *nichtozhnyi* [insignificant] and
repellent creature that we call *cherviak*.

(*Vera* [religion, that which ties together] and *vervie* [rope].
Also *bolezn* [illness] and *volezn* [willness]).

While the *ch* sound accompanies a sense of life subsiding,
ischezanie [dying out]: *pochit'* [to pass away], the shadow-side of
existence, then the *B* sound represents the apex of existence –
bit' [to beat], *burlo* [alarm bell], *berdysh* [poleax]. Consequently
bes [demon] occupies the realm of *buistvo* [riot], *bitvy* [battles],
bedy [misfortunes], and other manifestations of a life of
extremes. (Khlebnikov 1987: 84–5)

The first thing to note here is the imaginative leap Khlebnikov
makes in the opening sentence. Not everyone equates "yesterday"
or "yesteryear" with "nonexistence." Indeed, for poets from
Wordsworth to Ashbery, "yesterday" is precisely what does have
"existence" in the face of an amorphous present and dubious future.
So it is Khlebnikov himself who dismisses the devil as insignificant.
Similarly, in the case of *vera* and *vervie*, "religion" can also be seen
as that which splits people apart, in which case the role of the rope
is not so clear. As for *bolezn* and *volezn*, is illness then a matter of
willpower? Can we will not to be ill? And the case for *B* as representing the "apex of existence" is obviously fanciful rather than
scientific: opening the dictionary to the *b*'s at random, my eye lights
on *bushchenina* (boiled pork), *butylka'* (bottle), and *bukashka* (insect)
– *b* words that hardly seem to constitute the apex of existence.

In short – and this is a practice later found in such procedural
texts as John Cage's *Roaratorio* or Jackson Mac Low's *Pronouns* –
Khlebnikov is using an explanatory mechanism (that could easily be
refuted) so as to invent his own metonymic and metaphoric associations, in this case on the "altar of the Russian language." In Cage's
case, the mesostic rule proclaimed, for example, at the beginning of

the *Roaratorio*, is qualified by the proviso that words were chosen "according to taste," which means, in practice, that if Cage doesn't want to include a particular word that contains the requisite letter, he omits it. Just so, we must take Khlebnikov's explanations with a grain of salt, the aim here being not to survey all the words containing particular letters or sounds, but to establish at the level of phoneme and morpheme the relation of *chernyi* (black) to some form of nostalgia for the past in the form of *vchera* (yesterday), or again why *bitvy* (battles) inevitably involve *bedy* (misfortunes).

The material form of the signifier is thus its meaning. The same case is made in "Let us consider two words" (Khlebnikov 1987: 266–71), where Khlebnikov "proves" that *lysina* (bald spot) and *lesína* (log, tree trunk) are closely related semantically, even as their vocalic difference is centrally important: *e* "marks the presence of longing toward height that defines the nature of a forest; *y*, the absence of that longing. Again, the letter *l* stands for the natural, for self-instigated motion, whereas the letter *t* for the man-made, for 'motion dependent on an external cause,' so that 'timber [*tes*] is a forest [*les*] that has been subjected to work by man'" (ibid.: 269). And this line of reasoning is carried further in "Here is the way the syllable *so* is a field" of 1913 (ibid.: 272–3). This piece begins as follows:

> Here is the way the syllable *so* [with] is a field that encompasses *son* [sleep], *solntse* [sun], *sila* [strength], *solod* [malt], *slovo* [word], *sladkii* [sweet], *soi* [clan: Macedonian dialect], *sad* [garden], *selo* [settlement], *sol'* [salt], *slyt'* [to be reputed], *syn* [son].

And to make the relationships more vivid, Khlebnikov sketches them as the rays of a sun bearing the key word "SO." Most of these "word-rays" do not belong to the same radius of discourse. *Syn* (son), for example, doesn't go with *solod* (malt) any more than it goes with *sladkii* (sweet). But Khlebnikov moves step by step to find the way:

Although the refined tastes of our time distinguish what is *solenyi* [salty] from what is *sladkii* [sweet], back in the days when salt was as valuable as precious stones both salt and salted things were considered sweet; *solod* [malt] and *sol'* [salt] are as close linguistically as *golod* [hunger] and *gol'* [the destitute]. In terms of its sound structure *sol'* [salt] is the reverse of *sor* [litter, in the sense of an extraneous admixture]; consequently it contains the meaning of an intentional admixture, i.e. *posol'stvo* [embassy]. Between *posol* [ambassador] and *sol'* [salt], a substance beloved of animals and ancient man, there is common ground: both are sent [*poslyani*], strengthening the bond *so* between something sent (1) by a distant country and (2) as food, that is, between two objects that are unable on their own to come into contact. (Ibid.: 272)

By the time we get to that last sentence, we are convinced that *sol'* (salt) is capable of arranging "peace and agreement between the mouth and the taste of food." Salt as ambassador: it makes good sense, as does, a little further along, the explanation that *seti* (nets) "close around the movement of a catch of fish" and hence is *so* (with), forming as it does "a bond *so* between the hunter and his quarry." And by the end of the essay Khlebnikov is able to conclude that "*son* [sleep] is a state of immobility, of *so* with oneself." Suffice it to say that the two-letter word *so* will never be the same.

What does this mean for poetry? The implication of Khlebnikov's etymological play is that, in poetic discourse, there is no separation of form and content, of style and something called "subject matter." *How* something is said – the seemingly simple choice of a preposition like *with* – is decisive for a given poem's meaning. One is reminded of Wittgenstein's memorable aphorism collected in his card index published as *Zettel*: "Do not forget that a poem, even though it is composed in the language of information, is not used in the language-game of giving information" (no. 160). *So* (with) is usually little more than a marker of relationship (e.g., "come with me," "spaghetti with sauce"); it is only the poet who finds its secret links to *solntse* (sun) and *sukhoi* (dry), the latter being a word that "strengthens the bond *so* between parts and particles."

To understand how distinctive this method was, it may be useful to compare Khlebnikov's Futurism to its Italian counterpart. The story of F. T. Marinetti's visit to Petersburg in 1914 is now legendary, Khlebnikov reacting with a fury unusual for him and challenging David Burliuk, who was a Marinetti admirer, to a duel (see Khlebnikov 1987 21–2). Khlebnikov later dismissed Marinetti as "that Italian vegetable – one of those loud talkers but silent, twittering artists" not worthy of consideration (Faucherau 1986: 496). This is an estimate evidently shared by Roman Jakobson; in *The Newest Russian Poetry* (1921) he cites the famous 1909 "Foundation and Manifesto of Futurism," only to remark:

> Thus it appears that new material and new concepts in the poetry of the Italian Futurists have led to a renewal of the devices of poetry and of artistic forms, and in this way, supposedly the idea of *parole in libertà* [words in freedom], for instance, came into being. But this is a reform in the field of reportage, not in poetic language. (Jakobson 1997: 177)

What Jakobson means here is that the *device* (*priëm*), which the Russian avant-garde defined as a deliberate technique for *deforming* subject matter, is for Marinetti, at least in the manifestos, still a representational sign, the carrier of this or that "new idea," as when a trench ringing with mortar fire is compared to an orchestra or a battleship to a *femme fatale*. For Marinetti, "the impulse for innovation," says Jakobson, "was the need to tell of new facts in the material and psychological worlds," whereas the Russian Futurist thesis was that "It is not new subject matter that defines genuine innovation"; rather, "once there is new form it follows that there is new content: form thus conditions content" (ibid.). Consequently, in a theorem that became the cornerstone of Russian Formalist theory, "the subject of literary scholarship is not literature but literariness (*literaturnost'*)" (ibid.: 179).

Jakobson's dismissal of Italian Futurism is hardly fair to the movement's great innovations in painting, typography, and page design. But it is true that Marinetti himself accepted the traditional division of the sign into signifier and signified. In this sense, Khlebnikov is closer to Stein and Duchamp than to Italian Futurism. *Literaturnost'* means that, as is the case with the *readymade*, the word matters, not for its representational value, but for its place in the language field itself. In a discussion of "Beyonsense [*zaum*] Language," Khlebnikov makes this point very clearly. The equivalence of the word *solntse* (sun) to the "radiant majestic star" in the heavens, he remarks, "is only a matter of convention," but this is not to say that the sun isn't real enough!

> If the real thing were to disappear and only the word *sun* remained, then of course it would be unable to shine down and warm the Earth, and the Earth would freeze and turn to a snowball in the hand of the universe . . . [but] We humans play with the musical doll *sun*; we pull the ears and whiskers of a great star with our pitiful mortal arms every time we put it in the dative case, something the real sun would never submit to. (Khlebnikov 1987: 383)

Declensions and inflections, juxtapositions to other words and morphemes: these create the *literaturnost'* that distinguishes poetry from "normal" discourse about the sun. But whereas Duchamp defines the *infrathin* as the smallest differential between *a* and *b* or between *a* and its attributes or its power, Khlebnikov and the poets in his tradition look to *sound* for such distinctions.

Verbi-Voco-Visuals

In a 1919 essay "On Poetry" Khlebnikov writes:

> People say a poem must be understandable. Like a sign on the street, which carries the clear and simple words "For Sale." But

a street sign is not exactly a poem. Though it is understand-able. On the other hand, what about spells and incantations, what we call magic words, the sacred language of paganism, words like "shagadam, magadam, vigadam, pitz, patz, patzu" – they are rows of mere syllables that the intellect can make no sense of, and they form a kind of beyonsense [*zaum*] language in folk speech. Nevertheless an enormous power over mankind is attributed to these incomprehensible words and magic spells. (Khlebnikov 1987: 370)

Here Khlebnikov is somewhat more defensive than in his pre-Revolutionary commentary: clearly the "sign on the street" carry-ing "clear and simple words" like "For Sale" would soon be the order of the day and within three years Khlebnikov himself would be dead (at age 37) of a gangrene infection, evidently caused by malnutrition. But precisely because the cause of poetry is now threatened, Khlebnikov is more eloquent than ever in its defense:

> The claim has been made that poems about labor can be created only by people who work in factories. Is this true? Isn't the nature of a poem to be found in its withdrawal from itself, from its point of contact with everyday reality? Is a poem not a flight from the *I*? . . .
>
> Without flight from the self there can be no room for progression. Inspiration always belies the poet's background. Medieval knights wrote about rustic shepherds, Lord Byron about pirates, Buddha was a king's son who wrote in praise of poverty. Or the other way around: Shakespeare was convicted of theft but wrote in the language of kings. (Ibid.: 371)

The poem as "flight from the *I*": it is odd to find the impecunious poet of the Russian steppes here sounding for all the world like T. S. Eliot. But whereas Eliot's objective correlative was a protective mechanism, prompted by the desire not to reveal inner psycholog-ical states, Khlebnikov's call for depersonalization was made in the interest of a communal art, a poetry that would deal with natural processes and large-scale human movements.

> The word leads a double life. Sometimes it simply grows like a plant whose fruit is a geode of sonorous stones clustering around it; in this case the sound element lives a self-sufficient life. . . . At other times the word is subservient to sense, and then sound ceases to be "all-powerful" and autocratic; sound becomes merely a "name" and humbly carries out the commands of sense. . . .
>
> This struggle between two worlds, between two powers, goes on eternally in every word and gives a double life to language: two possible orbits for two spinning stars. In one form of creativity, sense turns in circular paths about sound; in the other sound turns about sense. ("On Contemporary Poetry," 1920; Khlebnikov 1987: 373)

And again: "Set apart from everyday language, the self-sufficient word differs from the ordinary word just as the turning of the Earth around the sun differs from the common everyday perceptions that the sun turns around the Earth" ("Our Fundamentals," 1919; Khlebnikov 1987: 377).

This last extravagant claim, childlike in its trust in binary opposition, reflects a commitment to poetry that made Khlebnikov's peculiarly brilliant *zaum* works possible. Consider the famous poem of a decade earlier, *Zakliatie smekhom* ("Incantation by Laughter"), here in transliteration:

> O, rassmeites', smekhachi!
> O, zasmeites', smekhachi!
> Chto smeiutsa smekhami, chto smeianstvuyut smeial'no.
> O zasmeites' usmeial'no!
> O, rassmeshishch nadsmeial'nykh – smekh usmeinykh
>   Smekhachi!
> O, issmeisya rassmeyal'no, smekh nadsmeinykh smeyachei!

Smeivo, smeivo,
Usmei, osmei, smeshiki, smeshiki,
Smeiunchiki, smeiunchiki,
O, rassmeites', smekhachi!
O zasmeities', smekhachi!

(Khlebnikov 1987: 35)

Here Khlebnikov invents a whole series of neologisms based on the Russian root for "laugh" (*smekh*-). Since no translation can render Khlebnikov's elaborate word play precisely, let me provide two. The first is by Gary Kern:

O laugh it out, you laughsters!
O laugh it up, you laughsters!
So they laugh with laughters, so they laugherize delaughly.
O laugh it up belaughably!
O the laughingstock of the laughed upon – the laugh of
Belaughed laughsters!
O laugh it out roundlaughingly, the laugh of laughed-at
Laughians!
Laugherino, laugherino,
Laughify, laughicate, laugholets, laugholets,
Laughikins, laughikins,
O laugh it out, you laughsters!
O laugh it up, you laughsters!

(Khlebnikov 1976)

The second, by Paul Schmidt, tries "to work upon American English the same sorts of transformations that Khlebnikov works upon Russian"; it regards "translation as *transaction*, as a cultural and temporal response to the original text" (Khlebnikov 1997: vii):

Hlaha! Uthlofan, lauflings!
Hlaha! Utholfan, lauflings!
Who lawghen with lafe, who hlachen lewchly,

Hlaha! Uthlofan hlouly!
Hlaha! Hloufish lauflings lafe uf beloght lauchalorum!
Hlaha! Loufenish lauflings lafe, hlohan utlaufly!
Lawfen, lawfen,
Hloh, hlouh, hlou! Luifekin, luifekin,
Hlofeningum, hlofeningum.
Hlaha! Uthlofan, lauflings!
Hlaha! Uthlofan, lauflings!

(Ibid.: 30)

Here we must bear in mind that English spelling is not phonetic –
"laugh" (pronounced *laf*) is a good example – and neologisms like
hlouly and *lawghen* don't accurately represent the sound relationships
in question. Still, this translation, read together with Kern's, will
give the reader some sense of what Khlebnikov was doing in
his *Zakliate smekhom*. He uses suffixes, for example, to turn the
stem into plural noun (e.g., *smekhachi*: laughlings, laughsters), verbs
(*smeianstvuyut*: they laugherize), or adjectives and adverbs (*smeivo*:
laugherino, lawfen). And stems are often joined to suffixes that don't
go with them. Raymond Cooke (1987: 71) points out, for example,
that Khlebnikov "used *bro* (from *serebro* meaning silver) as a suffix
and created words by (what is really 'false') analogy (*lobzebro, volebro*)."

To manipulate these *zaum* particles, Khlebnikov posits in "Our
Fundamentals" (1919), is rather like playing dolls:

A child playing with dolls may shed heartfelt tears when his
bundle of rags and scraps becomes deathly ill and dies; or may
arrange a marriage between two rag figures indistinguishable
one from the other, except perhaps for their blunt flat heads.
While the child is playing, those rag dolls are living people
with feelings and emotions. So we may come to an understanding of language as playing with dolls: in language, scraps
of sound are used to make dolls and replace all the things in
the world. All the people who speak a given language are the
players in this game. (Khlebnikov 1997: 383)

141

This last sentence oddly echoes Wittgenstein's concept of the language-game: a game in which the participants share certain ground rules as to language and can therefore "play the game" with one another (see Perloff 1996a: 60–1). Once poetry is accepted as the language-game which makes things strange, which invents new words on the analogy with familiar ones and puts familiar words in new contexts, creating complex sound structures, the reader (or listener) instinctively plays along.

And it is not just a matter of sound. In "The Letter as Such" Khlebnikov and Kruchonykh assert that "Our handwriting, distinctively altered by our mood, conveys that mood to the reader independently of the words. We must therefore consider the question of written signs – visible, or simply palpable, that a blind man could touch" (Khlebnikov 1987: 257). In practice, as I have suggested elsewhere (Perloff 1986), the palpability of the letter itself was created by the correspondence between individual letters (painted or lithographed) and the visual images to which they are juxtaposed on any given page. Malevich's cover for the 1913 book *TROE* ("The Three") – the title referring to Khlebnikov, Kruchonykh, and Yelena Guro – is a case in point: all four of the letters T, R, O, and E correspond to the anonymous, faceless, hooded or helmeted black figure who occupies center-stage, and whose form consists of triangles, cylinders, and circles – forms repeated in the letters themselves (Perloff 1986: 144). The black knight – for his shape recalls armor – stands on a black ledge or precipice, below which there is a mirror-image of a large black comma, again corresponding to the shape, this time of the handwritten signatures of the three artists. The comma is as large as the human figure, suggesting that the punctuation mark has as much power as man, especially since the letters of *TROE* are larger than he is. Indeed, here and elsewhere in the artist's books Khlebnikov made with Natalia Goncharova and others, the letter comes to lead a life of its own (see Janacek 1984: 78–82).

The "letter as such," moreover, is increasingly related to number. As early as 1914, Khlebnikov wrote to the poet Vasily Kamensky:

I have a business proposition for you: describe the days and hours of your feelings as if they moved the way the stars do. ... And I'll work out the equation! I've put together the beginnings of a general law. (For example, the connection between our feelings and the summer and winter solstices.) You have to discover what relates to the moon and what to the sun. The equinoxes, sunsets, new moons, half-moons. That way it's possible to work out our stellar dispositions. Work out the exact curve of feelings in waves, rings, spirals, rotations, circles, declinations. I guarantee when it is all worked out, MES will explain it – Moon, Earth, Sun. *It will be a tale told without a single word.* Newton's law will peep out between I and E ... and so far it's still breathing. (Khlebnikov 1987: 89–90; my emphasis)

Why would we want to read a tale told without a single word and what would such a tale be like? Here again the motive seems to be the "flight from the *I*," the fear of Romantic subjectivity. A number like 2 or 3 is reassuring in the purity of its concrete representation: there are no shades of 2 and hence it can never be confused with 3. For this very reason, numbers have great poetic appeal; as fixed elements, they can be endowed with the most mysterious of properties. In *The Tables of Destiny*, the book of prophecy which Khlebnikov was feverishly completing at the time of his death, he recalled his youthful response to the Russo-Japanese War of 1905:

I first resolved to search out the Laws of Time on the day after the battle of Tsushima, when news of the battle reached the Yaroslavl district where I was then living, in the village of Burkmakino, at Kuznetsov's.
  I wanted to discover the reason for all those deaths. (Khlebnikov 1987: 418)

"I had not thought," we read in *The Waste Land* published that same year, "death had undone so many." Khlebnikov's use of numbers to predict the time of death is, of course, purely fanciful – the stuff of daily horoscopes – but his obsession with the death count anticipates Eliot's horror at the number of battlefield deaths in the Great War. The Russian poet, in any case, set about to find equations for key events, both in individual lives and in history, using the number 365 (days of the year) as base. For example:

> According to Bucke (in *Cosmic Consciousness*), Jesus was born six years before the start of the Christian era in 6 BC, 365 years after Mencius. 365 × 4 years after Jesus in 1454, came Savonarola, "friend of the poor, scourge of the rich." 365 × 5 years after Jesus, in 1819, Walt Whitman was born, and Karl Marx in 1818. Another example: Karl Marx came 365 × 8 years after the Brahmin Buddha, according to the *Bhagavata Purana*.
>
> So Whitman is identical with Jesus, spattered by sparks from the factory workbench rather than by seaspray and the dust on the road. (Khlebnikov 1987: 411)

These reincarnations – Christ as Savonarola as Marx as Whitman, Christ as factory worker as well as humble peasant – seem to satisfy Khlebnikov's need to make sense of the Revolution, to view it as part of a larger meaningful structure. When in *The Tables of Destiny* the arithmetical scheme described above gave way to the theorem that "the true nature of time consists in the recurrent multiplication of itself by twos and threes" (ibid.: 420), Khlebnikov was able to plot the relationship of the 1905 to the 1917 Revolution and map the great events of history according to elaborate charts derived from algorithms, specifically based on n to the second and third power. "When the future becomes clear thanks to these computations," he wrote a friend, "the feeling of time disappears; it is as if you were standing motionless on the deck of foreknowledge of the future. The feeling of time vanishes, and it begins to resemble a field in front of you and a field behind; it becomes a kind of space" (ibid.: 137).

Such freezing or spatialization of time is, we know, one of the central characteristics of modernism. The "shoring" of fragments in the collage structure which is *The Waste Land*, the system of repetitions in Stein's prose texts, and the interchangeable assemblage of images in Duchamp's *Green Box* produce a similar avoidance of temporality. In part, this is a response to Einsteinian theorems and non-Euclidean geometry, but no doubt the utopianism of the avant-garde is also related to the fear of what the actual future was to offer.

Khlebnikov, in particular, composed his later poems and *Tables of Destiny* in the shadow of war, revolutionary crisis, and the birth of the Soviet police state. It was in Baku during the Civil Wars, when he was living in a maritime dormitory and working on propaganda posters for the cultural section of the Volga–Caspian fleet, that Khlebnikov formulated his fundamental algorithms. A letter to his sister Vera (January 2, 1921) poignantly admits that his "visions of the future," recently read as "a report at scholarly meeting at Red Star University," had fallen on deaf ears:

> Those whose self-esteem goes no further than getting a pair of boots as a reward for good behavior and loyal thoughts have drawn away from me, and now watch me with terrified eyes. But all the same the die is cast, and the serpent will be thrust through the very belly. Until that moment, though, life is caught in the coils of his slimy body, and its baleful patterns of the death of body and soul. (Khlebnikov 1987: 125)

Such pessimism is rare for Khlebnikov, but it stands behind a curious paradox, one that is again characteristic of avant-garde poetics. In the famous 1931 essay "On a Generation that Squandered its Poets," Jakobson (1987) traces the conflict between utopianism and what is known as *byt* (everyday life), between the "creative urge toward a transformed future" and the "stagnating slime, which stifles life in its tight, hard mold" (ibid.: 277) that animated – and finally destroyed – Mayakovsky's poetic life. But in Khlebnikov's work it took a different, less pessimistic form.

145

On the one hand, as in the case of the late verse plays *Bogi* ("Gods") and in his "supersaga" *Zangezi*, Khlebnikov increasingly relies on what he calls *ptichi iazik* (bird language) and *iazik bogov* (the language of the gods), both of which represent onomatopoeic poetry at it most non-referential. Here, for example, is a dialogue between Eros and Juno in the second scene ("Plane 2: The Gods") of *Zangezi*, as rendered with approximate English spelling by Paul Schmidt:

Eros	Emch, amch, oomch!
	*Doom*chee, *dam*chee, *dom*chee,
	Maka*rako* keeo*cherk!*
	Tseetseeleetsee tseetsee*tsee!*
	Kooka*ree*kee keekee*koo*
	*Ree*chee, *chee*chee, tsee-tsee-*tsee.*
	Olga, Elga, Alga!
	Peets, patch, *potch! Ekhamchee!*
Juno	Pee*rara* – peeroo*rooroo!*
	Lay*lola* Vooaroo!
	Veeche*holo* sehseh*seh!*
	*Ve*chee! *Ve*echee! *ee* bee-*bee!*
	Zeeza*zee*za eeza*zo!*
	Eps, Aps, Eps!
	*Moo*ree-*goo*ree reeko*ko!*
	Mio, *Mao*, Moom!
	Ep!

(Khlebnikov 1989: 334)

Generically, this lyric is a form of *charm*, the magic incantation, as Andrew Welch (1978) defines it, "carried on the singsong voice of a magician at work." The root of charm is the Latin word *carmen*, which means song but also magic formula or incantation. In primitive societies charms were "closed, secret, and hidden"; their words were likely "to involve a special language." Again, "whereas songs are organized by the external rhythms of music . . . the rhythm of charms, on the other hand, grows out of the internal rhythms of the words themselves" (ibid.: 135–6). Repetition, both rhythmic and verbal, is central to the charm; Welch gives as an example a charm of the Trobriand Islands that inaugurates a new planting season with the clearing of the land for the next year's yam-gardens:

> Vatuvi, vatuvi,
> Vatuvi, vatuvi
> Vitumaga, I-maga
> Vatuvi, Vatuvi,
> Vatuvi, vatuvi,
> Vituola, I-lola.
> (Ibid.: 141)

Here lines 1–2 and 4–5 repeat the imperative "Show the way," the third line reads "Show the way groundwards, into the deep ground," and the sixth, "Show the way firmly show the way to the firm moorings."

In the Khlebnikov passages cited above, referential elements, as in the use of the proper name "Olga" in line 7 of Eros's speech, serve to ground the *zaum* words, as does the approximate cock cry in line 5 and the cat's miaow in line 17. The tightly structured stichic stanza, with its phonemic and phrasal repetition, begins with three heavy stresses ("Emch, amch, oomch!") and then modulates into a seven-syllable line in which two trochaic feet are followed by an amphimac, as in "Kookka*ree*kee keekeek*oo*" or "*Ve*chee! *Vee*chee! *ee*-bee-*bee*" (/x/x/x/). Welch points out that both charm and chant (the latter relying more fully on what are truly "nonsense" sounds or rather sounds which make only rhythmical sense) invariably have communal associations, "creating a voice larger than the individual"; as such, these ancient forms are admirably suited to Khlebnikov's hero Zangezi, whose name combines two rivers, the Zambezi and the Ganges, which constitute the African and Asian coordinates of the poet's worldview. "In Khlebnikov's 'Alphabet of the Intellect,'" notes Ronald Vroon, "the letter *z* signifies reflection and reflected light and is associated with words that signify sight, mirrors, eyes, stars, and even the earth itself (*zemlia* in Russian). Zangezi, in short, is a seer." And further: "The image of Zangezi as an itinerant prophet is based in part on the poet's own life of wandering, but also on the life of the great ninth-century sage, Sankara . . . who traveled throughout India, preaching and gathering disciples for his reformed sect of Hinduism" (Khlebnikov 1989: 397).

Vision, prophecy, "supersaga," whose "characters" are birds, gods, or even stars: this is perhaps the major strain in Khlebnikov's late work. In Plane 9, called "Thought," Zangezi declares: "Sound the alarm, send the sound through the mind! Toll the big bell, the great tocsin of intelligence! All the inflections of the human brain will pass in review before you, all the permutations of OOM!" And we read, in Paul Schmidt's version:

> GO-OOM
> OUR-OOM
> OOW-OOM
> EAR-OOM
> WITH-OOM of me
> and those I don't know
> MO-OOM
> BO-OOM
> DAL-OOM
> CHE-OOM
> BOM!
> BIM!
> BAM!
>
> (Ibid.: 345)

And it continues in this vein for another forty-odd lines. But this seemingly "primitive" chant is qualified by Khlebnikov's notes, which give his sound poetry a personally inflected semantic underpinning: GO-OOM, for example, refers to "The mind that towers like those celestial trinkets unseen by day, the stars." "When rulers fall," he further explains, the word GO-OOM "picks up their fallen staff GO." Or again, DEV-OOM means "The mind of discipleship and true citizenship, of a spirit of devotion," DA-OOM equals "Affirmative" and NO-OOM "argumentative" (ibid.: 346–7).

But – and here is the paradox I spoke of above – even as Khlebnikov presents "All the inflections of the human brain" as "permutations of *OOM!*" (ibid.: 345), he is also writing surprisingly "simple," colloquial autobiographical lyrics in which neologism is replaced by everyday speech, fantasy image, and wildly comic hyperbole. Here, for example, is "Russia and Me" (*Ia i Rossiia*):

Russia has granted freedom to thousands and thousands.
It was really a terrific thing to do,
People will never forget it.
But what I did was take off my shirt
and all those shiny skyscrapers the strands of my hair,
every pore
in the city of my body,
broke out their banners and flags.
All the citizens, all the men and women
of the government of ME,
rushed to the windows of my thousand-winnowed hair,
all those Igors and Olgas
and nobody told them to do it,
they were ecstatic at the sunshine
and peeked through my skin.
The Bastille of my shirt has fallen!
And all I did was take it off.
I have granted sunshine to the people of ME!
I stood on a beach with no clothes on,
that's how I gave freedom to my people
And suntans to the masses.

                    (Khlebnikov 1997: 94; cf. 1968: II, 304)

149

This droll and absurd fantasy where the Russian Revolution is figured as the poet's shedding of his shirt and taking a sunbath, the "shiny skyscrapers" of his hair standing up and erupting at "every pore in the city of my body," prefigures Frank O'Hara in its burlesque humor: one thinks of "A Pleasant Thought from Whitehead," where the poet, sitting at his desk, imagines that his writings are flooding the skies where "the improving stars / read my poems and flash / them onward to a friend" (O'Hara 1995: 23–4) or "Poem (Khrushchev is coming on the right day!)," in which the poet-lover's buoyancy momentarily lifts him above the fray so that "joy seems to be inexorable," even with the dark and dour figure of Khrushchev, pictured as he arrives at Pennsylvania Station (ibid.: 340).

True, Paul Schmidt, a good friend of O'Hara's, leans toward the casual register in his translation. But even if we read "Russia and Me" in a literal rendition, the irreverence of the central metaphor is startling: it recalls the jaunty hyperbole of the young Mayakovsky (e.g., "A Few Words about Myself"), but here the issues at stake are nothing if not serious. Can the political turmoil of the Revolution really be translated into the momentary ecstasy of the declaration that "I have granted sunshine to the people of ME!"? And what has happened to the desired escape from the self, the need Khlebnikov insists on in the critical prose of this period to get rid of the lyrical ego?

The answer, I believe, is that Khlebnikov's late poetry, threatened as it was by material and psychological constraints, dispenses with all theories as to what poetry should be. "Russia and Me" is poetry on the edge: one more minute, it seems when one reads the opening assertion, and the pretty picture will dissolve totally, and the "suntans" the poet is proffering the "masses" of his body will be more real than the freedom "granted" to the "thousands and thousands" by the new Red government. At such moments, Khlebnikov suggests, the power to design elaborate neologisms from the sea of etymology no longer matters. In a neighboring poem, "When I was young I went alone" (*Ia vyshel iunoshei odin*), the poet recalls an adolescent moment in the forest when, in a fit of ecstatic rage, he set his hair on fire, committing "Arson in Khlebnikov Acres!" "I burned my fields and trees / and things felt better." So he now longs to "depart / with flaming hair, not as I, but WE" – in order to escape a horror never described in the poem, a horror so enormous that even "Our Rhineland enemies / fear the stink of famine and disease across our border" (Khlebnikov 1997: 103).

"When I was young" dates from 1921; in January of that year Khlebnikov writes sadly to his sister: "I have forgotten the world of poetry and sound, I have cast them as sacrifices into the bonfire of numbers. But a little while longer and the sacred gift of speech will return to me" (ibid.: 126). And in February to Mayakovsky: "The writer's inkwell is dry, and the fly was *not* amused when it dove in for a swim." He takes some comfort in his new "mastery" of numbers but declares that "instead of a heart I seem to have something resembling a chunk of wood or a kippered herring. I don't know. No more songs" (ibid.: 128).

The reference to "kippered herring" here is interesting because the poet who claimed that "the writer's inkwell is dry" was writing an amazing series of poems about hunger, specifically about village life at the time of the famine in 1920–1. Unlike the *zaum* poems of the same period, these short, graphic, free-verse poems are entirely accessible, documentary, and imagistic. Here is the opening of "Hunger" (*Golod*), whose first section is called "In the Woods":

> Why do the elk and the rabbits run,
> abandon the woods in autumn?
> People have eaten the bark of the aspens,
> the green shoots of the fir trees.
>
> Women and children wander the woods,
> gathering leaves from the birch trees
> for soup: birch borscht, birch-bouillon.
>
> The tender tips of fir branches, the silvery moss –
> Food from the forest.

They'll start getting teeth like the elk
from eating the trees. . . .

The children are wasting away:
their mouths stretch hugely from ear to ear,
their eyes like sunglasses – blue glasses, brown glasses –
glint in their faces like shiny reflectors;
their noses sharpen to knife-points,
like candles set out on a grave.
(Khlebnikov 1997: 104–5; cf: 1968, III, 75–6)

This documentary image of starvation and human degradation seems disarmingly "simple," its syntax straightforward, its mode that of "straight" description, using images familiar to anyone. But the poem's perspective is very much Khlebnikov's, beginning with the terrifying merger of elk (*losi*) and people (*liudi*) in the opening stanza. The *device* of "making strange," in this case, is not, at least overtly, sound play, although the stanza about the children fore-grounds the letter *g*, as in *glaza golubimy* (eyes of blue) and *groba* (graves). These are, in Khlebnikov's system, variants on *golod*; in "The Warrior of the Kingdom," we recall, the alphabet table gives us "G [*g*] – too little as a result of a situation of insufficient force, hunger" (Khlebnikov 1987 294). But if the *g* network of this stanza provides its secret structure, the surface narrative surely speaks to a wide audience. The poet's "I" is absent in what looks like documentary reportage, but what the "I" defamiliarizes is the common adage, "Some people are no better than animals." In the face of starvation they *are* animals, taking away the vegetable food supply of the elk and rabbits and, having ingested the bark of the aspens and the "green shoots of the fir trees," they actually *become* animals, acquiring elk teeth. The other pole of dehumanization is man-made commodity. The starving children's glassy eyes are "like sunglasses – blue glasses, brown glasses," they "glint in their faces like shiny reflectors. Their thin little noses "sharpen to knife-points," melting to nothing "like candles set out on a grave" – their own grave of course.

In portraying what is potentially the most sentimental of subjects – starving peasant children – Khlebnikov avoids all sentimentality. Rather than standing outside the frame, weeping for the poor in this moment of crisis, he concentrates on what hunger does to human beings. In the manic pursuit of any edible substance – birchborscht, barbecued worms, fried caterpillars, skunk cabbage – human beings lose all "humanity." Hence they become, in what is the poem's cruel irony, things, commodities like those sunglasses they could never afford and the candles so scarce that they too may soon be melted and eaten. From *golod* to *groba*: the image is terrifying in its poignancy, especially when we remember that the poet himself would soon die from an infection brought on by malnutrition.

In his "Self-Statement" of 1919, let's recall, Khlebnikov declared it his first aim "To find – without breaking the circle of roots – the magic touchstone of all Slavic words, the magic that transforms one into another, and so freely to fuse all Slavic words together" (Khlebnikov 1987: 147). That magic touchstone remained elusive, but the possibilities of Khlebnikovian morphology have been tested by late-century poets from *Oulipo* and Brazilian Concrete poets to Jackson Mac Low's *Pronouns*, John Cage's *mesostics*, to Susan Howe's book, named in what is an almost Khlebnikovian gesture, *Articulation of Sound Forms in Time*. Indeed, at the turn of the twenty-first century, the possibilities of chant and charm, *zaum* and word magic, largely dormant in the "rationalist" and personalist years of mid-century, are once again invoked. "Beyonsense language," remarked Khlebnikov in a moment of childlike simplicity, "means language situated beyond the boundaries of ordinary reason, just as we say 'beyond the river' or 'beyond the sea' (Khlebnikov 1987: 383). "Literature" is thus "Word-work" or "Letter-ature," the composer a "Sound-stirrer" and the poet a "Cloud-climber" or "Sky-scraper" (ibid.: 79–80). As for the poet's reward, "Human happiness is a secondary sound; it twists, turns around the fundamental sound of the universe."

5

"Modernism" at the Millennium

The Imagiste movement was made with four or 5 poems of Hilda [Doolittle]'s, three or four of Richard [Aldington]'s and one ole Bill Water Closet W[illiam]'s, plus y.v.t. or if you like manipulated by y.v.t. whereto were added about the same amt. of stuff that wdn't damage (i.e. one hoped it wdn't damage the effek).

Prob[lem] ain't now the same . . .

You (on the other foot.) have got to disentangle a far more multitudinous etc. etc.

                                    plenty of chaps meaning
What they say (with no lit. capac.) . . .

plus mess caused by reaction against these dilutes. I mean the Tennysonian sonnet etc. now being done, and NOT so well done as in 1898 . . .

        Ezra Pound to Louis Zukofsky, October 25, 28, 1930

The business of Art . . . is to live in the actual present, that is the complete actual present, and to completely express that complete actual present.

                        Gertrude Stein, *How to Write*

Recalling the London poetry scene of the 1890s, W. B. Yeats (1966: 164) remarked: "I had already met most of the poets of my generation." This was no doubt true, at least so far as Anglo-American poets were concerned. A century later, no poet could make such a boast; indeed, today no New York poet is likely to know (or have read) even his or her fellow New York poets, much less those of San Francisco or Sydney, Los Angeles or London. In the US a mass society with a large university-educated population inevitably breeds an "official verse culture" (Bernstein 1986: 246–49) – a culture whose discourse is as conventionalized and institutionalized as any other mass discourse from advertising to political campaign rhetoric to legal language. Indeed, surprising as it may seem, given the enormous political, demographic, and cultural changes of the post–World War II era, in the mainstream poetry press the lyric paradigm has remained remarkably constant. Consider the following examples, each of them by a well-established, widely admired American poet:

> Tired and unhappy, you think of houses
> Soft-carpeted and warm in the December evening,
> While snow's white pieces fall past the window,
> And the orange firelight leaps.
>
>   A young girl sings
> That song of Gluck where Orpheus pleads with Death;
> Her elders watch, nodding their happiness
> To see time fresh again in her self-conscious eyes:
> The servants bring the coffee, the children retire,
> Elder and younger yawn and go to bed,
> The coals fade and flow, rose and ashen
> It is time to shake yourself! And break this
> Banal dream, and turn your head
> Where the underground is charged, where the weight
> Of the lean buildings is seen,
> Where close in the subway rush, anonymous
> In the audience, well-dressed or mean,
> So many surround you, ringing your fate,

155

"Modernism" at the Millennium

Caught in an anger exact as a machine.
(Delmore Schwartz, "Tired and Unhappy, You Think
of Houses," *In Dreams Begin Responsibilities*, 1938)

It is raining here.
On my neighbor's fire escape
geraniums are set out
in their brick–clay pots,
along with the mop,
old dishrags, and a cracked
enamel bowl for the dog.

I think of you out there
on the sandy edge of things,
rain strafing the beach,
the white maturity
of bones and broken shells,
and little tin shovels and cars
rusting under the house.

And between us there is – what?
love and constraint,
conditions, conditions,
and several hundred miles
of billboards, filling-stations
and little dripping gardens. . . .

O my dear, my dear,
today the rain pummels
the sour geraniums
and darkens the grey pilings
of your house, built upon sand.
And both of us, full grown
have weathered a long year.
Perhaps your casual glance
will settle from time to time

on the sea's travelling muscles
that flex and roll their strength
under its rain-pocked skin.
And you'll see where the salt winds
Have blown bare the seaward side
Of the berry bushes,
and will notice
the faint, fresh
smell of iodine.

(Anthony Hecht,
"Message from the City,"
The Hard Hours, 1968)

I remember the greasy moon floating
like a tire over the highway, the last
stars flecked like dust on the window
of my father's garage. For years I've walked
away from the concrete fields of a lousy
childhood, the damp haze of life in Chester.

but now I've come back to follow the
moon through the toothed stacks of chimneys,
through the back alleys lit up by shabby
yellow lanterns. I've come here to stand
like a pilgrim before the tin shacks
holding their tin ears on the highway

while trucks roar by without stopping
and factories clack their fat tongues
together in the wind. . . .

(Edward Hirsch,
"How to Get Back to Chester,"
For the Sleepwalkers, 1981)

This sequence of poems, spanning the decades from the 1930s to the
near-present, exhibits a gradual move toward a greater informality

and everyday language as we turn from Schwartz to Hecht to Hirsch, but otherwise the poetics in question are remarkably constant. I am thinking not of bio-cultural determinants – all three of these poets happen to be white, male, and Jewish – nor of such obvious thematic markers as the shared urban themes, the mixing of memory and desire, the frustrated longing for love and approval – but of the premises that govern the form these poems take.

First and most obviously, it is assumed that "poetry" involves lineated verbal – and only verbal – text (no mixed media permitted). Second, lineated though it is and orderly as it looks on the page as a text column with white space around the stanzas, the "modern" poem must avoid meter and fixed rhyme scheme – sound features too rigid to represent the phenomenology of individual consciousness. Third, lyric is understood to be the expression of a particular subject (whether designated as "I" in Hecht and Hirsch or "you" in Schwartz), whose voice provides the cement that keeps individual references and insights together. Fourth, "modern" language should not be stilted or formal (shades of "poetic diction") but rather "natural" and colloquial, even as (fifth), a poem conveys its feelings and ideas only by means of indirection – which is to say, by metaphor and irony.

Thus in "How to Get Back to Chester" the "greasy moon float[s] like a tire over the highway," chimney-stacks are "toothed," and the "tin shacks" hold their "tin ears" while "factories clack their fat tongues / together in the wind" and the poet breathes in the "deep blasts from an old furnace." The inanimate world is consistently animated even as the human world is marked by death. In Hecht's "Message from the City" it is the sea that is personified, exhibiting its "travelling muscles / that flex and roll their strength / under its rain-pocked skin." And the "white maturity / of bones and broken shells" at the beloved's beach house points up the poet's own immaturity, his refusal to give up on what he knows is a love affair that can't go anywhere. And in Schwartz's "Tired and Unhappy" the vision, whether memory or dream, of a young girl singing at the piano by the firelight in a warm and cosy drawing room, is contrasted to the oppressive "machine" of the anonymous "subway rush" within which the poet himself is hopelessly "caught." And not only the poet, for, in a characteristic Schwartz linkage of metaphor and irony, even the song the young girl is singing in the "warm and soft-carpeted" interior is Gluck's aria in which "Orpheus pleads with Death." And – another irony – even the "lean buildings" crush the lyric speaker with their "weight."

Eliot's "objective correlative," that "set of objects," "situation," or "chain of events" that serves as a "formula" for the poet's particular emotion (Eliot 1958: 145), would seem to be alive and well in these poems: look at that "faint, fresh / smell of iodine" with which Hecht's poem ends – the smell literally blown in by the sea air but referring, of course, to the poet's attempt to allay the pain of his loved one's absence. Again, in Hirsch's grimy Chester, the "last stars" are "flecked like dust on the window / of my father's garage," while the "tin shacks" in this sad industrial town "hold their tin ears on the highway." Such imagery recalls Eliot's "Preludes"; indeed, Hirsch's tradition, like Schwartz's or Hecht's, is broadly speaking the "metaphysical" modernism traceable to Eliot as filtered through the "New Critical" poetry of Allen Tate and John Crowe Ransom, Robert Penn Warren and Randall Jarrell, that dominated the mid-century. "Hirsch owes much to T. S. Eliot in the way of irony, self-detachment, and quick shifts of logic" (Christensen 2001: 532).

The connection seems reasonable until one actually rereads "Preludes" or "Prufrock." For consider Eliot's wrestling to find the *mot juste* – his refusal to use a single word that doesn't *work* – and his inspired sound/meaning conjunctions, as in his modulation of the *st/ts* cluster in

> Of restless nights in one-night cheap hotels
> And sawdust restaurants with oyster-shells

or

> Streets that follow like a tedious argument
> Of insidious intent . . .

159

The language-game in question is one Delmore Schwartz never quite mastered. "Tired and unhappy": these adjectives, like "soft-carpeted" in the next line, are not exactly graphic or sonically charged. Indeed, Schwartz's images often border on cliché, as when the predictably "orange" firelight predictably "leaps" and when, in line 10, "the coals fade and glow, rose and ashen." In other cases, word choice seems inept: can snow really be said to fall in "white pieces"? And why are the elders who listen to the young girl's song "nodding their happiness"? Their approval, perhaps, or their pleasure at the event, but happiness is a larger state of mind, one that isn't "nodded."

What all this means, of course, is that the state of mind ostensibly described remains something of a blur. Why is the poet so lost and unhappy? Did he once frequent a "soft-carpeted" house and listen to his beloved play Gluck? Is he himself the Orpheus figure who has lost his Eurydice? And what is the relation of the more conventional ten-syllable lines (e.g., "So many surround you, ringing your fate") to those that are longer and shorter? Why is the poem written in complete sentences? And, most important, how does the "you" used throughout distance the subject from Delmore Schwartz himself?

The same strictures apply to the other two poems. In the case of Hecht, the casual immediacy of "It is raining here" invites instant participation on the part of the reader. But the banal details that follow – the geraniums "set out" in their "brick-clay pots, / along with the mop" and "old dishrags," and such obvious symbolic properties as that "cracked enamel bowl" set out "for the dog" – do little to inspire interest in this lover's condition or complaint. For what is the rain said to be doing at the beach town where the woman is all too predictably perched "on the sandy edge of things"? Unsurprisingly, it "strafes the beach." And what separates Manhattan from the beloved's summer cottage? "Several hundred miles / of billboards, filling-stations, and little dripping gardens." No wonder that the woman in question, predictably perched "on the sandy edge of things," isn't too interested in the poet's "message."

160

The free verse of "Message from the City" often modulates into a three-stress line that recalls the trimeter of such W. H. Auden poems as "September 1, 1939," but whereas Auden's emphatic, impassioned lines ("As the cléver hópes expíre / Of a lów, dishónest décade") are intrinsic to his dirge, such trimeters as "Yésterdáy was níce" or "Perháps your cásual glánce" seem arbitrary; they could easily be longer or shorter without doing much to change the poet's rueful expression of love and regret. Such arbitrariness is carried even further in "How to Get Back to Chester," whose stanzaic structure is merely visual. Its six-line stanzas have roughly the same number of syllables per line (the range is seven to twelve), but since there is little internal sound play or rhyme and the lines are almost invariably enjambed, the effect is that of prose. Indeed, it is not clear what would be lost, if the text were transposed as follows:

I remember the greasy moon floating like a tire over the highway, the last stars flecked like dust on the window of my father's garage. For years I've walked away from the concrete fields of a lousy childhood, the damp haze of life in Chester.

Perhaps Hirsch designed his verse form so as to create tension between the tight visual frame and the "prosaic" syntax, but in that case, why use such "poetic" phraseology as "the concrete fields of a lousy childhood"? Too often, in poems like this one, lineation seems to act as no more than a guarantee that the narrative contained is special and, at least in this case, culminates in the closure of the poet's punch-line: the ironic thrust of the father's poignant last words, "Don't come back, son. And welcome."

Most poetry currently written continues to follow the basic assumptions that govern the works just discussed. A generic "sensitive" lyric speaker contemplates a facet of his or her world and makes observations about it, compares present to past, divulges some hidden emotion, or comes to a new understanding of the situation. The language is usually concrete and colloquial, the ironies and metaphors multiple, the syntax straightforward, the rhythms muted and low-key. Generic and media boundaries are rigorously observed: no readymades or word sculptures here, no *zaum* explorations of etymologies, no Steinian syntactic permutations. As for Eliot's objective correlative, it emerges, in the mainstream poetry before us, as little more than a faint echo, an ironic tic:

> Today the rain pummels
> The sour geraniums
> And darkens the grey pilings
> Of your house, built upon sand.
> (Hecht 1968: 8)

"The ordinary man's experience," Eliot observes in "The Metaphysical Poets" (1921), "is chaotic, irregular, fragmentary. The latter falls in love, or reads Spinoza, and these two experiences have nothing to do with each other, or with the noise of the typewriter or the smell of cooking; in the mind of the poet these experiences are always forming new wholes" (Eliot 1958: 287). Just how "chaotic, irregular [and] fragmentary" "ordinary" experience would turn out to be when the typewriter came to be replaced by cyber-text and the smell of cooking by those odorless packaged foods snatched on the run in the mall or at the airport in the age of hypermechanized fast-food reproduction, is something Eliot couldn't have predicted, but he understood, as did Stein, that the process of signification was itself undergoing a sea-change. In Stein's words in "What are Master-Pieces" (1936):

> The tradition has always been that you may more or less describe the things that happen but nowadays everybody all day long knows what is happening and so what is happening is not really interesting, one knows it by radios cinemas news-papers biographies autobiographies until what is happening does not really thrill any one. . . . The painter can no longer say that what he does is as the world looks to him because he

cannot look at the world any more, it has been photographed too much and he has to say that he does something else. (Stein 1998 II: 357)

Something like Duchamp's *With Hidden Noise*, for instance, or the *Tzanck Check*. And we come back to the great question of Duchamp's Notebooks: "Can one make works that are not works of 'art'?"

In the visual arts, in musical composition, and especially in architecture, the notion of *doing something else* has been widely accepted: witness the success of Frank Gehry's Guggenheim Bilbao or Daniel Liebeskind's Holocaust Memorial in Berlin. But the verbal arts – perhaps because we all use language and hence feel we somehow own it and know what it is – are more problematic and in poetry, as in the novel and drama, a topical "subjective" realism always reasserts itself as the path of least resistance:

> In Yellowbird's Store, the tart tinge
> of something sour boggles my nose.
> Overpriced cans of Spaghetti-Os
> and Spam on the sad shelves
> are powdered with Great Plains dust.
> (Adrian C. Louis, 1997)

Or

> I always had a thing for Natassja Kinski.
> My Sorbonne clique and I went to see her latest film. Giant
> billboards all over Paris: Natassja – legs spread, her
> lover's face lost in between.
> I watched *Paris, Texas* twice, living with
> the eternal memory of those lips
> biting into a fleshy strawberry in *Tess*.
> Thank you, Roman Polanski.
>
> (Ana Castillo, 1991)

Here is poetry approaching the condition, not of music, as Walter Pater famously held, but of journalism – a form of writing as harmless as it is ephemeral. Meanwhile, the avant-garde momentum of the early decades of the twentieth century has found new channels – channels mediated, as I have argued elsewhere, by a succession of avant-gardes from the Objectivists of the 1930s to the John Cage circle and its intersection with New York poetry/painting and Black Mountain in the 1950s and 1960s, to the performance poetries and ethnopoetics of the 1970s. These movements have inevitably positioned themselves as *postmodern*, with the understanding that they have exceeded modernism or at the very least have distinguished themselves from what looked, to the 1960s, like an elitist and politically suspect white male culture.

But as we move into the twenty-first century, the modern/postmodern divide has emerged as more apparent than real. "Prufrock" and *Tender Buttons, With Hidden Noise* and Khlebnikov's manifestos – these oddly strike us as more immediate and "contemporary" than the fabled postmodern "breakthrough" of Robert Lowell's *Life Studies* or Charles Olson's *Maximus*. The modernist challenge, perhaps most common-sensically stated by Pound when he warned, "Do not imagine that a thing will 'go' in verse just because it's too dull to go in prose" (LE: 6), remains open. To see how this process works, I want to take up some distinctive poems of the past decade – poems usually considered anything but "modernist" – so as to reassess what I take to be the special relationship between the early twentieth century and the early twenty-first.

"A Sort of Border Life"

My first example, Susan Howe's *Thorow*, which appears in *Singularities* (1990), is what Pound called, with reference to the *Cantos*, a "poem including history." It is also a poem including geography, specifically the Lake George (upstate New York) area, where Howe,

so her headpiece tells us, spent the winter and spring of 1987 teaching a poetry workshop:

> The town, or what is left of a town, is a travesty. Scores of
> two-star motels have been arbitrarily scrambled between gas
> stations and gift shops selling Indian trinkets, china jugs shaped
> like breasts with nipples for spouts, American flags in all shapes
> and sizes, and pornographic bumper-stickers. There are two
> Laundromats . . . a Howard Johnson . . . a fake fort where a real
> one once stood, a Dairy-Mart, a Donut-land, and a four-star
> Ramada Inn built over an ancient Indian burial mound. (Howe
> 1990: 41)

But it is not a case of simple degradation of a once pristine mountain wilderness. For the 28-mile long lake and its surrounding forest
was, in the 1750s, the scene of some of the fiercest battles of the
French and Indian Wars. The lake (a sheet of ice in winter) marked
the void between two encroaching frontiers: to the north, Fort
Carillon, the French fortress, represented the gateway to Canada; to
the southeast, on the Hudson, stood Fort Edward, the northern
terminus of the English headway into the forest. When the Anglo-
Irish commander William Johnson defeated the French in 1755 he
renamed the Lac du St. Sacrement, as it had been called, Lake
George and built Fort William Henry on its shores. Within two
years the French retaliated. After a long siege a truce was declared
only to be broken by the raids of the restive Indian tribes who in
turn attacked and massacred the French and English, and forced a
massive retreat. Many soldiers fled into the forest, many were cap-
tured by the Indians.

This is the "background" of Howe's twenty-page poetic sequence,
which is, on one level, a passionate critique of "paternalist colonial
systems" (ibid.) and their victimization of the native peoples. But it
is also much more. The impetus for the poem, Howe has remarked,
was "the sight of the single word *Thorow*," which the poet came

across in Sir Humfrey Gilbert's *A New Passage to Cataia*: "To prove
that the Indians aforenamed came not by the Northeast, and that
there is no thorow passage navigable that way" (Howe 1990: 42).
Then, too, Thorow = Thoreau, the great nineteenth-century medi-
tator on the natural world, whose French name places him in an
equivocal position *vis-à-vis* the French–British conflict playing itself
out in the Adirondacks – a locale, so Howe tells us, the New
England Thoreau was never to visit (ibid.: 42). Thoreau is in one
sense the poet's guide; he acts as "scout" for her meditation. But she
is skeptical about his "domain of transcendental subjectivity" (ibid.:
43), his trust in that "First precarious Eden" of Lost Pond (ibid.:
52). Further: *Thorow* also means *throw*, as in "Irruptives / thorow
out all / the Five Nations" (ibid.: 46). Living alone in a cabin on
the deserted lake, surrounded by ugly motels and junk shops closed
for the winter, the poet is *thrown into* a particular circumstance: "The
Adirondacks *occupied* me" (ibid.: 41).

The layering of *Thorow* is thus extremely complex; in its allu-
siveness, its collaging of the journals of William Johnson, of
Thoreau's *Ktaadn* and *Walden*, of different speech registers, spellings,
proper names (the Indian Swegachey and Kittaning, the alluvial
Flatts north of Albany occupied by Dutch and German settlers), this
is an Eliotic poem. Eliotic too is its ambivalence to "the literature
of savagism / under a spell of savagism" (ibid.: 49) and its studied
"impersonality." Except for its headnote, *Thorow* supplies no direct
references to the poet, whose consciousness is known only through
the text's network of references. The objective correlative is very
much in evidence in lyrics like the following:

> Most mysterious river
> On the confined brink
>
> Poor storm
> all hallows
>
> and palings around cabin
>
> Spring-suggesting light

Bustle of embarkation
Guides bewildered

Hunt and not the capture

Underthought draws home
Archaism

Here is dammed water

First trails were blazed
lines

Little known place names

tossed away as little grave
pivot bravura

(Ibid.: 53)

These isolated three and four-stress lines and uneven couplets, composed largely of noun phrases, are linked together even more tenuously than are the sections of "Prufrock" or even the bulk of *The
Waste Land*, but the basic mode is similar. Words, to begin with, are
charged with complex meanings. We don't, for example, usually
think of the "brink" of a river as being "confined"; on the contrary,
the brink is the edge of something beyond, something unknown.
But "confined" is the *mot juste* here because this river's brink is far
from free, owned as it is by one or another occupying colonial
power. Similarly, on this stormy All Hallows Eve, the "palings"
(fences) around the poet's cabin connote pallor and hence bring in
the "Spring-suggesting light." A sketchy mysterious rout – 'Bustles
of embarkation / Guides bewildered' – one in which there is "Hunt
and not the capture," leads literally to trail blazing along the
dammed (damned) water. The old place names like Swegachey –
little known by those who now live in this Kitschville – have been
"tossed away as little grave" – both the little graves of the one-time
warring factions but also because those who toss them away are
only "little grave" about it all, they don't take the historic presence

167

seriously. Or again, "grave" may be an adjective modifying "pivot." As for the final line, Howe herself has suggested in a letter: "Pivot bravura is one of my favorite images. Pivot as a word is a deed. Sharp short t stop again. And *p* as opposed to *b* to clash with the openness and hubris of 'bravura.' So many names in upstate NY State are full of desperate pivot bravura. Rome, Troy, Attica, Fonda, Cairo. Thoreau had a names obsession."

Here is what we might call the *côté* Khlebnikov of Susan Howe, although I am not positing any form of direct influence. To begin with, *pivot bravura* is not in fact an image but a play on words. A pivot is "a central point or shaft on which something swings or turns"; it is a "deed," not literally, but in the sense that ensuing events will depend on its function. Howe's linking of *pivot*, its short vowels framed by voiceless stops, to the word *bravura*, with its voiced *b*, open vowels and trilled *r*'s, ironizes the power of this "pivot bravura" – a bravura Howe evidently associates with Thoreau's endowment of a bunch of cold and ugly upstate towns – "Rome," "Troy," "Attica," "Fonda," "Cairo" – with classical Mediterranean names. Her own response to proper names is much more tentative: in *Thorow* concrete names thus repeatedly give way to abstraction.

From the first lyric where the sounds and letters of *Thorow* reappear in "snow," "two," and "now," where "Thorow" rhymes with the initial "Go" and the final line's "So," and where the snow at the Fort (William Henry) "falling very deep / remained a *fort*night" (ibid.: 43), we see sound used very much as Eliot relates those "*restless* nights" of "Prufrock" to "saw-dust *restaurants*." The poem moves from its initial paratactic lyric sequences to the non-linear visual criss-cross composition of the last few pages and the sibylline fragments of the conclusion. By this time Howe has turned from linearity to *calligramme*, and, within the visual format of clashing diagonal lines and spacing, a focus on the individual word or, more specifically, the morphemes within the word, and what Khlebnikov called the *letter as such*, both as sound and as visual element. After the mirror pages with their heightened war images (ibid.: 56–7), we have the following configuration:

168

You are of me & I of you, I cannot tell

Where you leave off and I begin

       selving

       forfending
            Immeadeat Settlem
       but wandering
            Shenks Ferry people
       unhoused
            at or naer Mohaxt
       elect
            Sacandaga vläie
       vision
            Battoes are return
       thereafter
            They say
       resurgent
            "Where is the path"
       laughter

       ankledeep

       answerable

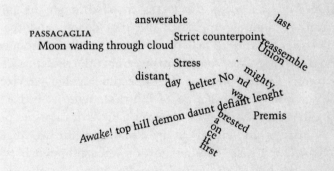

PASSACAGLIA   Strict counterpoint last
Moon wading through cloud reassemble Union
      Stress
distant day helter No nd mighty,
          wa lenght
Awake! top hill demon daunt defiant Premis
           brested
           a
           on
           ce
           first

Plate 5.1   Extract from Susan Howe's *Thorow.*

The first two lines are straightforward enough, except that we cannot quite say who the "I" and "you" are. The poet and Thoreau? The poet and William Johnson, the author of the journal from which she quotes? One fugitive to another or to her captor? Or especially, as seems most likely, the present-day world of the poet and the ones she invokes and reimagines? "Selving," in any case, cannot quite take place in the "unhoused" condition of the "Shenks Ferry people . . . at or near Mohaxt." Their wandering is now imaged not only as a time of suffering, but surprisingly as "laughter / ankledeep / answerable." And the poem ends with a verbal–visual "PASSACAGLIA" or "Strict counterpoint," in which the image of the "Moon wading through cloud" is crossed by the diagonal line-fragments detailing the march of a reassembled Union army in Thoreau's day. This diagonal is in turn crossed by an intersecting line that reads, "*Awake!* top hill demon daunt defiant lenght."

When I first read that last word I thought it was a misprint and queried the poet about it. "Length," she responded, "is misspelled on purpose. It was some old spelling probably but the reason I use it is that it makes one stop (sound of the *t*) as if the sound were a wall. A stop. And it reverses the *th* that is all through the poem. When I read it aloud I emphasize the *t* of defiant and the *ght* together (a kind of rhyme or match). *Th* is not *t* when pronounced." It is as if old spellings like "lenght" make visible the violence of the wars, the terrors of the forest. At the same time, spelling deviations emphasize the palimpsestic nature of Howe's poem, its verbal and visual strata that the "scout" must uncover. This, at least, is the poet's "Premis" – that word set off all by itself at a further angle – "Premis," which she calls "another stop or wall" although here the word ends on the hiss of a spirant. Whose "premises" are these? Can the "unhoused" occupy them? And "where is the path?" By this point, the poet's absorption into the ambiguous Lake George landscape is complete.

The relation of sound to meaning, of morpheme to neighboring morpheme, is thus reminiscent of Khlebnikov's *zaum*, where the semantically unrelated "salt" and "sun" are linked by poetic fiat:

anthen   uplispth   enend

  adamap   blue wov   thefthe

folled   floated   keen

                                Themis

thouscullingme
Thiefth

The first word of the final ideogram, "anthen," sounds like "anthem" but also "and then." The next, "uplispth" (an echo of "Till tousendsthee. Lps." in the last line of *Finnegans Wake*), connects "anthen" to the *th* of "thefthe," "Themis," "thouschulling me," and the final all but unpronounceable "Thiefth." The lisping stutter of these words measures the shards of history that are recoverable in the present. The broken references to the Battle of Lake George, the story of Fort William Henry, the Indian rout, the scattering of the settlers, to the contrasting sense of wilderness found in Thoreau's writings, and the up-to-date absurd honky-tonk town – all these coalesce in an "enend" that is less end than *emend*, an "adamap" (*adamant*) moment, or is it *a day map*, an added map that is needed? There is "theft," barely named and breaking down linguistically into "the the" (an echo of the last line of Wallace Stevens's "The Man on the Dump"). The vestiges of the dead are no more than scraps of "blue wov[en]" cloth that "folled" (*fooled*) the public and "f'loted" (*floated*), thus culminating in what is an Irish "keen[ing]" or wake. But the conclusion is not all negative, for Themis (Urania) appears, the wise and honest daughter of Uranos and Gaea who is responsible for upholding justice in human affairs. The scales in her left hand represent fairness; the sword and chain in her right hand are symbols of severely enforced justice. Even Zeus, we know from various myths, trusted Themis's advice. Themis is "keen" and protective ("thousculling me"). But the word also contains the paragram *the miss*, and the final word of the poem is "Thiefth (see ibid, 59)."

Here all the *th* sounds come to a head. The French and English colonists are thieves who have stolen the Indians' land. The Indians, in turn, are literally thieves, stealing the army's booty. Thoreau is a thief, wanting the wilderness somehow to be *his*. And the poet has thieved her materials from many sources, has stolen documents and recycled their lines. A descendant of the very British settlers who occupied Lake George, she takes *thiefth* very seriously. Indeed, it is an impossible word to pronounce fully and so "Thorow" ends with spatial dislocation and language that has become no more than inarticulate lisp.

"Till human voices wake us and we drown." The last line of "Prufrock" is apposite as is the "Gull against the wind" of "Gerontion." Howe's is a dark lyric reenactment of historical matter that nevertheless expresses a fascination with the savage and violent world so wholly Other in the context of present-day Lake George. The poem's language hoard, at the outset of the poem not unlike Prufrock's ("I have snow shoes and Indian shoes"), turns bit by bit into the extreme sound play, pun, neologism, and etymological word formation found in the poetry and manifestos of Khlebnikov, even as her page layout, following, like her first book, *Hinge Picture* (1974), Duchamp's plan to "develop in space the PRINCIPLE OF THE HINGE in the displacements 1st in the plane 2d in space" (Howe 1996: 31), comprises mirror fragments, doubling, and shards of found text. Eliot's "These fragments I have shored against my ruins" is thus intricately refigured in the "thouscullingme / thiefth" crescendo of *Thorow*.

An Art of Adjacency

A very different response to Eliot's verbal density is found in the poetry of Charles Bernstein. His extraordinary *dysraphism* – the title of one of Bernstein's finest poems, meaning "a dysfunctional fusion of embryonic parts," a "mis-seaming" (Bernstein 1987: 44) – the collaging of items that are not only disparate but have different syntactic orders, shifting voices, sources, and multiple allusions, is combined with a penchant for punning and word play that recalls the Duchamp of *Ovaire tout la nuit* and *La Bagarre d'Austerlitz* (see Antin 1972: 70). Even in Bernstein's essays we are likely to find constructions like the following: "Is prose justified? Or aren't you the kind that tells? That's no prose that's my default. Default is in our sorrow not in our swells" (Bernstein 2000: 47). Here the punning on prose that is "justified," that is with a fixed right margin, and the incongruous question asked when sexual secrets are at stake, gets transferred into computer-talk (and of course one of the commonest defaults is setting the margin) and then the spoof – with a New York accent – on *Julius Caesar*: "The fault, dear Brutus, is not in our stars, / But in ourselves." Further: "swells" rhymes with "tells" to give this "justified" prose a nice poetic twist.

But isn't *poetry* more than this stand-up comic routine? And does Bernstein's sound play really have a place in the great modernist tradition? A poem from *Dark City* (1994) called "The Lives of the Toll Takers" may provide some answers. The title, reminiscent of *Lives of the Poets* or *Lives of the Rich and Famous*, is immediately arresting: what sorts of lives do toll takers, those anonymous persons who operate the tollbooths at freeway checkpoints and bridges, have, and why would anyone write about them? Pondering this question, I went online and came up with surprisingly many items, the most apposite one being a piece in the *San Francisco Chronicle* (May 31, 1999) called "Toll Takers Don't Let Their Job Take Its Toll" by Carolyne Zinko. It begins as follows:

There's the slap, the snatch, and the ball of change.

These are the moments that make up a day in the life of a Bay Area toll taker. Five hundred times an hour, eight hours a day, as the cars approach endlessly, like lemmings to the sea.

Toll collectors must make change with as few bills as possible, and balance the cash drawer at the end of each shift.

They must count cars and axles that come through their lane. They must give directions. They must be happy. And above all, no matter how cranky the motorists are, they must never, ever snap back.

173

And the discussion continues with the story of one particular toll taker, Peter Klein, 60, who has held this job for 26 years and says he has come to enjoy observing and classifying the various toll payers who pass through his booth.

Bernstein, whose poem was written some years prior to this particular article, is obviously interested in the play on toll takers and "taking its toll," as well as in the terrible routinization of modern life where many jobs are of the order described above. But of course his poem is no more a "narrative of lives of the toll takers" than *The Waste Land* is the "story" of the typist and the "young man carbuncular" or of Albert and Lil. Here is the opening of the poem:

> There appears to be a receiver off the hook. Not that
> you care.
> > > Beside the gloves resided a hat and two
> pinky rings, for which no
> finger was ever found. Largesse
> > > with no release became, after
> not too long, atrophied, incendiary,
> > > > > stupefying. Difference or
> *differance*: it's
> the distinction between hauling junk and removing
> rubbish, while
> I, needless not to say, take
> > out the garbage
> > > (pragmatism)
>
> Phone again, phone again jiggity jig.
> > I figured
> they do good eggs here.
> > > Funny $: making a killing on
> junk bonds and living to peddle the tale
> > > (victimless rime)

(Bernstein 1994: 9–10)

The poem opens with an omen of sorts: the receiver that is off the hook. No one can "get a message" or send one; there is no communication, no sense of identity or proportion so that it is not the ring that is missing from the finger but conversely the finger that should be inside the "pinky ring." In this contemporary milieu – the world of media, junk bonds, deals, and money-making schemes – language is reduced to cliché and stock response. "Not that you care" in the opening line, for example, is absurd in the context. What is the nameless "you" supposed to do to show that he or she cares? Hang up the receiver? Find who took it off the hook? No answer is given and the poem quickly shifts to the stilted rhetoric and rhyme of "Largesse with no release became, after / not too long, atrophied, incendiary, / stupefying." Just what is "largesse with no release"? The gesture of a too-fond lover rebuffed by his mistress? The largesse of a too generous friend whose gifts no one wants? The parenthetical "after / not too long," in any case, injects a burlesque note into the narrative. For how long is "not too long"? And at what point does largesse become "incendiary"?

The "toll takers" of the poem are surely all of us, engaged as we are in the daily round of meaningless, repetitive activity – activity that generates money but never really gets anywhere. The circularity of everyday experience induces futile attempts to make distinctions like the Derridean one in line 8 between "difference and *différance*" (deferral), which modulates – comically enough – into "the distinction between hauling junk and / removing rubbish, while / I, needless not to say, take / out the garbage." The parenthetical word "pragmatism" is appropriate in this context. It is pragmatic to grant that whatever we want to call the activity in question, it still involves the removal of trash. A rose by any other name. On the other hand, "pragmatism" also involves the irony that there *is* a distinction – indeed, a kind of Duchampian *infrathin* – between "hauling junk," which requires a vehicle and is usually done by someone else one has hired, and "tak[ing] out the garbage," which is a routine individual act. And further: pragmatism forces us to recognize that in the world of junk bond "killings," the poetic

175

function itself is treated as "atrophied, incendiary" – just so much language laid waste and consigned, as it will be later in the poem, to the trash.

Where is the lyric subject positioned in this seemingly "mad" monologue, whose "justified" left margin cannot contain its words and phrases so that they form visual units that block all forward linear momentum the speech might have. "Stupefying" is aligned with "incendiary" as if to say that these are synonyms. The silly Derrida question – "Difference or –" is left hanging. And the line "out the garbage" puns on the practice of "outing individuals," whereas "I figured," isolated in its line, applies to almost everything that follows. The spatial disposition of words and phrases further complicates the question as to who is actually "speaking" in lines like "I figured / they do good eggs here" (the prelude to a business breakfast in the city). Identifying *the* speaker of "Toll Takers" is obviously impossible, but we should note that, vocal shifts notwithstanding, the language devices establish an overriding tone that is staccato, nervous, self-deprecating, parodic, sophisticated – a jaded Manhattan tone as different as possible from *Thorow*'s chant-like rhythms and proper-name invocations.

Bernstein's "injected songs" like "Phone again, phone again jiggity jig" (which plays, of course, with the second line of the nursery rhyme "To market, to market to buy a fat pig") are poles apart from "Go on the Scout they say / They will go near Swegachey." But the unstated reference "To market, to market" (the stock market) followed by the talk of "Funny $: making a killing on / junk bonds and living to peddle the tale (victimless rime)" recalls, say, "Mr. Eugenides, the Smyrna merchant / Unshaven, with a pocket full of currants / C.i.F. London: documents at sight" (*The Waste Land*). *Funny money* – the term originally referred to coins from the British colonies, money that wasn't authentically minted – is also "funny $" because it is derived from a prospective "killing" on / junk bonds" – a killing that leads, in a nice paradox, to the possibility of "living" – and living not just to tell the tale but, appropriately, to "peddle" it. Manipulating money – an innocent enough activity for the real toll takers who take our bills and coins and give us change – is at the very heart of contemporary life. Is it a "victimless rime"? Yes, in that poetry, as Auden taught us, makes nothing happen, but the junk bond killing is hardly without its victims, even though, as the unstated rhyme word suggests, this is a "crime" whose perpetrators are as difficult to nail down as its victims are everywhere.

The "lives of the toll takers," it seems, are indeed taking a toll, not wholly unlike the sinister lunch invitation of Eliot's Smyrna merchant. In the course of Bernstein's poem everyone talks at cross-purposes, proposes get-rich-quick schemes, makes jokes at other people's expense, and converses in platitudes. The mode of stark juxtaposition without authorial intrusion that characterizes *The Waste Land* is here complicated by the Duchampian punning and word play in such works as *Why not Sneeze Rrose Sélavy?* or *Fresh Widow*. But whereas Duchamp's innuendos are always sexually charged, Bernstein is more interested in the problem of information overload, the "noise" that increasingly blocks all communication in our society. "It seems someone has taken the phone off the hook." Indeed, and the buzz and static that results, the background noise that is essential to language as we now know it, has created a more and more complex empirical differentiation. As Michel Serres puts it:

> At the extreme limits of empiricism, meaning is totally plunged into noise, the space of communication is granular, dialogue is condemned to cacophony, the transmission of communication is chronic transformation. Thus the empirical is strictly essential and accidental *noise*. . . . Consequently, for dialogue to be possible one must close one's eyes and cover one's ears to the song and beauty of the sirens. (Serres 1982: 70)

"Dialogue" here refers to scientific discourse, the mounting of a logical argument which must purge itself of as much "noise" as possible in order to communicate. But, Serres says,

> To exclude the empirical is to exclude differentiation, the plurality of others that mask the same. It is the first movement

177

of mathematization, of formalization . . . one must eliminate cacography, the wavering outline, the accident of the mark, the failure of a gesture, the set of conditions that ensure that no graph is strictly of the same form as any other. (Ibid.: 69)

But the case of poetry is almost the opposite: here the wavering outline, the accident of the mark, the failure of a gesture may all contribute to what is the text's *poeticity*. In Serres's words:

The object perceived is indefinitely discernible: there would have to be a different word for every circle, for every symbol, for every tree, and for every pigeon; and a different word for yesterday, today, and tomorrow; and a different word according to whether he who perceives it is you or I, according to whether one of the two of us is angry, is jaundiced, and so on *ad finitum*. (Ibid.: 69–70)

Here is the "pictorial nominalism" we met in Duchamp, the *infrathin* distinction which separates "eat" from "ate" or "chair" from "chairs." In his quest to capture the *infrathin* aspects of things, Bernstein is nothing if not a Duchampian.

Such a move is not without its dangers. If "the object perceived is indefinitely discernible," if "meaning is totally plunged into noise," what prevents a given poem from being entirely chaotic, formless, and hence meaningless? To put it another way: how does the *infrathin* avoid the anarchy of pure nominalism, of wholesale empiricist differentiation? Perhaps, as in the case of Duchamp's *With Hidden Noise*, a poet like Bernstein binds his materials with a set of elaborate threads – threads he is at pains not to show so as to "keep it moving" (Charles Olson's words), keep up the urgency of the performative stance. Thus, throughout *Dark City* "business" and "poetry" are viewed as frighteningly equivalent in our culture. "Poetic opportunities, however" we read in "Lives of the Toll Takers," "do not fall into your lap, at least not / very often" (Bernstein 1994: 22). And again, in a riff on Pound's Imagist credo, "Poetry

178

services provide cost savings / to readers, such / as avoiding hospi-
talizations . . . minimizing / wasted time (*condensare*), and reducing
adverse idea interactions" (ibid.: 23).

But Bernstein is also a New York poet, although his city, unlike
Ashbery's and O'Hara's, is a Jewish Upper West Side New York
where "real" business (e.g., selling a product) goes with finding
restaurant bargains ("you could get steak & eggs for breakfast for
under ten / & change"), overachieving mothers and children, Jewish
jokes, computing frenzy, elaborate letter-writing, advertising cam-
paigns, and especially talk talk talk – talk in the morning at breakfast, in the afternoon on the subway, in the street, or in the
neighborhood bar. And just as Duchamp's readymades and boxes use
the most unlikely material in the making of "art," so Bernstein never
moves too far from language that is not so much *heard* as *overheard*
and then recycled in formal patterns:

> Is the Pope Polish? Does 3 + 5 equal 5 + 3?
> is Lincoln buried in Grant's Tomb? Is
> the South Bronx a WASP enclave? Will this
> burn at Fahrenheit 451? Is Napoleon the President
> of the Bahamas? Is Communism finished? Do
> hearts break when you don't touch them?
> are the rich getting richer or are you just
> glad to see me?
>
> ("Reveal Codes," ibid.: 122–3)

This seemingly absurd catalogue, delicately skewing actual items
overheard, say, on the subway, is a marvelously accurate image of
current cultural confusion and half-knowledge. Take the question
"Is Napoleon the President / of the Bahamas," which confuses the
former British colony, whose prime minister still reports to Her
Majesty, the Queen of the Commonwealth, with Haiti's successful
revolt against Napoleon and French rule in 1804. The import of the
ridiculous question is thus complex. Who can distinguish between
those exotic little vacation islands "down there" in the Caribbean?

Didn't I read that one of them had a president named Napoleon something? And so on. Not surprisingly, the stanza concludes with an equation of sex and money (the play on the current idiom, "Is that a rocket in your pocket or . . . ") that, in a nice twist, does not undercut the pathos of the preceding question. "Hearts," after all, do "break when you touch them" – a truth made evident in François Truffaut's's great science-fiction film *Fahrenheit 451.*

What seems at first reading sheer "noise" or information glut can thus be read as a heightened version of the Prufrockian "It is impossible to say just what I mean!" The real questions, this poem implies, remain unanswered, try as we may to turn to the "Help" menu on our computer screens and press the "Reveal Codes" key which gives this poem its title. For the toll takers in the "Dark City," it seems, the moment when "human voices wake us and we drown" – a more public moment than Prufrock's very private agony – has always already occurred.

Hazards That Hope

If Charles Bernstein's poetry is one of "undecorous" excess, a poetry of purposeful "exaggeration, attention scattering, distraction, digression" (see Bernstein 1992: 29), its Blakean Contrary, in the scheme elaborated in Bernstein's own "Artifice of Absorption," would be the "word to word halting" of Gertrude Stein (ibid.: 56), the "immersion in language, where language is not understood as a code for something else or a representation of somewhere else" but, in its concentration on word as object, "a revelation of the ordinary as sufficient unto itself" (ibid.: 143). Some of Bernstein's own early poems like "Parsing" (1976) are exercises in adapting the Stein sentence, as are Ron Silliman's *Ketjak* and *Tjanting*, but the poet who has, I think, most fully taken up the challenge of Stein's poetics is Lyn Hejinian, in such books as *My Life*, *The Cell*, and *Happily*, a poetic sequence that meditates, with a Khlebnikovian passion for etymology, on the single word of its title.

Happily, published as a pocket-size paperback (Hejinian 2000a) and reprinted the same year in a new collection of Hejinian's essays (Hejinian 2000b), consists of 250 sentences, ranging from single words like " 'You!'/ 'Me?' " and fragments like "We the wall," to eight lines, arranged as strophes, in which all lines after the first are indented. These strophes are, in turn, organized into irregular stanzas, perhaps on the model of Stein's *Stanzas in Meditation*. The combination of short line fragments and long sentence units gives the page an open, exploratory look, as if to say we cannot tell what might come next.

And indeed we can't. In the *Nichomachean Ethics* (1097b) Aristotle defines happiness as the one thing "we choose always for itself and never for the sake of something else." "Honor, pleasure, reason, and every excellence we choose . . . for the sake of happiness, judging that through them we shall be happy. Happiness, on the other hand, no one chooses for the sake of these, nor, in general, for anything other than itself." Precisely because happiness is thus a final and complete good, no man, says Aristotle, can be called "happy" while he lives, for at any moment his fortune may change. On the other hand, it would be absurd to call a dead man "happy," and so, it seems, no ideal exemplar of happiness presents itself.

Wittgenstein (1979: 74) seems to have solved this dilemma when he writes, in his wartime notebook, "Only a man who lives not in time but in the present is happy." Time is the enemy of happiness in that both memory and anticipation of the future point to the death that is to come. For Wittgenstein, happiness is thus an inner state of mind, independent of external circumstances and the chance contingencies of position or fortune. In a famous aphorism, repeated in the *Tractatus* (6.43), we read: "The world of the happy is a *different* world from the world of the unhappy. But the difference can't be defined; there is only tautology: 'The world of the happy is *a happy world*' " (Wittgenstein 1979: 78). And further, "if I *now* ask myself: But why should I live *happily*, this of itself seems to me to be a tautological question; the happy life seems to be justified, of itself, it seems that it *is* the only right life" (ibid.).

181

What complicates this notion of happiness as outside time is that the adjective "happy" has the same root as the verb "happen" – and if something *happens* it marks an event in time. The root of both words, according to the OED, is the Old English *hap* meaning "Chance or fortune (good or bad) that falls to anyone." More specifically (definition 2), *hap* is "An event or occurrence which befalls one; a chance, accident, happening; often an unfortunate event, mishap, mischance." But it can just as well mean (3) "Good fortune, good luck; success, prosperity," so that the element of *hap* that came to be stressed was (4) "Absence of design or intent in relation to a particular event; fortuity; chance." The root *hap*, in any case, gives us *hapless* ("unlucky"), *haphazard* ("without design, random"), and especially *happen*, "to come to pass, to take place." "Happen," according to the OED, is "the most general verb to express the simple occurrence of an event, often with little or no implication of chance or absence of design." But a subsidiary and now obsolete meaning of "happen" is "to chance to be or to come," "to turn up," as in "Two Officers asked how we happened abroad so late," and "happen on" or "happen upon" continue to mean "to come upon by chance," as in "Just then, I happened upon him." And so the chancy element of happenings is central. As for "happy," its first, now obsolete meaning was "coming or happening by chance; fortuitous," and the notion of luck, chance, or fortune has never disappeared. "Having good 'hap'" meant "to be lucky, fortunate, favoured by lot, position, or other external circumstances." As for "happily," it was originally *haply*, "By chance; perchance," which soon came to mean, "With or by good fortune, fortunately, luckily, successfully."

Not until the Renaissance does happiness come to be seen in Aristotelian terms as a state of mind not necessarily controlled by external fortune. Happiness (OED definition 2), in modern parlance, is "the state of pleasurable content of mind, which results from success or the attainment of what is considered good." "Happily" thus means "with mental pleasure or content," and "happy" comes to be a synonym for "glad" and "pleased." And further (definition 5), "Successful in performing what the circumstances require; apt, dexterous, felicitous." "What," asks Wittgenstein, "is the objective mark of the happy, harmonious life? Here it is again clear that there cannot be any such mark, that can be *described*." Accordingly, one can only say, with childlike tautology, "The world of the happy is *a happy world*." The German word for happy is *glücklich*, which literally means "lucky": happiness, in this scheme of things, is always tied up with what *happens*, especially what happens by luck or chance.

It is this etymological paradox – the tension between a conception of happiness as a state of mind independent of time and circumstance, and a conception of happiness as chance-ridden and fortuitous – that animates Hejinian's *Happily*. In *The Language of Inquiry*, *Happily* is preceded by a piece called "A Common Sense," which is Hejinian's meditation on the meaning of the everyday or commonplace in Gertrude Stein's *Stanzas in Meditation*. "It was through participation in the everyday with its 'inevitable repetition,'" writes Hejinian, "that Gertrude Stein first came to understand the metaphysical as well as compositional force of habit" (Hejinian 2000b: 361). And she points to the sentence in *Portraits and Repetition* where Stein says, "No matter how often what happened had happened any time anyone told anything there was no repetition."

To recount the past, Hejinian suggests, is to freeze it; to say "this happened" leaves no room for contingency. Repetition in a continuous present, on the other hand, assures difference, for no repetition, whether of word or deed, can ever produce an exact replica of a now lost original. The resulting free play, she posits following William James, is equivalent to "The Will to Live." "And," she adds, "it is what here I am going to risk calling happiness"(ibid.). Happiness – and there is a footnote to this effect – not as the usual condition of "privilege bestowed by fortune (in the form either of luck or of money)," but happiness as the awareness of "what happens, happens as effects to beings – things that exist" (ibid.: 362). Whether these things are good or bad is not at issue; what matters is that it is the contemplation of *happening* that arouses the "wonder at mere existence" – in Stein's case, an "alertness to the liveliness of the present and the everyday, the mode of being that for Stein constituted 'complete living'" (ibid.: 363). "Happiness" is thus "a complication, as it were, of the ordinary, a folding in of the happenstantial. . . . In this respect, it is *un*like *un*happiness . . . since unhappiness is a marked condition, firmly attached to plots (that of good vs. evil, of love and loss)" (ibid.: 371), whereas happiness is an attentive awareness to the sheer contingency of happenings.

Like Wittgenstein, Hejinian thus relates happiness to *presence*. It involves "taking a chance . . . into the present," getting *in time* rather than meditating *on* time. Here the root *hap* comes in: Hejinian cites Nietzsche as saying "Happiness arises out of chance, hazard, accident, events, fortune, the fortuitous." Its very contingency is a sort of blessing. "In its very ordinariness, [it] says *yes*" (ibid.: 378). What Hejinian doesn't say in "Common Sense" – although she alluded to it at a 1998 conference, where she aired this talk – is that her meditation on happiness was triggered by a bout with cancer from which she had recently recovered. In one sense, then, *Happily* is her poetic response to reprieve, to the happiness the poet experiences in recognizing her reinsertion into a state of happening. The sequence, as Hejinian says in her headnote to the *Language of Inquiry* version, was designed as "an affirmation of thinking, of thinking's substance and context (what happens) and of writing as the site of such thinking" (ibid.: 384). Writing, in this instance, is less "an aid to memory", as in Hejinian's first major book, than a mode of transformation whereby what the poet calls a "marked condition" – the *what happened* – is absorbed into the continuous present of happen*ing* and such related present participles as *persevering* and *knowing*: witness what the poet calls her "accordioning" sentences, "ones with solid handles (a clear beginning and a clear end) but with a middle that is pleated and flexible" so as "to allow for the influx of material that surges into any thought, material that is charged with various and sometimes even incompatible emotional tonalities" (ibid.).

Such sentences pay homage to Stein's precepts, such as "beginning again and again" and the "continuous present," as well as to

Stein's insistent charging of a single word, even as the word "gay" is charged and recharged in "Miss Furr and Miss Skeene." But, in the end, *Happily* strikes me as perhaps less Steinian than, as was the case with *Oxota*, Hejinian's long parodic Russian "epic" based on Pushkin's *Eugene Onegin*, an oblique homage to the etymological poetics of Khlebnikov and his circle. In *The Language of Inquiry* Hejinian frequently cites the Russian Formalist theorists – Jakobson, Schlovsky, Tinyanov – from whom she traces her own concern for the materiality of language and its ability to effect *ostranenie* (making strange). *Ostranenie*, as Hejinian remarks in a recent essay on translation, posits *relatedness* as the primary quality of poetic discourse. Relatedness can be imagistic or syntactic, but, in the poetry of Ilya Kutik and Arkadii Dragomoschenko which she has translated, Hejinian finds it primarily in "a high degree of wordplay, often of a type that is dependent on etymological associations" (Hejinian 2000b: 303).

It is here that Hejinian parts company with Stein, whose unit of composition is the sentence rather than the word as such (*slovo kak takovoe*). Like Susan Howe, Hejinian is fascinated by dictionaries where "words in storage . . . seem frenetic with activity, as each individual entry attracts to itself other words as definition, example, and amplification" (Hejinian 2000b: 51). One thinks of Khlebnikov tracing the lineage of *so* ("with") in *sol'* ("salt") and *solntse* ("sun"). Similarly, at the end of "Common Sense," Hejinian probes the definition of the word "meditation" in Webster's *Ninth Collegiate Dictionary*: "a discourse intended to express its author's reflections or to guide others in contemplation" (Hejinian 2000b: 375). But, she adds, "the word 'meditation' comes from the Latin, *modus* (measure), and from the Old English, *metan* (to measure), and for Stein it appears to mean a prolonged present cogitation." And *Happily* is clearly motivated by the fact that "happy" and "happen" both derive, as I mentioned earlier, from the root *hap*, and that even the word "habit," which has so much to do with "happening," begins with the letters "ha." Indeed, the poetic sequence orchestrates these words, together with a carefully plotted set of synonyms. "Happen" gives us "take place," "arrive," "come," "recur"; *hap* generates "chance," "accident," "hazard," "event." But – and this is the beauty of the poem – the word "happily" – the adverbial form is preferable to the noun "happiness," since modification is much more likely to produce contingency than is nominalization, which suggests a state of being – is always just "happily" and it appears only three times in the sequence, as compared to some twenty-odd uses of "happen." No synonym, it seems, can do "happily" justice.

Now consider the opening pages of *Happily*:

Constantly I write this happily

Hazards that hope may break open my lips

What I feel is taking place, a large context, long yielding, and
    to doubt it would be a crime against it. . . .

We came when it arrived

Here I write with inexact straightness but into a place in place
    immediately passing between phrases of the imagination

Flowers optimistically going to seed, fluttering candles lapping
    the air, persevering saws swimming into boards, buckets
    taking dents, and the hands on the clock turning – *they*
    aren't melancholy. . . .

The day is promising

Along comes something – launched in context

In context to pass it the flow of humanity divides and on the
    other side unites

All gazing at the stars bound in a black bow

I am among them thinking thought through the thinking
    thought to no conclusion

Context is the chance that time takes

Our names tossed into the air scraped in the grass before
   having formed any opinion leaving people to say only that
   there was a man who happened on a cart and crossed a
   gnarled field and there was a woman who happened on a
   cart and crossed a gnarled field too

Is happiness the name for our (involuntary) complicity with
   chance?

Anything could happen

A boy in the sun drives nails into a fruit a sign (cloud) in the
   wind swings

A woman descends a ladder into mud it gives way
                              (Hejinian 2000a: 3–6)

"Constantly" in the first line immediately provides us with a key
to this complex meditation. Its primary meaning – "continuously,"
"always" – gives way to the secondary sense of "faithfully," "un-
waveringly," as in Somerset Maugham's *The Constant Nymph*. The
writing is happy because it is dedicated, committed: "to doubt it
would be a crime against it" (ibid: 3). But "happily" in line 1 is
followed by "hazards," so as to remind us how "haphazard" these
moments of writing, these "Hazards that hope may break open my
lips," really are. To say "this is happening," to place oneself *inside*, is
to proceed "happily." And here the notion of being in the midst
of *existence* is opposed to the linear narrative of "We came when it
arrived." To be inside happening is to be attentive to contingency
and chance, and to forestall the downward spiral toward closure, here
imaged as flowers going to seed, "fluttering candles," "persevering
saws swimming into boards," "buckets taking dents," and of course
"the hands on the clock turning" – all these familiar items of everyday life but defamiliarized by surprising modifiers, as when the
flowers "optimistically" go to seed or the saws swim into rather than
lacerate the boards they cut.

"Context," we read in the next stanza, "is the chance that time takes." And, a few lines later (ibid: 5), "Is happiness the name for our (involuntary) complicity with chance?" Yes, but not because of the truism "Anything could happen," but because when something does happen, we cannot define what it is. The "marked condition" of plot – "there was a man who happened on a cart and crossed a gnarled field and there was a woman who happened on a cart and crossed a gnarled field too" – cannot yield happiness. For to look at *what happened* this way is to objectify events and thus to undermine the world of the happy, to become aware that "A boy in sun drives nails into a fruit," that "A woman descends a ladder into mud it gives way" (ibid: 5).

"There is really no single poem," Hejinian remarks in a 1995 dialogue with the Serbian poet Dubravka Djuric. And she cites Jack Spicer's (1975) letter to Robin Blaser in *Admonitions*: "Poems should echo and reecho against each other. They should create resonance. They cannot live alone any more than we can" (Hejinian 2000b: 168). This affords an apt description of the mode of *Happily*, whose accordion sentences, interrupted by aphorisms and pithy statements, mime the processes of mind whereby the poet tries to remain in the suspended state of existing *happily* in a state of contiguity – of metonymy rather than metaphor. The very notion of the individual poem – closed, confined, surrounded by white space and hence marked – goes against the notion of contingency so central to Hejinian's ethos. Yet – and this gives her meditation its edge – even in an open sequence like *Happily* there can't help being lapses into linearity:

> I can always wait sometimes, other times impatience overcomes
> me like a disease effacing the fingerprints of the naked hand
> on my inner nature which chance bothered to put there,
> beauty scratched out, and history answered in the affirmative
> (2000a: 12)

Impatience and insistence are blocking factors, as is nostalgia:

> Nostalgia is another name for one's sense of loss at the thought
> that one has sadly gone along happily overlooking some-
> thing, who knows what (ibid: 15)

Avoid, this meditation suggests, clear definition, doctrine, rigid
dialectic. And so the poem avoids overt connections – meter, rhyme
scheme, a structure of images, controlling metaphor – in favor
of those hidden connections produced by those variants on
hap and their synonyms and homonyms. Hence sentences are
left incomplete, pronouns like "it" remain undefined, prepositions
signaling time and space relations are indeterminate, and
sentences don't directly connect and are, at any rate, eminently
interruptable, whether by questions, maxims, narrative interludes,
or merely non-sequitur. "The world of the happy," no longer quite
the "happy world" of Wittgenstein, is subject to everything that
happens.

In this context, uncertainty (the word and its cognates appear frequently toward the end of the poem) is a virtue: "Of each actual-
ity I'm uncertain and always was uncertain and such uncertainty
is certain" (ibid: 36). Chance teaches the poet to trust finitude, to
dwell, as Emily Dickinson put it, in possibility. The sentence "It's
between birth and death our commonality and *our own* birth and
death we are incapable of experiencing" (ibid: 29), obliquely points
to Wittgenstein's terse formulation, "Death is not an event of life.
Death is not lived through" (*Tractatus* 6.4311). True, near the end of
Happily there is a chill in the air: "Come winter," we read, "I see
particularly the foreshortened perspective / disguise retreat and in
no way get arranged" (ibid: 37). And as the poem ends, the talk is
of "preparation for what will come next." "That," says the poet, "may
be the thing and logically we go when it departs" (ibid: 39). The
rupture seems definitive – a long way from *happening* and *happily*.
But it's only "logically" that "we go when it departs," and logic has
been abandoned from the beginning. So the death note is muted,
a poignant reminder even as "happily I'm feeling the wind in its
own right."

189

Chances are that the cycle will continue: "Every moment was better later and it greatly changed appearance" (ibid: 38). Like Stein's anticipation of that "magnificent asparagus and also a fountain" at the conclusion of "Rooms" (see chapter 2, this volume), *Happily* faces toward the future, toward those "beginnings that reason can motivate but not end." In its enactment of the Flaubertian principle that "sentences" should be "erect while running" (ibid: 7), as an ode to a "happy" contingency, *Happily* stands in the tradition of Stein's "A Valentine Sherwood Anderson," with its modulations of "very fine" and "very mine."

Ataraxia in Vortex State

If Hejinian's *Happily* takes its inspiration from the etymology of a single word, Steve McCaffery's poems, sound texts, and verbal–visual pieces, from *'Ow's Waif* (1975) to *The Cheat of Words* (1991), have always played with the paragrammatic dimension of language as well as its visual properties. His four-page text called "Four Versions of Pound's 'In a Station of the Metro'" from *Modern Reading* (1990), now available in *Seven Pages Missing* (2001: 378–81), is a case in point and brings us back, full circle, to the avant-garde movements of the *avant guerre*. But "circle" is something of a misnomer: McCaffery's is a visual poem that reconceives Pound – very respectfully, to be sure – through Duchampian eyes.

Let's recall the genesis of Pound's most famous Imagist poem. In the *Fortnightly Review* for September 1, 1914 (see Ruthven 1969: 152–3), Pound explained:

> Three years ago in Paris I got out of a "metro" train at La Concorde, and saw suddenly a beautiful face, and then another and another, and then a beautiful child's face, and then another beautiful woman, and I tried all day to find words for what this had meant to me, and I could not find any words that seemed to me worthy, or as lovely as that sudden emotion.

And that evening, as I went home along the Rue Raynouard, I was still trying and I found, suddenly the expression. I do not mean that I found words, but there came an equation . . . not in speech, but in little splotches of color. . . .

That evening, in the Rue Raynouard, I realized quite vividly that if I were a painter . . . I might found a new school . . . "non-representative painting," a painting that would speak only by arrangements in colour. . . . "The one image poem" is a form of super-position, that is to say, it is one idea set on top of another. I found it useful in getting out of the impasse in which I had been left by my metro emotion. I wrote a thirty-line poem, and destroyed it because it was what we called work "of second intensity." Six months later I made a poem half that length; a year later I made the following hokku-like sentence:

> *In a Station of the Metro*
> The apparition of these faces in the crowd;
> Petals on a wet, black bough.

In its first appearance in *Poetry* (April 1913), as Ruthven (1969: 152) notes, the lines were spaced as follows:

> The apparition   of these faces   in the crowd
>   Petals   on a wet, black   bough.

Pound's early insistence on the visual meaning of spacing, typography, and the spatial disposition of letters and words in a given poem looks ahead to his fascination with the Chinese ideogram first formulated in his edition of Ernest Fenollosa's manuscript *The Chinese Written Character as a Medium for Poetry* (1919). The superiority of the Chinese ideogram to Western alphabetic writing, Pound was to insist throughout his life, is that the ideogram doesn't *represent* something else but *is* that thing. Thus, as he declares in *ABC of Reading* (1934), whereas in English "red" is defined as a color and color, in turn, as "a vibration or a refraction of light, or a division of the spectrum," in Chinese, the ideogram for "red" juxtaposes the words for "Rose," "Cherry," "Iron Rust," and "Flamingo" (Pound 1960: 19). Thus, "The Chinese 'word' or ideogram for red is based on something everyone KNOWS" (ibid.: 22). It respects the concreteness – the thingness of the things.

And further: the "ideogrammatic method" accords with Vorticism. In his memoir of the Vorticist sculptor *Gaudier-Brzeska* (1916), in which the anecdote about "In a Station of the Metro" reappears (Pound 1970: 86–7, 89), Pound defines the image as "a radiant node or cluster . . . a VORTEX, from which and through which, and into which ideas are constantly rushing" (ibid.: 92). And again, "The image is the poet's pigment"; it is "the furthest possible remove from rhetoric." And Pound cites its "artistic descent *via* Picasso and Kandinsky (ibid.: 86, 83, 82).

Now suppose we take Pound at his word when he insists that "if I were a painter . . . I might found a new school . . . of 'non-representative' painting" (Ruthven 1969: 153). This is what Steve McCaffery does in his "Four Versions." Taking Pound's claim literally, he decides to produce a visual rendition of "In a Station of the Metro," but not by producing an image of a subway, much less a picture of petals on a wet, black bough or some similar "pretty" Japanese-print image. On the contrary, just as Pound reinvents China, so McCaffery reconceptualizes Pound's exemplary Imagist haiku.

"The apparition of these faces in the crowd": McCaffery's first page (see plate 5.2) presents us with a Caucasian woman's rounded eye as the middle item of the second line in a grid of Chinese ideograms – or rather some are bona fide ideograms because at least three of the fourteen (2, 8, 10) look bogus. McCaffery says he doesn't remember from where he took these "ideograms" but that a Chinese friend thinks it must have been a children's book. But of course the whole point here is that the "apparition" (the mysterious eye), seen by the reader's eye, far from being a definable concrete thing (cherry tree) or action ("Man sees horse"), is equivocal. How, McCaffery asks, does the Western European eye (whether seen or seeing) relate to the Eastern (not quite Chinese) script? And,

Plate 5.2 Steve McCaffery, "Four Versions of Pound's 'In a Station of the Metro'," panel 1.

Plate 5.3 Steve McCaffery, "Four Versions of Pound's 'In a Station of the Metro'," panel 2.

more important, how does the depicted eye – an ideogram among ideograms – relate to the generic lyric "I" which McCaffery, like Pound before him, takes pains to displace. No first-person expression here and no apparition of a face, but only an eye that is an object among objects, indeed a thing. For all his talk of thingness, Pound never anticipated such dehumanization! And the other three panels carry on this replacement of "I" by "eye."

In the second panel (plate 5.3) the eye reappears, but this time in inverted form and instead of the plucked eyebrow of no. 1, here the hairline is covered by what might be a veil. At the lower right is the head and upper torso of a man, his back to the reader, his face invisible. And surrounding these two photographs are shards ("petals"), presumably of paper, with writing on them, the letters unreadable because they are cut off. Thus at the bottom we have what looks like half an *S* next to an *I* on its side; the third letter-image in this row is not identifiable as more than a white column in a grid. The apparition of these faces in the crowd thus remains enigmatic. They don't light up the atmosphere and the black "petals" are more attractive than the inverted eye or the back of the man's head.

The third panel (plate 5.4) depicts an Olympus camera bearing the name of the manufacturer, F. Zuiko, thus again juxtaposing East and West. Inside, the lens (the camera eye) encloses the image of a contorted male face, perhaps a self-portrait. Is this the "apparition" of a face in the crowd? Can this camera see or only be seen? What is the relationship of self-portrait to the outlined profile below, which recalls the upturned faces of Picasso's *Guernica* as does the large offscale eye inside the face and the second eye inside the square on the right? And what about the diagrammatic fish tail in the right-hand grid under the eye? In Pound's Canto II, we read:

> So-shu churned in the sea.
> Seal sports in the spray-whited circles of cliff-wash,
> Sleek head, daughter of Lir,
>   Eyes of Picasso
>
> (Pound 1993: 6)

Plate 5.4 Steve McCaffery, "Four Versions of Pound's 'In a Station of the Metro'," panel 3.

The Chinese Han Dynasty poet, his name rendered in Japanese transliteration, juxtaposed to the playful seal, whose eyes, Pound notes, resemble those in a Picasso painting, and then to the Celtic sea-god Lir: here is the "super-position" of images that creates the Poundian Vortex, with its juxtapositions of East and West, ancient and modern, human and animal. McCaffery gives Pound's montage an interesting twist. Whereas Pound turns image – the thing seen – into verbal signifier, McCaffery turns the verbal signifier into a schematic pictorial image – an image that has to be *read* rather than merely seen like the "eyes of Picasso." Then, too, the allusions to Picasso provided an unstated link between Pound and Stein's various portraits of Picasso – a link that surely didn't escape McCaffery. The ideographic method, far from bringing us closer to *things*, thus opens the door for conceptual thought.

The same thing happens in the case of panel 4 (plate 5.5). McCaffery collages two anonymous portrait-heads (or is it four, since the heads above and below the horizontal strip of writing don't match?) on two columns of letters, both the portraits and the letters evidently taken from an art book or magazine. As in the other panels, the writing is not decipherable: letters are cut off and broken. The face on the left seems to be that of a generic Roman emperor – Augustus, perhaps, whose head looks as if it has been speared on the letter-pole (like a barber-pole) beneath his chin, if that is his chin. But the woman to his right seems unrelated – an African queen, perhaps, or other imposing black figure. The "crowd," in this case, is not a sea of faces within which those of beautiful girls stand out; it is a dehumanized "crowd" of semi-legible letters that compose no complete words. As for the small photograph at the lower right, beneath the verbal column or black bough, it looks like an urban scene (perhaps Paris, perhaps near the Metro station) in the rain. The street lights have haloes and are reflected in puddles of water on the pavement. A cab stands waiting on the left; two people, their backs to us, walk toward the right rear. The panel is thus quite an apparition, what with the ghosts of emperors and queens, again the "super-position" of East and West or African and

197

Plate 5.5 Steve McCaffery, "Four Versions of Pound's 'In a Station of the Metro'," panel 4.

European and the black strips covered with incomplete writing like tubes disappearing into the white tunnel of the page.

"The image," for Pound, "is a radiant node or cluster from which, and through which, and into which, ideas are constantly rushing." McCaffery takes this definition at face value. His images have little retinal interest; rather, as in Duchamp's case, they are designed to make the viewer/reader *think*. Like the Duchampian "delay in glass," McCaffery's "pictures" yearn to free themselves, not only from the retinal but also the tactile. Texture, in this scheme of things, is subordinated to conception. As McCaffery puts it in a brilliant poem called, in a sly allusion to Alain Resnais's great film, "Serbia mon amour":

> Each ideogram an excised tissue graft
> of chin ſtroked belly valves a furnace five
> and reckoning precision means
> demotic series
> puſtules peculiar to the ſtylus pad.
> Ataraxia in vortex ſtate
> to bifurcate theodicy.
>   (McCaffery 2001: 393)

"Serbia mon amour," written long before the Serbian–Kossovar conflict, alludes uncannily to projected conflict and war, to "the broken board / the liar's hunt," and "the module unreachable by pain / in the joints of common borders." An "ideogram," the poem suggests, is never just a lovely concretion of abstract thought: it has materiality, weight, substance – "pustules peculiar to the stylus pad, a coveit reference to the ligatures on the *st*'s." But that doesn't preclude the quizzical response evoked by the line "Ataraxia in vortex state." Ataraxia means "peace of mind, tranquillity, calm." How can there be ataraxia in a vortex state when the move is on "to bifurcate theodicy – to partition the city of God," which in this case may well refer to Belgrade or Kosovo or Zagreb? That, as the line's sound patterning – Ataraxia/vortex – suggests, is the unanswerable question, rather like the "identity" of Duchamp's *Fresh Widow*.

"Serbia mon amour" is at once impersonal and exuberant, rather like Khlebnikov's brilliant political poem "Russia and Me," discussed in chapter 4. As in Khlebnikov's case, the reader is guided by sound: a line like "of chin stroked belly valves a furnace five" conveys the horror and absurdity of war by means of sound and rhythm before we puzzle out its meanings. And a key to the poem is its modulation of *st* in the old spelling, joining "alarmiſt," "upſtream," "firſt," "inſtruct," "Cataſtrophe," "capitaliſt," "ſtroked," "puſtules," "ſtylus," "ſtate," "ſtatues," and "pointilliſtic." So frequent is the hissing *st* spirant/stop (supported here by the look of the letters on the page) that it forms its own Poundian ideogram: the key word, after all, is *cataſtrophe* – and a capitaliſt cataſtrophe at that.

"The word," Khlebnikov declared in 1920,

> leads a double life. Sometimes it simply grows like a plant whose fruit is a geode of sonorous stones clustering around it; in this case the sound element lives a self-sufficient life. . . . At other times the word is subservient to sense, and then sound ceases to be 'all-powerful' and autocratic; sound becomes merely a 'name' and humbly carries out the commands of sense. (Khlebnikov 1987: 373)

In mainstream lyric poetry the "commands of sense" may well continue to dominate the poetic field, even as they do in mainstream theater, where the topical realistic drama remains the staple, year in and year out, whatever the artistic and cultural currents of the time. But as the above examples testify – and there is now an impressive range and production of poetry in which language, sound, rhythm, and visual layout are, in Pound's terms, "charged with meaning" – ours may well be the moment when the lessons of early modernism are finally being learned.

Notes

1 Avant-Garde Eliot

1 A letter from Eliot to Eudo C. Mason, February 21, 1936 (see Eliot 1996: xv) contains the following information: 'J. Alfred Prufrock was written in 1911, but parts of it date from the preceding year. Most of it was written in the summer of 1911 when I was in Munich. The text of 1917, which remains unchanged, does not differ from the original version in any way. I did at one time write a good bit more of it, but these additions I destroyed without their ever being printed."

2 Schuchard (1999) reproduces for the first time in print Eliot's syllabi for the Modern English Literature course he gave in 1916, under the auspices of the University of London Joint Committee for the Promotion of the Higher Education of the Working People. In the case of Hardy, Eliot's focus was only on the novels, "particularly their fatalism as well as their absence of humour" (ibid.: 43–4).

3 Originally, Eliot used Arnaut Daniel's "Sovegna vos" from *Purgatorio* XXVI: see Eliot (1996: 39–41). The later epigraph was, of course, more appropriate to the psychology and narrative of "Prufrock": Guido da Montelfeltro, placed inside a flame in the eighth ring of the eighth circle of hell for his role as evil counselor, delivers an anxiety-ridden self-canceling monologue. Harrison (1987) argues that Guido's account of his past is made in bad faith, the character constantly trying to justify himself in his own eyes as well as in Virgil's and Dante's.

4 Gordon (1999) dismisses the very possibility that Eliot and Verdenal were more than friends, given that Eliot "denied . . . absolutely" the existence of such a relationship (ibid.: 52–4).

5 According to Ricks's tabulation, in late 1912 Eliot wrote the discarded "Prufrock's Pervigilium," only the first three lines of which made its way into "The Love Song of J. Alfred Prufrock" (see Eliot 1996: 43–4); in 1913 he wrote "The Burnt Dancer," "The Love Song of St. Sebastian," and "Morning at the Window." He was now working on his philosophy degree.

6 *Purgatorio* XXI, lines 133–6, my translation. Christopher Ricks notes that this epigraph appears in the Notebook (reprinted in Ricks 1996), suggesting an early date, but argues that this dedication and epigraph must have been a later addition, since it first appears in print in *Poems 1909–25*. The Notebook adds the previous line, "Tu se' ombra e ombra vedi," in which Dante warns Statius not to embrace Virgil because he is only a shadow (Eliot 1996: 3–4).

7 See, for example, Smith (1962: 74–7). Olney (1994: 9–11) relates the Hyacinth Girl to her earlier incarnation as "La Figlia che Piange," "Her hair over her arms and her arms full of flowers," and argues that she reappears as the "Eyes that last I saw in tears" in *Burnt Norton*. But I see more difference than similarity between the Hyacinth episode and the disembodied "moment" in the *Quartets*.

8 More accurately, *The Waste Land* was simultaneously published in two journals, the *Criterion* in England and the *Dial* in the US, and in December 1922 in book form by Boni & Liveright, which included, for the first time, Eliot's explanatory notes. See Rainey (1998: 78).

2 Gertrude Stein's Differential Syntax

1 The use of "gay" here and in related Stein texts like *A Long Gay Book* (1912) naturally suggests that Stein may have anticipated the contemporary meaning of "gay" as "homosexual." But there is no evidence that this was the case. Rawson (1981: 119–21) provides a very full etymology of "gay," from its early use (seventeenth century) as a euphemism for a "loose and immoral life," to its nineteenth-century designation of women of pleasure as "gay women" ("The *gay women* of this era were said to lead the *gay life*, to work in *gay houses*, to be *gay in the arse* . . . and to *gay it* [either sex might *gay it*, this simply meaning "to copulate"] to its underground meaning of "homosexual," first used in the 1920s in the private discourse of male homosexuals.

Would Stein have known of this usage? Ronald Butters, the editor of the journal *American Speech*, who kindly alerted me to Rawson's very helpful dictionary, thinks that in 1911 when Stein wrote "Miss Furr and Miss Skeene" she probably did not, and observes that Stein's close writer-friend Sherwood Anderson used the word "gay" as more or less synonymous with "crazy." Cf. Dydo (1993: 254), headnote to "Miss Furr and Miss Skeene."

3 The Conceptual Poetics of Marcel Duchamp

1 *Bottle Rack (l' Égouttoir)* is an ordinary bottle dryer (the French word *égoutter* means "able to drain drops" but also plays on the word *goût*, "taste") that Duchamp picked up at the Hôtel de Ville department store, but its multi-phallic form is obvious – a form ironized by the absence of those empty bottles that belong on its rods. I have discussed Duchamp's readymades in Perloff (1992: 5–15; 1996; 1999). Some of the material in these essays appears here in revised form.

2 Duchamp's now famous boxes have become important museum pieces. In 1998, for example, the Philadelphia Museum of Art and the Menil Foundation in Houston cooperated on an exhibition called "Joseph Cornell / Marcel Duchamp . . . in resonance," which exhibited Duchamp's intricate boxes and *boîtes en valise* in relationship to Cornell's own magical box constructions. The catalogue (Winkler and d'Harnoncourt 1998) is itself a work of art, reproducing each scrap of paper in actual size and in color.

3 Henderson (1998: 72–4). Both Henderson and Bonk (1998) note that Duchamp did alter the typeface inscription of one of the box labels from *Union Photographique Industrielle* to *15/16 Photographies Industrielles*, thus creating a slight off-note, but otherwise the artist remained scrupulously impersonal. Henderson's magisterial study of the *Large Glass*, together with her earlier *Fourth Dimension* (1983), are essential reading for anyone interested in Duchamp's "scientific" art-making.

4 Duchamp (1966: unpaginated; 1975: 74). The Hamilton, Bonk and Matisse "typotranslation" (1999) is a transcription that retains the original's graphic complexity. "To convey the information contained in the facsimiles," write the authors in their Afterword, "requires that the words, sketches, and diagrams be integrated into a new isomorph." But

since this is a very limited edition, and since the notes themselves, facsimiles like those of the *Box of 1914*, are reprinted in Sanouillet''s edition (Duchamp 1975), the translations here are somewhat different from those in the 1999 edition. The sentence here quoted, for example, is translated as "Can works be made which are not 'of art'?"

5 Duchamp (1975: 13). Cf. "Flirting at the Bon Marché" (Stein 1998 I: 304–5): "Why is everything changing. Everything is changing because the place where they shop is a place where every one is needing to be finding that there are ways of living that are not dreary ones, ways of living that are not sad ones, ways of living that are not dull ones, ways of living that are not tedious ones."

6 See Duchamp (1975: 49, 71). For a discussion of Duchamp's use of Jarry's pataphysics, see Henderson (1998: 47–9, 95–6). Cf. Tomkins (1996: 122–42).

7 Duchamp (1975: 26); cf. Hamilton (1976). In his postface (unpaginated), Hamilton notes that since it was impossible to make a complete analogy between Duchamp's calligraphy and the printed version, his own version uses color coding (red) to capture Duchamp's revisions.

8 In Duchamp (1975: 103–19) these are grouped under the heading "Rrose Sélavy & Co." *Ovaire tout la nuit* turns the common phrase "ouvert tout la nuit" into an all-night ovary. "The poet Ron Padgett wittily translates it as 'We never clothe'" (ibid.: 111). *La bagarre d''Austerlitz* (1921), literally "the brawl at Austerlitz" (an allusion to the famous Napoleonic battle), puns on "la gare" (the station), specifically the Paris terminal, the Gare d'Austerlitz. David Antin (1972: 70–1) suggests that the title can be broken down to *La Bague, Garde d''Austères Lits* ("The Ring, Keeper of Austere Beds").

9 Joselit writes: "On the surface of the work language is reified while at its center a thing regresses from the status of a commodity to a primitive form of exchange, the exchange of sound. In an extraordinary double move – or double *inscription* – language becomes a commodity, as a commodity becomes language" (Joselit 1998: 84). This is an intriguing reading, but it gives *With Hidden Noise* a more negative tone than I think Duchamp intends. The "double *inscription*" exists but I take it as a comical reminder that "noise" is always a form of language.

10 Joselit (1998: 151, 228) remarks that the window's "odd shade of greenish-blue suggestive of tropical seas" has an air of "kitsch."

11 Nesbit (1986: 63) further notes that "The claim to copyright [by Rose Sélavy] brings the interrogation by the shop window to a different halt: Duchamp has claimed a copyright for a window that is not only plagiarized but by definition not eligible for copyright. . . . The copyright was a bluff. But with it, Duchamp subjugated the culture of the patent in no uncertain terms." For a disagreement with this interpretation, see Joselit (1998: 228–9).

12 See Bonk (1998: 100–1) and Naumann (1999: 111–17). The previously unpublished letter to Arensberg is cited in Winkler and d'Harnoncourt (1998: 111). In the end, Duchamp used only 93 manuscript notes as opposed to the projected 135 and made only 300 copies of the regular edition, 20, as planned, of the deluxe.

13 The notes are reproduced as facsimile scraps, with the French and English print versions at the bottom of the page. Forward slash marks (/) indicate the end of the line in the handwritten original; back slashes (\) indicate that the word is above a crossed-out word. Duchamp sometimes hyphenates infrathin, sometimes not, as if to say that even the word itself cannot remain the same. Similarly, he sometimes ends an entry with a period, sometimes with a dash, sometimes with no punctuation. The book is unpaginated but the notes are numbered.

4 Khlebnikov's Soundscapes: Letter, Number, and the Poetics of Zaum

1 Except for proper names, the transcription I have used here and throughout is based on the Library of Congress system. When citations don't follow that system, I regularize their spelling in the interest of consistency.

Bibliography

Altieri, Charles. *Painterly Abstraction in Modernist American Poetry.* New York: Cambridge University Press, 1989.

——"Eliot's Impact on Twentieth-Century Anglo-American Poetry." In *The Cambridge Companion to T. S. Eliot,* ed. A. David Moody, Cambridge: Cambridge University Press, 189–209, 1994.

Andrews, Bruce. "Jeopardy." In *Wobbling,* New York: Roof, 90–3, 1981.

Antin, David. "Duchamp: The Meal and the Remainder." *Art News* 68–71, October 1972.

——"Some Questions about Modernisms." *Occident* 7, new series, spring 1974.

Ashbery, John. *Self-Portrait in a Convex Mirror.* New York: Viking, 1975.

——"The Impossible." In *Poetry* 1957. Reprinted in *Gertrude Stein Advanced: An Anthology of Criticism,* ed. Richard Kostelanetz. Jefferson, NC: Macfarland, 108–11, 1990.

Benjamin, Walter. "The Work of Art in the Age of Mechanical Reproduction" [1936]. In *Illuminations,* ed. Hannah Arendt. New York: Schocken, 217–51, 1968.

Bernstein, Charles. *Content's Dream: Essays 1975–1984.* Los Angeles: Sun & Moon, 1986.

——"Dysraphism." In *The Sophist,* Los Angeles: Sun & Moon, 44–50, 1987.

——*A Poetics.* Cambridge, MA: Harvard University Press, 1992.

——*Dark City.* Los Angeles: Sun & Moon, 1994.

——*My Way: Speeches and Poems.* Chicago: University of Chicago Press, 2000.

—— "Common Stock." In *With Strings*, Chicago: University of Chicago Press, 2001.

Bloom, Harold. *Yeats*. New York: Oxford University Press, 1970.

Bonk, Ecke. "Delay Included." In *Joseph Cornell/Marcel Duchamp . . . in resonance*, ed. Paul Winkler and Anne d'Harnoncourt. Catalogue of the Exhibition. Houston: Menil Foundation, 95–112, 1998.

Bürger, Peter. *Theory of the Avant Garde*, trans. Michael Shaw. Minneapolis: University of Minnesota Press, 1984.

Cabanne, Pierre. *Dialogues with Marcel Duchamp*, trans. Ron Padgett. New York: Viking, 1971.

Cage, John. "Questions." *Perspectiva*, 1967.

Cameron, Eric. "Given." In *The Definitely Unfinished Marcel Duchamp*, ed. Thierry de Duve, Cambridge, MA: MIT Press, 1–29, 1992.

Castillo, Ana. "Seduced by Natassja Kinski." In *Anthology of Modern American Poetry*, ed. Cary Nelson, New York: Oxford University Press, 1181–2, 2000.

Cendrars, Blaise. "Contrasts" [1919]. In *Complete Poems*, trans. Ron Padgett, Berkeley: University of California Press, 58–9, 1992.

Christensen, Paul. "Edward Hirsch." In *Contemporary Poets*, 7th. edn., ed. Thomas Riggs. Detroit: St. James, 532–3, 2001.

Clover, Joshua. "The Rose of the Name." *Fence* 1 (Spring 1998) 35–41.

Cooke, Raymond. *Velimir Khlebnikov. A Critical Study*. Cambridge: Cambridge University Press, 1987.

Cowan, Laura (ed.). *T. S. Eliot: Man and Poet*, 2 vols. Orono: National Poetry Foundation, 1990–1.

Dalton, F. T. Review (anon.) of *Prufrock and Other Observations* in the *Times Literary Supplement*, June 21, 1917. Reprinted in *The Modern Movement: A TLS Companion*, ed. John Gross. Chicago: University of Chicago Press, 1992.

Davidson, Michael. "From Act to Speech Act." *Aerial* 8, 1995. Reprinted in *An Anthology of New Poetics*, ed. Christopher Beach. Tuscaloosa: Alabama University Press, 70–6, 1998.

Davie, Donald. *Thomas Hardy and British Poetry*. New York: Oxford University Press, 1972.

de Campos, Haroldo. *Ideogramma: Lógica/Poesia/Linguagem*, 2nd. edn. São Paulo: Editora da Universidade de São Paulo, 1986.

de Duve, Thierry. *Pictorial Nominalism: On Marcel Duchamp's Passage from*

Painting to the Readymade [1984], trans. Dana Polan with the author. Minneapolis: University of Minnesota Press, 1991.

——(ed.). *The Definitely Unfinished Marcel Duchamp.* Cambridge, MA: MIT Press, 1992.

d'Harnoncourt, Anne and Kynaston McShine (eds.). *Marcel Duchamp.* New York: Museum of Modern Art; Philadelphia: Philadelphia Museum of Art, 1973.

Duchamp, Marcel. "Stance 69 des 'Stances de meditation.'" *Orbes* 4, 63–4, winter 1932–3.

——Interview with Michel Sanouillet: "Dans l'atelier de Marcel Duchamp," *Les Nouvelles littéraires,* December 16, 1954.

——*À l'Infinitif. Manuscript Notes of Marcel Duchamp 1912–1920*, trans. Cleve Gray in collaboration with the author, ed. Richard Hamilton and Ecke Bonk. Limited edition of facsimile reproductions with an original silkscreen print on vinyl of *The Glider* (from the *Large Glass*). New York: Cordier & Ekstrom, 1966.

—— *The Essential Writings of Marcel Duchamp: Marchand du sel – Salt Seller,* ed. Michel Sanouillet and Elmer M. Peterson, London: Thames & Hudson, 1975.

——*Notes,* presentation and trans. Paul Matisse. Paris: Musée National d'Art Moderne, Centre Georges Pompidou, 1980; rpt. Boston: G. K. Hall, 1983

Dydo, Ulla E. (ed.). *A Stein Reader.* Evanston, IL: Northwestern University Press, 1993.

Eliot, T. S. "Charleston, Hey! Hey!" Review of Rose Macauley's *Catchwords and Claptrap*, John Rodker's *The Future of Futurism*, Basil de Selincourt's *Pomono: or the Future of English*, Gertrude Stein's *Composition as Explanation*, in *Nation & Atheneum* 595, January 29, 1927.

——*Selected Essays.* London: Faber & Faber, 1953. Cited as SE.

——"Hamlet and his Problems." In *Selected Essays*, London: Faber & Faber, 141–6, 1958.

——"Reflections on Vers Libre" [1917]. In *To Criticize the Critic*, New York: Farrar, Straus & Giroux, 1965.

——*Collected Poems 1909–1962.* New York: Harcourt, 1970. Cited as CP.

—— *The Waste Land: A Facsimile and Transcript of the Original Drafts including the Annotations of Ezra Pound*, ed. Valerie Eliot. London: Faber & Faber, 1971.

Bibliography

—— *The Letters of T. S. Eliot. Volume 1: 1898–1922*, ed. Valerie Eliot. New York: Harcourt, 1988. Cited as L.

—— *Inventions of the March Hare*, ed. Christopher Ricks. New York: Harcourt, 1996.

Faucherau Serge. "Khlebnikov." In *Futurism and Futurisms*, ed. Pontus Hulten, New York: Abbeville, 496, 1986.

Flaubert, Gustave. *Letters of Gustave Flaubert*, ed. and trans. Francis Steegmuller. Cambridge, MA: Harvard University Press, 1980.

Gordon, Lyndall. *T. S. Eliot: An Imperfect Life*. New York: Norton, 1999.

Guttman, Yair. "Conceptual Art and Philosophy." In *Encyclopedia of Aesthetics*, ed. Michael Kelly, New York: Oxford University Press, 414–27, 1998.

Hamilton, Richard. *The Bride Stripped Bare by her Bachelors, Even. A Typographic Version of Marcel Duchamp's Green Box*, trans. George Heard Hamilton. New York: Jaap Rietman, 1976.

Hamilton, Richard, Ecke Bonk, and Jackie Matisse. *À l'Infinitif. A Typography*. Paris: Succession Marcel Duchamp/ADAGP, 1999.

Harrison, Robert. "Comedy and Modernity: Dante's Hell." *Modern Language Notes* 108, 1050–2, 1987.

Hass, Robert (ed.). *A Primer for the Gradual Understanding of Gertrude Stein*. Santa Barbara, CA: Black Sparrow, 1976.

Hecht, Anthony. *The Hard Hours*. New York: Atheneum, 1968.

Hejinian, Lyn. *Happily*. Sausalito: Post-Apollo Press. Reprinted in *The Language of Inquiry*, Berkeley: University of California Press, 383–405, 2000a.

—— *The Language of Inquiry*, Berkeley: University of California Press, 296–317, 2000b.

Henderson, Linda Dalrymple. *The Fourth Dimension and Non-Euclidean Geometry in Modern Art*. Princeton, NJ: Princeton University Press, 1983.

—— *Duchamp in Context: Science and Technology in the Large Glass and Related Works*. Princeton, NJ: Princeton University Press, 1998.

Hirsch, Edward. *For the Sleepwalkers*. New York: Alfred A. Knopf, 1981.

Howe, Susan. *Articulation of Sound Forms in Time*. Windsor, VT: Awede, 1987.

—— *Thorow*. In *Singularities*, Hanover, NH: Wesleyan Press, 39–59, 1990.

—— "Hinge Picture" [1974]. In *Frame Structures: Early Poems 1974–1979*, New York: New Directions, 31–56, 1996.

Hulten, Pontus (ed.). *Marcel Duchamp: Work and Life.* Cambridge, MA: MIT Press, 1993.

Jakobson, Roman. "Subliminal Verbal Patterning in Poetry" [1970]. In *Language in Literature,* ed. Krystyna Pomorska and Stephen Rudy, Cambridge, MA: Harvard University Press, 250–66, 1987.

——*My Futurist Years,* ed. Bengt Jangfeldt and Stephen Rudy, trans. Stephen Rudy. New York: Marsilio, 1997.

Janacek, Gerald. *The Look of Russian Literature: Avant-Garde Visual Experiments 1900–1930.* Princeton, NJ: Princeton University Press, 1984.

Joselit, David. *Infinite Regress: Marcel Duchamp 1910–1941.* Cambridge, MA: MIT Press, 1998.

Joseph, Branden W. "'A Duplication Containing Duplications': Robert Rauschenberg's Split Screens." *October* 95, 3–28, winter 2001.

Jouffroy, Allain "Conversations avec Marcel Duchamp." In *Une Revolution du regard: A propos de quelques peintres et sculpteurs contemporains.* Paris: Gallimard, 107–24, 1964.

Joyce, James. *The Portrait of the Artist as a Young Man* [1916]. New York: Penguin Books, 1992.

Judovitz, Dalia. *Unpacking Duchamp: Art in Transit.* Berkeley: University of California Press, 1995.

Kenner, Hugh. *The Invisible Poet: T. S. Eliot.* New York: Harcourt, 1959.

Khlebnikov [Xlebnikov], V. V. *Sobranie sochinenii [Collected Writings],* 4 vols. Slavische Propyläen, Texte in Neu-und Nachdrucken. Munich: Wilhelm Fink, 1968.

Khlebnikov, Velimir. *Snake Train: Poetry and Prose,* ed. and trans. Gary Kern. Ann Arbor, MI: Ardis, 1976.

——*Collected Works of Velimir Khlebnikov,* 3 vols, trans. Paul Schmidt. Vol. 1: *Letters and Theoretical Writings,* ed. Charlotte Douglas, 1987; Vol. 2: *Prose, Plays, and Supersagas,* ed. Ronald Vroon, 1989; Vol. 3: *Selected Poems,* ed. Ronald Vroon, 1997. Cambridge, MA: Harvard University Press, 1987–97.

Knowles, Sebastian D. G. and Scott A. Leonard (eds.), *Annotated Bibliography of a Decade of T. S. Eliot Criticism 1977–86, T. S. Eliot: Man and Poet,* Vol. 2. Orono, ME: National Poetry Foundation, 1991.

Kosuth, Joseph "Art after Philosophy" [1969]. In *Art after Philosophy and After: Collected Writings, 1966–1990,* ed. Gabriele Guercio, Cambridge: MIT Press, 13–45, 1991.

Bibliography

Kozloff, Max "Three-Dimensional Prints and the Retreat from Originality." *Artforum* 4, 4, 26–7, December 1965.

Kuh, Katherine. *The Artist's Voice: Talks with Seventeen Artists.* New York: Harper 1962.

Lawton Anna (ed.). *Russian Futurism through its Manifestos 1912–1928*, trans. Anna Lawton and Herbert Eagle. Ithaca, NY: Cornell University Press, 1988.

Lebel, Robert. *Marcel Duchamp*, trans. George Heard. New York: Paragraphic, 1959.

Lewis, Wyndham. *Blasting and Bombadiering: An Autobiography (1914–1926)*. London: Calder & Boyers, 1967.

Louis, Adrian C. "Petroglyphs of Serena." In *Anthology of Modern American Poetry*, ed. Cary Nelson, New York: Oxford University Press, 1134–41, 2000.

Ma, Ming-Qian. "A 'no man's land!': Postmodern Citationality in Zukofsky's 'Poem beginning "The." ' " In *Upper Limit Music: The Writing of Louis Zukofsky*, ed. Mark Scroggins, Tuscaloosa: Alabama University Press, 129–53, 1997.

Mac Cormack, Karen. "French Tom." In *The Tongue Moves Talk*, Tucson, AZ: Chax, 1997.

McCaffery, Steve. *North of Intention: Writings 1973–86.* New York: Roof, 1986.

McCaffery, Steve. *The Cheat of Words.* Toronto: ECW Press, 1996.

——*Seven Pages Missing. Volume One: Selected Texts 1969–1999.* Toronto: Coach House, 2001.

Markov, Vladimir. *Russian Futurism: A History.* Berkeley: University of California Press, 1968.

Mays, J. C. "Early Poems from 'Prufrock' to 'Gerontion.' " In *The Cambridge Companion to T. S. Eliot*, ed. A. David Moody, Cambridge: Camnridge University Press, 108–20, 1994.

Miller, James. E., Jr. "*Four Quartets* and an 'Acute Personal Reminiscence.' " In *T. S. Eliot: Man and Poet*, Vol. 1, ed. Sebastian D. G. Knowles and Scott A. Leonard, Orono, ME: National Poetry Foundation, 219–38, 1990.

Mink, Janis. *Duchamp.* Koln: Taschen, 2000.

Monk, Ray. *Bertrand Russell: The Spirit of Solitude 1872–1921.* New York: Free Press, 1996.

Moody, A. David (ed.). *The Cambridge Companion to T. S. Eliot*. Cambridge: Cambridge University Press, 1994.

Naumann, Francis M. *Marcel Duchamp: The Art of Making Art in the Age of Mechanical Reproduction*. New York: Harry N. Abrams, 1999.

Nelson, Cary (ed.). *Anthology of Modern American Poetry*. New York: Oxford University Press, 2000.

Nesbit, Molly. "Ready-Made Originals: The Duchamp Model." *October* 37, 53–64, summer 1986.

Nicholls, Peter. *Modernisms: A Literary Guide*. London: Macmillan, 1995.

O'Hara, Frank. *Standing Still and Walking in New York,* ed. Donald Allen. San Francisco: Grey Fox Press, 1977.

O'Hara, Frank. *The Collected Poems of Frank O'Hara*, ed. Donald Allen. Berkeley: University of California Press, 1995.

Olney, James. "Where is the Real T. S. Eliot? Or, The Life of the Poet." In *The Cambridge Companion to T. S. Eliot*, ed. A. David Moody, Cambridge: Cambridge University Press, 1–13, 1994.

Oppen, George. *The Selected Letters*, ed. Rachel Blau DuPlessis. Durham, NC: Duke University Press, 1992.

Ozick, Cynthia. "T. S. Eliot at 101." *The New Yorker*, 119–54, November 20, 1989.

Pater, Walter. "Style." In *Appreciations, With an Essay on Style*, London: Macmillan, 1925.

Perelman, Bob. *The Trouble with Genius: Reading Pound, Joyce, Stein, and Zukofsky*. Berkeley: University of California Press, 1994.

Perelman, Bob. "The Marginalization of Poetry." In *0–10: Selected Poems*, Hanover, NH: Wesleyan Press, 1999.

Perloff, Marjorie. *The Futurist Moment: Avant-Garde, Avant-Guerre, and the Language of Rupture*. Chicago: University of Chicago Press, 1986.

——— *Radical Artifice: Writing Poetry in the Age of Media*. Chicago: University of Chicago Press, 1992.

——— *The Dance of the Intellect: Studies in the Poetry of the Pound Tradition*. Evanston, IL: Northwestern University Press, 1995.

——— *Wittgenstein's Ladder: Poetic Language and the Strangeness of the Ordinary*. Chicago: University of Chicago Press, 1996a.

——— "Of Objects and Readymades: Gertrude Stein and Marcel Duchamp." *Forum for Modern Language Studies* 32, 2, 137–54, 1996b.

——*Frank O'Hara: Poet among Painters*. Chicago: University of Chicago Press, 1997.

——"Dada without Duchamp/Duchamp without Dada: Avant-Garde Tradition and the Individual Talent." *Stanford Humanities Review* 7, 1, 48–78 summer 1999a.

——*The Poetics of Indeterminacy: Rimbaud to Cage* [1981]. Evanston, IL: Northwestern University Press, 1999b.

Pitchford, Nicola. "Unlikely Modernism, Unlikely Postmodernism: Stein's Tender Buttons." *American Literary History* 11, 642–67, winter 1999.

Pound, Ezra. *Selected Letters of Ezra Pound 1907–1941*, ed. D. D. Paige. New York: New Directions, 1950.

——"A Retrospect" [1918]. In *The Literary Essays of Ezra Pound*, ed. T. S. Eliot, London: Faber & Faber, 1954. Cited as LE.

——*ABC of Reading* [1934]. New York: New Directions, 1960.

——*Gaudier-Brzeska* [1916]. New York: New Directions, 1970.

——*Personae: The Shorter Poems*, revd. edn., ed. Lea Baechler and A. Walton Litz. New York: New Directions, 1990.

——*The Cantos of Ezra Pound*. New York: New Directions, 1993.

Pound, Ezra and Louis Zukofsky. *Selected Letters of Ezra Pound and Louis Zukofsky*, ed. Barry Ahearn. New York: New Directions, 1987.

Power, Kevin. "An Interview with George and Mary Oppen." *Montemora* 4, 1978.

Pritchard, William H. "Eliot, Frost, Ma Rainey and the Rest." *New York Times Book Review* 10–11, April 2, 2000.

Rabaté, Jean-Michel. "Tradition and T. S. Eliot." In *The Cambridge Companion to T. S. Eliot*, ed. A. David Moody, Cambridge: Cambridge University Press, 210–22, 1994.

Rainey, Lawrence. *Institutions of Modernism: Literary Elites and Public Culture*. New Haven, CT: Yale University Press, 1998.

Rawson, Hugh. *Dictionary of Euphemisms and Other Doubletalk*. New York: Crown, 1981.

Reed, Brian. "Hart Crane's Victrola." *Modernism/Modernity* 7, January 2000, 99–125.

Robinson, E. A. *Collected Poems*. New York: Simon & Shuster, 1937.

Rothenberg, Jerome. "New Models, New Visions: Some Notes Toward a Poetics of Performance" [1971]. In *Performance in Postmodern Culture*, ed. Michel Benamou and Charles Caramello, Madison, WI: Coda Press, 11–17, 1977.

Ruthven, K. K. *A Guide to Ezra Pound's Personae (1926)*. Berkeley: University of California Press, 1969.

Sanouillet, Michel and Elmer Peterson (eds.). *The Essential Writings of Marcel Duchamp*. London: Thames & Hudson, 1975.

Schuchard, Ronald. *Eliot's Dark Angel: Intersections of Life and Art*. New York: Oxford University Press, 1999.

Schwartz, Delmore. *Selected Poems (1938–58)*. New York: New Directions, 1959.

Schwarz, Arturo. *The Complete Works of Marcel Duchamp*. New York: Harry N. Abrams, 1970.

Seigel, Jerrold. *The Private Worlds of Marcel Duchamp*. Berkeley: University of California Press, 1995.

Serres, Michel. "Platonic Dialogue." In *Hermes: Literature, Science, Philosophy*, ed. Josué V. Harari and David F. Bell. Baltimore, MD: Johns Hopkins University Press, 1982.

Sieburth, Richard. *Instigations: Ezra Pound and Remy de Gourmont*. Cambridge, MA: HarvardUniversity Press, 1978.

Silliman, Ron. *The New Sentence*. New York: Roof, 1987.

Smith, Grover. *T. S. Eliot's Poetry and Plays: A Study in Sources and Meaning*. Chicago: Chicago University Press, 1962.

Spender, Stephen. *Eliot*. London: Fontana Collins,1975.

Spicer, Jack. *Admonitions*. In *The Collected Books of Jack Spicer*. Santa Barbara, CA: Black Sparrow, 1975.

Stead, C. K. *The New Poetic: Yeats to Eliot*, revd. edn. Philadelphia: Pennsylvania University Press, 1987.

Stein, Gertrude. "The Fifteenth of November." *New Criterion* 4, 71–5, January 1926.

——*Everybody's Autobiography* [1937]. New York: Vintage, 1964.

——"Sentences." In *How to Write* [1931]. Los Angeles: Sun & Moon, 1995, 119–228.

——*How to Write* [1931]. Los Angeles: Sun & Moon, 1997.

——*Writings Volume 1: 1903–1932*, New York: Library of America, 1998. Cited as 1998 I.

——*Writings Volume 2: 1932 –1946*, New York: Library of America, 1998. Cited as 1998 II.

——*Stanzas in Meditation*. In *Writings Volume 2: 1932 –1946*, New York: Library of America, 1–145, 1998 II.

—— *Tender Buttons.* In *Writings Volume 1: 1903–1932*, New York: Library of America, 313–55, 1998 I.

—— *The Autobiography of Alice B. Toklas* [1933]. In *Writings Volume 1: 1903–1932*, New York: Library of America, 653–913, 1998 I.

Teasdale, Sara. *Helen of Troy and Other Poems.* New York: Putnam, 1911.

Tomkins, Calvin. *Duchamp: A Biography.* New York: Henry Holt, 1996.

Waldrop, Rosmarie. "Thinking of Follows." In *Onward: Contemporary Poetry and Poetics*, ed. Peter Baker. New York: Peter Lang, 73–82, 1996.

Welch, Andrew. *Roots of Lyric: Primitive Poetry and Modern Poetics.* Princeton, NJ: Princeton University Press, 1978.

Wershler-Henry, Darren. *the tapework foundry andor the dangerous prevalence of imagination.* Toronto: House of Anansi, 2000.

White, Ray Lewis (ed.). *Gertrude Stein and Alice B. Toklas: A Reference Guide.* Boston: G. K. Hall, 1984.

Wilder, Thornton. "Introduction" to Gertrude Stein, *Four in America* [1934]. New Haven, CT: Yale University Press, 1947.

Winkler, Paul and Anne d'Harnoncourt (eds.). *Joseph Cornell / Marcel Duchamp . . . in resonance.* Catalogue of the Exhibition. Houston: Menil Foundation. 1998.

Wittgenstein, Ludwig. *The Blue and Brown Books, Preliminary Studies for the "Philosophical Investigations,"* 2nd. edn. New York: Harper, 1965.

—— *Zettel,* ed. G. E. M. Anscombe and G. H. von Wright, trans. G. E. M. Anscombe. Berkeley: University of California Press, 1970.

—— *Notebooks 1914–1916,* 2nd. edn. Chicago: University of Chicago Press, 1979.

—— *Culture and Value,* ed. G. H. von Wright, in collaboration with Heikki Nyman. Trans. Peter Winch. Chicago: University of Chicago Press, 1980. Cited as C & V.

—— *Tractatus Logico-Philosophicus* [1922], trans C. K. Ogden. London: Routledge, 1981.

Yeats, W. B. *A Vision* [1937]. New York: Macmillan, 1962.

—— *Autobiographies.* Macmillan: London, 1966.

Zukofsky, Louis. "Poem beginning 'The.'" In *Complete Short Poetry*, Baltimore, MD: Johns Hopkins University Press, 9–20, 1991.

Index

Italic page references refer to plates; bold page references indicate sections focusing on a particular writer or work.

Aiken, Conrad   27, 31–2
Aldington, Richard   35
Allen, Donald   2
Altieri, Charles   24, 27
Andrews, Bruce   5, 121, 123
Antin, David   5, 18, 101, 173, 205 n.8
Apollinaire, Guillaume   1, 5
Arensberg, Walter   111, 206 n.12
Aristotle   182–3
Armantrout, Rae   5
Arnheim, Rudolf   88
Ashbery, John   2, 5, 12, 25, 133, 179; "Tarpaulin"   7–8, 59
Auden, W. H.   2, 161, 177

Bakhtin, M.   38
Balla, Giacomo   3
Baraka, Amiri   2
Bateson, Gregory   88
Baudelaire, Charles   15, 26, 50
Beats, the   2

Beckett, Samuel   1
Benda, Julien   40
Benjamin, Walter   40, 109–11, 113
Bergson, Henri   28, 88
Bernstein, Charles   4, 5, 8, 10, 13–14, 28, 121; "Artifice of Absorption"   12–13, 53, 104, 155, 181; My Way   13–14; "Reveal Codes"   180–1; "Dysraphism"   173; "Lives of the Toll Takers"   103, **173–9**
Biely, Andrei   129
Binyon, Laurence   39
Bishop, Elizabeth   10, 25
Black Mountain   2, 164
Blaser, Robin   189
Bloom, Harold   12
Bök, Christian   87
Bonk, Ecke   81, 109, 113, 204 nn.3–4, 206 n.12

Braque, Georges   53, 66, 74
Brathwaite, Kamau   126
Breslin, James E. B.   2
Breton, André   52
Browning, Robert   24
Bürger, Peter   83–4
Burliuk, David   127, 131, 136
Burliuk, Vladimir   131
Butters, Ronald   203–4 n.1

Cabanne, Pierre   77, 84–8
Cage, John   5, 87, 93, 110, 133–4,
    153, 164
Cameron, Eric   89
Carlyle, Thomas   39
Carrà, Carlo   3
Carruth, Hayden   2
Castillo, Ana   163
Cendrars, Blaise   5, 12, 37
Césaire, Aimé   126
Cézanne, Paul   52, 54, 73–4
Christensen, Paul   159
Clover, Joshua   1
Cocteau, Jean   51–2
Coleridge, Samuel Taylor   16,
    72–3
Concrete Poetry   129, 153
Constructivism   26
Cooke, Raymond   141
Coolidge, Clark   13
Corbière, Tristan   15
Cornell, Joseph   204 n.2
Courbet, Gustave   84, 88
Crane, Hart   25
Cratylus   124
Creeley, Robert   2, 25
Criterion   11, 28, 39–42, 75
Cubism   25, 36, 54, 71

Dada   33, 40, 83–5, 93, 126
Dalton, F. T.   27
Dante Alighieri: *Inferno*   24;
    Purgatorio   34, 202 n.3,
    203 n.6
Davidson, Michael   9–10
Davie, Donald   12
Da Vinci, Leonardo   81
De Campos, Augusto   129
De Campos, Haroldo   23, 129
De Duve, Thierry   84, 89, 116–17
Delaunay, Robert   3
Derrida, Jacques   176
Dickinson, Emily   190
Djuric, Dubravka   189
Dostoievsky, Fyodor   40
Dove, Rita   4
Drucker, Johanna   87
Duchamp, Marcel   3, 5, 37, 41,
    52, 64, 68, 74, 76, **77–120**,
    121, 127, 137, 163, 173,
    178, 198, 204–6 nn.3–13;
    Bottle Rack (l'Egouttoir)   79,
    204 n.1; *Box of 1914*   81,
    82, 109–10, 118; *boîtes en
    valise*   84, 108, 111, 113, 114,
    114, 204 n.2; *Etant données*
    98, 101; *Fresh Widow*   107–
    9, *106*; *Green Box*   87,
    90–1, 95, 101, 102, 111, 118;
    Infrathin   114–20, 126, 176,
    179; *Large Glass (The Bride
    Stripped Bare by her Bachelors,
    Even)*   79, *80*, 86–7, 99, 111,
    112, 113–14, 118, 119, 130;
    Readymades   84–6, 95,
    101, 109, 117, 137, 180;
    Rendezvous 1916   95–101,

Duchamp, Marcel *cont.*
  96; "Rrose Sélavy" 85–6,
  107–8, 205 n.8, 206 n.11;
  The *92*, 93–7; *Tzanck Check*
  89–90, *90*, 163; *White Box
  (A l'Infinitif)* 81, 87, 91,
  101, 116–19; *Why not Sneeze
  Rrose Sélavy?* 85, 98, 117;
  With Hidden Noise 101–7,
  100, *104*, *105*, 163–4, 179,
  205 n.9
Duncan, Isadora 47
Duncan, Robert 2
Dydo, Ulla 203–4 n.1

Eliot, T. S. 2, 4, 5, **7–43**, 44–7,
  53, 61–2, 64, 66–9, 71, 75–8,
  88, 94, 98, 126, 128, 138, 159,
  166–8, 172, 202 nn.2–4; "Ash
  Wednesday" 75; "Gerontion"
  32, 35–7; "Love Song of J.
  Alfred Prufrock" 14, **18–28**,
  41–2, 55–6, 159–60, 164, 172,
  180–1, 202 n.1, 203 nn.5, 6,
  7, 8; "Metaphysical Poets,
  The" 10, 13, 162; "Second
  Caprice in North
  Cambridge" 7–8; "Tradition
  and the Individual Talent"
  10, 28, 47, 89; *The Waste Land*
  37–9, 77, 89, 129–30, 143,
  145, 174, 177–8, 203 n.8

Fauchereau, Serge 136
Fenollosa, Ernest 23, 192
Flaubert, Gustave 4, 22–4, 53–5,
  61, 74, 190
Ford, Ford Madox 16

Foucault, Michel 118
Frankfurt School 1, 128
Fraser, Kathleen 103
Frost, Robert 15

Gehry, Frank 163
Ginsberg, Allen 2, 4, 10, 13–14
Goldsmith, Kenneth 87
Goncharova, Natalia 142
Gordon, Lyndall 27, 202 n.4
Gray, Cleve 117
Greenberg, Clement 52
Gris, Juan 66, 74
Guro, Yelena 127, 131, 142
Guttman, Yair 83

Haigh-Wood, Vivienne 34–5
Hall, Donald 2
Hamilton, Richard 108, 204 n.4,
  205 n.7
Hardy, Thomas 12, 17, 25
Harrison, Robert 202 n.3
Hass, Robert 54
Hecht, Anthony: "Message from
  the City" 156–62
Hejinian, Lyn 5, 9–10, 25, 54–5,
  71, **181–90**, 191; *Happily*
  181–90; *Oxota* 185
Henderson, Linda Dalrymple 81,
  87–8, 99, 102, 130, 204 n.3,
  205 n.6
Herbert, George 5
Herrick, Robert 71
Hesse, Herman 40
Hirsch, Edward: "How to Get
  Back to Chester" 157–61
Howe, Susan 5, 87, 121, 123,
  153; *Thorow* **164–72**, 177

Hughes, Langston   129
Hulten, Pontus   101

Jakobson, Roman   97, 121–5,
    127–8, 136–7, 145, 185
James, William   184
Janacek, Gerald   142
Jarrell, Randall   2, 25, 159
Jarry, Alfred   205 n.6
Johnson, Lionel   15
Johnson, William   166, 170
Joselit, David   97, 103, 108,
    205–6 nn.9–11
Jouffroy, Allain   79
Joyce, James   10, 25, 45, 63;
    Finnegans Wake   171; *Portrait
    of the Artist as a Young Man*
    49–50; *Ulysses*   40–1
Judovitz, Dalia   99

Keats, John   70, 72
Kenner, Hugh   25
Kern, Gary   140–1
Khlebnikov, Velimir   4, 5–6, 64,
    68, **121–53**, 164, 168, 170,
    172, 201; "Grasshopper"
    (*Kuznechik*)   122–5;
    "Hunger" (*Golod*)   151–3;
    "Incantation by Laughter"
    (*Zakliate smekhom*)   139–41;
    "Russia and Me"   149–50,
    200; *Tables of Destiny*   143–5;
    Trap For Judges, A   127;
    "Word as Such, The"   131;
    Zangezi   146–9; *zaum*   123,
    126, 138–9, 151, 153, 162,
    170
Knowles, Sebastian D. G.   15

Kosuth, Joseph   83
Koteliansky, S. S.   40
Kozloff, Max   111
Krauss, Rosalind   89
Kruchonykh, V.   123–4, 127,
    131–2, 142
Kuh, Katherine   79
Kunitz, Stanley   4

Laforgue, Jules   15, 20
Larbaud, Valery   40
La Rochelle, Drieu   40
Lawrence, D. H.   94
Lawton, Anna   127, 131
Leiris, Michel   13
Leonard, Scott A.   15
Lévi-Strauss, Claude   122
Lewis, Wyndham   35
Liebeskind, Daniel   163
Livshits, Benedikt   131
Lobachevsky, N.   130
Louis, Adrian C.   163
Lowell, Robert   2, 164
Loy, Mina   37

Ma, Ming-Qian   94
Mac Cormack, Karen   4; "French
    Tom"   42–3
Mac Low, Jackson   87, 93, 118,
    133, 153
McCaffery, Steve   5, 10, 13, 87,
    126, **191–201**; "Four Versions
    of Pound's 'In a Station of
    the Metro'"   191–201, *194,
    195, 197, 198*; "Serbia mon
    amour"   200–1
MacGill, Patrick   16
Mackey, Nathaniel   129

Malevich, Kasimir   131, 142
Mallarmé, Stephane   4, 50, 74
Marinetti, F. T.   33, 84, 136–7
Markov, Vladimir   130
Masefield, John   73
Matisse, Paul   114
Maugham, Somerset   188
Mauriac, François   40
Mayakovsky, Vladimir   127, 131,
     150–1
Mays, J. C.   25
Meredith, George   16
Mink, Janis   85
Monro, Harold   27
Monroe, Harriet   27
Moore, T. Sturge   39
Mullen, Harryette   4, 129

Naumann, Francis   81, 95,
     110–11, 206 n.12
Nesbit, Molly   108, 206 n.11
New York School   1, 2, 164, 179
Nicholls, Peter   12
Niedecker, Lorine   5

O'Hara, Frank   2, 4, 5, 11, 26,
     50–1, 150, 179
O'Sullivan, Maggie   126
objective correlative   27, 71, 159
Objectivists   1, 164
Olney, James   202 n.7
Olson, Charles   2, 164, 179
Oppen, George   5, 26, 64
Oulipo   23, 87, 93, 153
Ozick, Cynthia   11–12

Padgett, Ron   205 n.8
Pater, Walter   22

Perelman, Bob   42, 46
Perloff, Marjorie   7, 54, 64, 71,
     126, 142, 204 n.1
Phillips, Tom   87
Picabia, François   41, 52, 85
Picasso, Pablo   41, 47, 49–53, 66,
     73–4, 85, 110, 193, 196, 198
Pignatari, Decio   129
Pinsky, Robert   4
Pitchford, Nicola   66
Poincaré, Henri   130
Pound, Ezra   5, 10, 18–19, 23, 27,
     31, 33, 38, 40–1, 45, 50,
     52–3, 56, 64–5, 69, 77, 94,
     126, 154, 164, 191–3, 198,
     201; *Cantos*   64–5, 196;
     "In a Station of the Metro"
     191–8; "Paracelsus in
     Excelsis"   18–19
Power, Kevin   64
Pushkin, Aleksandr   129, 185

Quinn, John   35

Rabaté, Jean-Michel   33
Rainey, Lawrence   203 n.8
Ransom, John Crowe   159
Raworth, Tom   25
Ray, Man   99, 110
Reed, Brian   25
Resnais, Alain   200
Rhode, Werner   111
Ricks, Christopher   8, 203 nn.5,
     6
Rivers, Larry   50
Robinson, Edward Arlington   17,
     19, 25
Ruthven, K. K.   191–3

Saintsbury, George   39
Sanouillet   130, 203–4 n.4
Saussure, Ferdinand de   124, 126
Schlovsky, Vikto   185
Schmidt, Paul   122–3, 140–1,
    146–8, 150
Schuchard, Ronald   15
Schwartz, Delmore   2; "Tired and
    Unhappy"   155–61
Schwarz, Arturo   93, 102, 108
Seigel, Jerrold   108
Seitz, William C.   88
Serres, Michel   177–8
Shapiro, Karl   2
Sieburth, Richard   22–3
Silliman, Ron   26, 55–7, 181
Sinclair, May   39–40
Smith, Grover   202 n.7
Smithson, Robert   87
Spender, Stephen   22–3
Spicer, Jack   2, 189
Stead, C. K.   16
Stein, Gertrude   1, 4, 5, 13, 37,
    41, **44–76**, 85–6, 105, 126,
    128, 137, 154, 162, 181,
    183–6, 190, 203–4 n.1; "A
    Box"   79–81; *Autobiography
    of Alice B. Toklas, The*   44–5,
    52, 63–4; *Everybody's
    Autobiography*   46–7, 50–2;
    "Fifteenth of November"
    44–5, 75; "Flirting at the Bon
    Marché"   205 n.5; "Glazed
    Glitter"   68–71, 118; "Lifting
    Belly"   85; "Miss Furr and
    Miss Skeene"   45–6, **56–63**,
    185; "Orta, or One Dancing"
    47; "Picasso"   47, 49–50;

"Poetry and Grammar"
    55–6, 65; "Portraits and
    Repetition"   67; "Rooms"
    72–3, 190; *Tender Buttons*
    63–76, 79–81, 164; "What are
    Master-Pieces"   46–8, 162–3;
    "What is English Literature"
    52
Steiner, Rudolf   129
Stevens, Wallace   5, 56, 171
Stieglitz, Alfred   109
Surrealism   25, 40, 52
Swinburne, Algernon   16, 39

Tate, Allen   159
Teasdale, Sara   17, 19, 73
Thoreau, David Henry   166, 168,
    170–1
Tinyanov, Juri   185
Tomkins, Calvin   99
Troe (The Three)   142
Trubetskoy, Nikolay   122
Truffaut, François   180
Turner, Michael   76

Verdenal, Jean   28–35, 39, 202 n.4
Verlaine, Paul   15
Villon, François   94
Virgil   34, 202 n.3
Vroon, Roland   147–8

Wagner, Richard   38
Waldrop, Rosmarie   5, 8, 10
Warren, Robert Penn   159
Watson, William   16
Welch, Andrew   71, 146–7
Wellmann, Mac   5, 126
Wershler-Henry, Darren   76

Index

White, Ray Lewis   63
Whitman, Walt   39
Wilbur, Richard   2
Wilder, Thornton   52–3
Williams, William Carlos   1, 5,
     11–12, 41, 66
Wittgenstein, Ludwig   1, 6, 9, 12,
     21, 23, 41, 56, 110, 116, 135,
     142, 182–3, 185, 190

Woolf, Virginia   40, 73
Wordsworth, William   16, 133

Yeats, W. B.   15, 16–17, 132, 155

Zinko, Carolyne   174
Zukofsky, Louis   5; "Poem
     Beginning 'The'"   93–5,
     154

DATE DUE

HIGHSMITH #45115

222